# How to Heal Your Inner Child

## Overcome Past Trauma and Childhood Emotional Neglect

Simon Chapple

sheldon PRESS

First published by Sheldon Press in 2021
An imprint of John Murray Press
A division of Hodder & Stoughton Ltd,
An Hachette UK company

5

A CIP catalogue record for this title is available from the British Library.

Trade Paperback ISBN 9781529383638
eBook ISBN 9781529383645

Typeset by KnowledgeWorks Global Ltd.

Printed and bound in Great Britain by Clays Ltd, Elcograf S.p.A.

John Murray Press policy is to use papers that are natural, renewable and recyclable products and made from wood grown in sustainable forests. The logging and manufacturing processes are expected to conform to the environmental regulations of the country of origin.

John Murray Press
Carmelite House
50 Victoria Embankment
London EC4Y 0DZ

Nicholas Brealey Publishing
Hachette Book Group
Market Place, Center 53, State Street
Boston, MA 02109, USA

www.sheldonpress.co.uk

*This book is dedicated to the many people who made it possible. The support, inspiration and guidance of these incredible individuals allowed me to heal, grow and believe in myself.*

# Acknowledgements

There are too many names to mention everyone who helped, suffice to say that you know who you are and will have had a part to play in my incredible, life-changing journey. Thank you for helping me become able to share it.

Dr David Perl – you have been an inspirational father figure. Without you this book would never have happened.

Ruth Perl – you helped me learn that lasting change is possible.

Michelle Chapple – my wife and an oasis of calm in the sandstorm of my life.

Robin Chapple – my son, your eyes see everything, may your dreams forever live.

Jackie McCarron – the mother I always wanted.

Annie Grace – you helped me push over the first domino.

Victoria Roddam at Hodder & Stoughton, for being patient, supportive and believing in me.

Deri, Neal, Allistair, David B, David W and Tom, 'The Wednesday Men' – my brothers, I am thankful for having you in my life.

Judy, Lois, Rob, Janet, Liam, Kate, Lisa, Kim, John and Jaqui – my sober 'ambassadors'.

My parents Pauline and Michael Chapple – who did the best they were able to do.

And my grandmother Betty Hackett – you allowed me to see that unconditional love is a reality.

# Contents

# About the author

For over four decades Simon Chapple struggled with feelings of depression, mood swings and emotional upset, he felt empty inside and disconnected from those who were closest to him. He experienced problems with relationships, careers, addiction and many areas of life that most people take for granted. Despite all of this he was somehow able to function and built a successful business, ran marathons and tried his best to be a father and a husband. But something was lacking in his life, he knew he wasn't the best version of himself; his life felt hollow and was slowly falling apart around him.

He chased happiness, and no matter where he looked it seemed to elude him. Meanwhile, his anxiety became worse and his mood became lower, causing him to turn to unhelpful and unhealthy behaviours as a method of coping.

It took time, but he eventually realised that the root of what he was experiencing was in his childhood. An anxious and insecure relationship with his parents had set him on course to destroy his life and what he had learned was not serving him in a way that was positive. He knew that something needed to change, but he didn't know what to do for the best.

Eventually, Simon embarked on a journey of self-exploration and went on to heal himself and discover a life of peace and happiness. Joy flowed back into his life for the first time since he was a child as he experienced the elation of living without constant emotional upset and anxiety. What Simon experienced was so profound that it became his mission to raise awareness and help others who feel stuck in a state of unhappiness and who don't understand why, or what to do for the best.

As well as sharing his own powerful story and inspiring people around the world, Simon is also a Certified Sobriety Coach and the founder of Be Sober, one of the largest quit drinking communities in the world. He has appeared on television and radio and spoken at live events in the US and the UK about his very personal journey from heavy daily drinking to becoming passionately sober. He has released two addiction-beating books: you can find these in the Resources section of this book. He has worked with thousands of people from all over the world in coaching programmes and helped them make a powerful and lasting change, not only to beat addictions, but to understand who they really are and what they need to do to thrive in life.

Simon has written this book to help anyone who has experienced childhood emotional neglect or past trauma. He draws on his considerable life experience, and the experiences of those he has helped in order to provide a structured path to healing.

Find out more at www.simonchapple.com

# Foreword

Many years ago, while training as a psychotherapist, a lecturer expressed a view that anything less than unconditional love expressed to a child while growing up was a form of child abuse. My initial feeling was this was a bit of an extreme viewpoint and that children were far more robust and durable than the lecturer was giving them credit for.

After all, at that time, I believed that my own father's emotional absence was largely due to being a child victim of both Auschwitz and Dachau Nazi concentration camps; and my mother's violence towards me as a child, because of her unconscious and uncontained anger, hadn't really had that much of an impact on my own emotional wellbeing while growing up and into adulthood.

With my increasing clinical experience, I have since witnessed all too often the impact of less than stellar parenting on my clients and the resulting damage caused to their adult lives, both with their inner psychological landscapes and how they relate in their interpersonal relationships. I've also come to appreciate that my own parents' ineptitude, along with their own trans-generational traumas, had traumatized me in many ways.

While the vast majority of our parents do not intentionally neglect us, it is more through a lack of awareness and ignorance that we, as children, are let down by them. As I was taught in my own training, children are often given too much of what they don't need (criticism, judgement, emotional distance and shaming) or not enough of what they do need (love without imparted conditions). Often, this emotional benign neglect is enough to deprive a child of the secure base that is so badly needed to enable us to grow up into whole and functional adults.

The evidence for this is overwhelming and well documented. Perhaps the most compelling is the American Adverse Childhood Experience study commenced in 1995, which looked at negative experiences in childhood and the impact on their later lives, on both their mental and physical wellbeing.

Adverse childhood experiences, or ACEs, are potentially traumatic events that occur in childhood, including witnessing violence in the home or community, or having a family member attempt, or die by, suicide. Also included are aspects of the child's environment that can undermine their sense of safety, stability and bonding, such as growing up in a household with substance misuse, mental health problems, instability due to parental separation or household members being absent.

ACEs can also negatively impact education and job opportunities. However measured, the evidence shows increased risk of cancer, diabetes, depression, anxiety, PTSD and suicide, higher rates of alcohol and drug abuse and earlier death for adults who have been impacted.

As a society, I am all too often perplexed as to why the failings of parents (myself included), are not put under the microscope more. The medical profession is woefully ignorant of the impact on children of later expressions of disease. My own training did not include any insight or education into such issues.

Even more problematic is the impact of more insidious poor parenting, often through ignorance as opposed to overt malice. Day in, day out, I now sit with clients struggling to hold down functional relationships, all too often because their own templates for healthy relationships have evolved from what they witnessed in their parents' own dysfunctional partnerships. After all, perhaps the most important task we will ever perform if we have chosen to have a child, that of being a parent, is one of the few jobs where no training, credentials, qualifications, certificate nor licence is required. And yet, the future of raising a more self-aware, conscious population is dependent on parents themselves being conscious and self-aware.

I started working with Simon in early 2020. I was immediately struck by his willingness to push past his own ego and take a searingly honest inventory of his own behaviours that had evolved from his childhood infused with emotional neglect. Being mindful of confidentiality, it is up to Simon to disclose what he chooses in the following pages and so I will say no more of the territories we have travelled through together.

In this book, Simon has used his gift of writing in a jargon-free and easy-to-read style on a topic that those in the psychological profession at times make too complex. It's refreshing to read a self-help book where the author is willing to be honest and share his own traumas as a way of illustrating concepts that needn't be difficult to understand.

This continues to be a curiosity for me, professionals who surround themselves with mystique through the use of impenetrable jargon. Having trained as a medical doctor and a psychotherapist, I have first-hand experience of two such professions where I believe many practitioners have a tendency to hide behind their own vulnerabilities by the use of impenetrable technical language. So how refreshing to see an author willing to share much of their own traumatic life experiences and to use these experiences to help others with no-nonsense practical and easy to understand suggestions and support.

The path to recovering our own self-respect and building back up our self-esteem is not a one-shot operation. It's the road less travelled and yet one, in my experience, that leads to many rewards. Simon's book will be, for many, an excellent embarkation point. For all those brave souls willing to embark into what may be unknown territory, I wish you safe travels.

Dr David Perl MB BS, Dip Counselling; Psychotherapy, Dip Coaching
Relationship coach, couple's counsellor and psychotherapist
Founder of limerence.net – an online resource for love addiction.

# Introduction

If you have picked up this book, then chances are that either you, or someone close to you, has identified issues relating to the past that have left them feeling empty, confused and emotionally stuck. I know how challenging this can feel and I want to help you find a solution that enables you to understand how to heal and become unstuck, once and for all.

I wrote this book to help anyone who is tired of being overwhelmed by painful emotions. I have been there, I know what it feels like, and I don't want experiences from your past to dictate the way that you feel and behave today.

You may have already identified that the way you feel, react and behave has been caused by Childhood Emotional Neglect (CEN) or by childhood trauma. If so, you have likely already begun to become much more self-aware and have taken a big step forward. You might even have started to pay more attention to uncomfortable feelings and emotions, asking yourself questions about where they have come from and what triggers them at a specific moment.

By opening this book and taking positive action, you have shown you have a desire and determination to overcome the issues that you have been facing. It is a brave step. Many people spend their entire lives stuck, never facing up to the fact that the sadness exists within them. They spend a lifetime in denial, often using unhealthy behaviours and addictions as an outlet to numb the pain and suffering. Congratulate yourself on making a courageous and powerful decision to face your challenges.

My previous books relate to topics around overcoming my alcohol addiction and offered self-help and advice about stopping drinking. As a speaker, life coach and certified sobriety coach, I help people who want to break free from the grip of alcohol, and over the years I have helped thousands to change their relationship with drinking. I have spoken at live events in the UK and the US and appeared on television and radio programmes discussing addiction and the best strategies for ending an unhealthy relationship with alcohol. I have a real passion for helping people reclaim their lives to become the very best version of themselves.

If you are a drinker, don't worry. I'm not going to ask you to quit alcohol or start preaching about sobriety. However, if this is an area of your life you are worried about, then I recommend reading one of my other books and exploring your relationship with alcohol in more depth.

# Why did I write a book about Childhood Emotional Neglect?

As a sobriety coach, I connect with thousands of people every year, in large online groups, as well as at live events and one-to-one coaching sessions. I hear stories of addiction from people all around the world, from a wide age range and diverse mix of different backgrounds. They all have one thing in common. Each and every one of them wants to cut alcohol out of their lives and become 'happy'.

Fundamentally, most people have one goal: to be happy. Yet we often fail to define what 'happiness' actually looks like. Likewise 'success'. Rarely do we give much thought to what 'success' and 'happiness' really mean and, even when we do, we may believe (falsely) that they are contingent on wealth and possessions. In my view, happiness and success come to us through peace, joy, connection with others, fulfilment in life and having a true sense of our self-worth, meaning and purpose.

Many of the people I work with are stuck with no idea how to get out of the trap they have found themselves in with alcohol, let alone become successful and happy. When they have additionally experienced CEN or trauma in childhood, it often leaves them with a compulsive need to soothe the pain, even though they don't know why they are suffering in the first place.

In addition to those with addictions, I also encounter people who find themselves over-achieving at work or in their hobbies; attempting to control other people; acting in an ego-centric way (showing off, for example); people-pleasing; experiencing angry outbursts; or avoiding conflict at all costs. These are all signs that something deeper is going on at a subconscious level.

Overcompensating and overachieving are common among people who have experienced CEN and trauma. I have worked with people who have reached the pinnacle of their career ladder, won awards, promotions and given huge salaries and responsibility. Yet they aren't even close to feeling happy or fulfilled. They tell me that each time they reach a new goal it feels like a disappointment. So they set the next target to work towards and re-focus their attention and energy towards it. Constantly striving is emotionally draining and another sign that deeper issues likely exist.

That's not to say everyone who has experienced CEN or past trauma is super-successful and egocentric. Some people can become withdrawn, isolated and deeply lacking in confidence. The tentacles of this invisible force can impact us in many different ways.

# Becoming naked

Through my sobriety work, I found that each individual has their own very personal and powerful story of addiction and the damage it has caused.

Ultimately, however, they have all become trapped by their beliefs about the benefits of drinking alcohol. The most common – false – beliefs I encounter are that alcohol is a reward that helps them relax or relieves their stress. It is these false beliefs that sit at the heart of the reason why so many people remain stuck in addictive behaviours, and my work involves inspiring people to change their beliefs to new, healthy and powerful statements that allow them to flourish and break free from alcohol for good.

Of course, there is much more to the process than simply changing beliefs, but these underpin the foundations of successful sobriety.

When people quit drinking I witness an incredible transformation, it is rather like a caterpillar transforming into a beautiful butterfly. They experience joy, they reconnect with old hobbies, evaluate what healthy relationships look like, set boundaries with people who might cause pain and, above all, become incredibly self-aware. They have usually used alcohol for years – decades in some cases – as a mask to hide from challenging emotions or thoughts. When the coping mask is removed people become naked, usually for the first time in a very long time. They strip away their unhealthy coping mechanism and end up left with no choice but to look at who they really are in the mirror, at the real version of themselves – naked.

For many people the fear of looking at the real version of themselves is too much. So they continue drinking, they suppress it and deny they have a problem in favour of keeping their mask firmly attached and the true version of themselves hidden away forever. Their natural human instinct to stay safe overrides their desire to get out of the deep hole they are in.

Getting naked doesn't come without a degree of discomfort in most cases. The good news is that it is the discomfort that becomes our saviour. When we find the courage to look into the mirror at who we really are without judgement, we begin to understand what shaped us as adults and we are able to accept our past and soften any pain it causes.

Often when people stop drinking (or other addictive behaviours), they feel great for a few months before noticing that there is something else going on, something much deeper, something they can't put their finger on. All they know is that it hurts, they want it to stop and they don't know why they have such a numbness within their soul.

I know exactly what this 'hollow' feeling is because I have experienced it, too. I was a heavy drinker for over twenty years, I believed alcohol was solving all my problems and that I needed to drink each day in order to be happy. When I got sober my life improved in many powerful and positive ways. But I still felt there was something fundamentally wrong with me, a sense that I wasn't whole, wasn't normal like other people.

My own journey took me along a path of discovery where I was able to uncover the roots of my emotional neglect and trauma from childhood, and learn how to pull them out of the ground so I never had to experience such pain again. I became whole, reconnected with my feelings and moved through my past issues. I have since helped many people do the same after they have become 'naked' and identified that there is more going on than just a problem with drinking. Alcohol was simply the effect, not the cause.

I am not a psychotherapist nor a doctor (although this book has been endorsed and approved by just such a clinician) and I don't have a magic formula. My qualification is that, through my work as a coach, I have helped people all over the world to face and move on from their CEN and trauma. More importantly, I lived for over 40 years with the very thing that you are experiencing. I spent more than two decades trying to figure out what was going on with my life and eventually, through trial and error (but not without thousands of pounds wasted on bad therapy), I was able to become free of the suffering for good. I want to share what worked for me with as many people as possible in order that they no longer have to suffer in silence.

This book isn't a standard 'self-help' book, but if you have experienced emotional neglect or trauma I am confident it will help you. It is made up of chapters that share the exact strategies I used in order to overcome my own CEN, alongside stories and experiences that will help you understand exactly how the adult that I went on to become was shaped, as a child, into an incomplete person who was unhappy, disconnected and fearful most of the time.

I know how hard it is to live with the effects of childhood emotional neglect and past trauma, I lacked the ability to connect emotionally with others and was unable to feel my feelings, express my emotions or enjoy healthy relationships. I was a 'victim' too, but I have come out the other side, I have managed to heal it, and so can you.

My hope for you as you move through this book is that the insights and experiences I share will enable you to heal, too. Millions of people live in daily discomfort because of the effects of CEN and trauma. Rarely is it spoken about, and very few people are aware of the problem or know how to address the issues.

Until we become aware, we will never get anywhere.

But you have become aware already. You have noticed what is going on and now you want to know how to heal. I will explain exactly what worked for me and the people who I have coached to help them overcome the same challenges you are facing.

Let's get started by understanding more about Childhood Emotional Neglect and trauma.

# 1 | What is Childhood Emotional Neglect and trauma?

Until a few years ago I hadn't heard of Childhood Emotional Neglect (CEN) and I thought trauma simply described the awful acts of physical violence or sexual abuse that I read about in the media. My head was firmly buried in the sand when it came to looking at my own past; something from deep within stopped me ever going near it, probably to protect myself from feeling pain. Still, my suffering was a daily burden. To an outsider it appeared that I had the perfect life: a decent job, a nice house, a perfect little family, and I enjoyed three or four holidays most years. I even had an expensive sports car, but none of it made me any happier.

Whenever I experienced difficult or painful feelings I would drink, downing bottles of red wine to blot it all out. I couldn't stand the pain. I was constantly over-analysing, critiquing and attempting to find solutions, 'big ideas' that I believed would make me successful, appreciated, loved and happy. The internal chatter never stopped.

My own journey to healing from CEN and trauma began after I successfully quit alcohol and found myself totally exposed to my feelings, insecurities and emotions without my coping mechanism. Sobriety felt like being dropped on a beautiful desert island, totally naked and completely vulnerable. It was simply beautiful, I was fully present and could walk barefoot in the white sand and paddle in the calm, turquoise sea. The sun warmed my skin as I sat, happy and contented, on the beach and gazed across the blue ocean toward the distant horizon.

But lurking in the dense jungle that jutted up against the soft sand was danger. Since childhood, I had lived with a sense that danger was never far away – on edge and jumpy, ready for a fight, flight or freeze response to overwhelm me at any moment. On my desert island of sobriety I knew that, if I wanted to stay healthy and happy, I had to venture into that jungle and seek out the danger, facing up to whatever demons and poisonous creatures lurked within my tropical paradise.

Certainly, my physical and mental health had dramatically improved after I got sober, but I also realized I needed to venture into the darker undergrowth of the jungle to discover and confront the deeper issues that existed at my very core.

I had no choice but to explore. I had taken the huge step of quitting alcohol and my ultimate goal was to be happy, but I wasn't there yet and I needed to keep searching. I didn't have a clue what I might find in the dense greenery behind the beach, but I knew that if I stayed where I was, then nothing would ever change and I would continue to carry unexplained pain and discomfort within me permanently.

I began to search online, read books, speak to counsellors and health professionals and talk to people who had been on similar journeys. I joined several private groups on Facebook where people shared their own experiences and talked openly about how they also felt like they had something wrong with them but couldn't understand why. This was my first breakthrough, as I realized I wasn't alone in feeling this way.

I hunted for information, uncovering more and more, with each new nugget of data forming part of an enormous jigsaw puzzle. Every time I found a new piece I would study it closely before carefully putting it into place, slowly seeing the picture of my life beginning to form.

# A diagnosis

As my search for answers continued I was diagnosed with Complex Post-Traumatic Stress Disorder (C-PTSD), a condition where sufferers experience some of the symptoms of classic PTSD, combined with additional complications.

Some of the symptoms that sufferers of C-PTSD might experience, in addition to those of PTSD include:

- feeling that nobody understands you;
- feeling as though you are different to everyone else;
- feeling unable to trust other people;
- feeling hostile towards the world;
- feeling empty inside;
- feeling hopeless;
- avoiding close friendships and intimate relationships;
- experiencing suicidal thoughts and feelings;
- difficulty controlling emotions.

My C-PTSD diagnosis was linked directly to my biological father abandoning me when I was around two years old. The more I thought about it, the more it began to make so much sense. Many of the episodes that had triggered me and caused an overwhelming flood of negative emotions were related to feeling abandoned or rejected when my father left me over four decades ago.

Something as innocuous as a barista being dismissive or rude when serving me in a coffee shop, a friend turning down my lunch invitation, or a client at work cancelling, would trigger a flood of intense negative feelings. When I became aware how it was linked to issues around abandonment and rejection, I began to see a very clear pattern in many of the episodes that were causing a strong emotional response.

Initially I believed that it was only my father's behaviour that had caused issues, but this wasn't the case. My mother didn't abandon me, but she was emotionally absent and failed to show enough compassion or support; she didn't ever truly bond with me. Among other things, this significantly affected my sense of self-worth and ability to connect with other people on an emotional level.

As I had never suffered violence or sexual abuse at the hands of my parents, I didn't immediately identify with terms like 'neglect' and 'trauma'. But as I continued to learn more about the impact of how our childhood experiences shape us in adulthood, it became glaringly obvious that I had experienced what can only be described as classic CEN (Childhood Emotional Neglect).

So what is it? Let's break this down into two sections, one for Childhood Emotional Neglect and one for trauma.

# Childhood Emotional Neglect (CEN)

CEN is usually (but not always) a consequence of a parent or primary caregiver failing to adequately meet the emotional needs of their child. It is important to understand that this is not necessarily physical or sexual abuse, it is subtle and often invisible – although some parents can be emotionally neglectful at the same time as being physically abusive.

Physical abuse is intentional, but CEN usually happens without anyone realizing it. We don't see it and we don't feel it fully until much later in our lives, when the effects leave us lost, confused and wondering why we feel so empty.

There is no 'one size fits all' with CEN, we have all experienced different behaviours and each of our stories are unique. But in every case there are common themes, symptoms and traits and, thankfully, a common way to heal, regardless of the extent or depth of the abuse or neglect. Unlike physical abuse, CEN is difficult to notice. My parents were not emotionally equipped or qualified for the job of raising a child. They didn't neglect me through conscious choice, they had simply taken on a role without understanding how to perform it.

CEN is a covert form of neglect, often referred to as benign emotional neglect by health professionals. In most cases there is no question that parents love their child, providing all the necessities in terms of food, shelter and clothing. Some parents go above and beyond in terms of making sure their children have all they could want on a material level. Most parents will also make sure their child shows up on time at school and for any important appointments or activities. But some are poor at providing emotional support, love, compassion and connection. This is where the damage takes place, usually without the parent having any idea that their behaviour is inflicting untold pain that will last long into the adult life of their child.

If you were to call out a parent who fails to provide adequate emotional support and tell them that their behaviour is emotional neglect, they would either be horrified or, more likely, try to defend their behaviour. However, I want to really emphasize the point that there is rarely any question that the parent doesn't love their child. In most cases they were simply grossly underqualified for the role that they have taken on.

Another way of describing CEN is to think of it in terms of what the parents didn't do, as opposed to what they did do. It is very often the case that CEN occurs through a lack of emotional support, bonding or connection rather than it being a case of the parent taking intentional action or carrying out a harmful act on purpose.

When parents withhold emotional support and connection it leaves a child deficient and devoid of the ability to fully experience and express their feelings, or handle emotions in a healthy manner. Because this neglect is covert, not overt, while the child knows there is something wrong, they can't pinpoint exactly what it is. As adults, they may seek out unhealthy coping mechanisms, such as addictions, as an anaesthetic to numb a constant, unexplainable internal pain.

Emotional neglect is a ghost, rarely seen or spoken about, that haunts us as we move into adulthood. Thankfully more and more people are using resources like this one to work out exactly what is going on, and with this awareness comes the gift of healing. Awareness gives us the gift of clear sight; when we understand what is going on we become able to see the enemy with complete clarity. The ghosts are no longer invisible or hidden and the more work we do, the less hiding places the enemy has.

Children of emotionally neglectful parents believe that their feelings are unimportant and, because of the way their parents interact with them, they can also convince themselves that they must be to blame and are, therefore, a bad person. Children don't have the ability to process information and behaviour patterns in the same way as adults, yet they still need to make sense of what is going on. With the wrong kind of parenting signals they will end up deciding they must be the one who is in the wrong and must, therefore, be flawed or 'bad'. This can lead to serious issues with self-esteem and their sense of worthiness.

Children need to find a way of coping with neglectful parents, so they will often suppress the feelings they don't feel safe expressing and keep them deep within. They may erect an emotional brick wall to stop anyone getting in, and anything getting out. This can serve them well when they are dealing with emotionally immature parents but, as they move into adulthood, the internal wall that blocks emotional connection causes problems with relationships and their ability to form meaningful, healthy bonds with people.

Putting up an emotional defence barrier causes children to 'translate' suppressed feelings and emotions, this in turn can create much greater problems. For example, a child who pushes away feelings of anger may find that, over time, the feelings translate into severe anxiety which may persist throughout their adult life.

Although CEN is mostly the result of our parents' behaviour, there are cases where other family members, siblings, older friends and acquaintances, or figures of authority, such as a teacher or group leader, have caused similar issues. Keep an open mind as you read this book and notice what comes up as you consider your own experiences. I mostly refer to CEN in the context of parents for ease of reference.

Early in my exploration of CEN I started keeping a daily journal where I wrote down everything I noticed in terms of my mood, thoughts and emotions. It served me very well and allowed me to get things out of my head and down on to paper. I found that I was able to get a different perspective on my discomfort when I wrote it out and thoughts or emotions that felt incredibly painful seemed to weaken as the ink dried on the paper in front of me. I would encourage you to journal each day as you move through this process. It is a powerful and cathartic tool on the path to healing.

In order to give you more insight and clarity into CEN, below are some examples of emotionally neglectful parenting that will help you identify with situations where parents have failed to meet the emotional needs of their child. This is far from being a comprehensive list, but my hope is that this will give you a clear picture of what an emotionally absent parent looks like.

## Lack of acknowledgement

Kelly's mother didn't acknowledge any of her achievements at school, even though she was achieving high grades and being selected for sports teams. No matter what she did her mother didn't notice: she missed parent and teacher meetings, school performances and plays, and would be absent from sports events that Kelly was taking part in. On the rare occasion Kelly's mother did make an appearance she would shame, criticize or embarrass her in front of the other children.

Kelly was left feeling that she was never good enough, despite constantly striving to impress people. This played out into adulthood where she built a successful career as a lawyer but struggled with self-esteem and intimacy in her relationships.

## Making a drama

Maisie falls from the bike she has been riding outside her house. As she cries out her father shouts at her: 'Pull yourself together and stop making such a fuss.' As Maisie runs towards her house where her father is standing in the doorway she hears: 'Don't be such a cry baby; it doesn't hurt that much.' Her father then inspects the damage to the bike and quickly attempts to move the drama into the house to avoid attention from the neighbours. He fails to give any attention to the scrapes and bruises on his daughter's arms and legs.

As she gets older Maisie develops a sense that she is not worthy of other people's affection, she feels like she is a pain to be around and would be better off alone. She constantly apologizes, even when she has done nothing wrong, and struggles with a lack of self-worth.

## Denying feelings

Richard felt sad and hurt after he was told off by his teacher for talking in class earlier in the day. It was actually his friend who had been talking, but he was the one who got in trouble. He feels upset that the teacher did not believe his version of events, especially as his friend refused to tell the truth. When Richard returns home and tells his mother how he feels she says, 'Don't be so silly, there's nothing to be sad about, just forget about it.' She denies his feelings and cuts off the conversation without further discussion. Similar belittlement happens on countless occasions throughout his childhood.

As the years go by Richard struggles with a lack of confidence when it comes to expressing himself, especially around women. He struggles with addictive behaviour and is unable to acknowledge the emotions he has spent years suppressing. He feels empty inside.

## Not noticed

Mary had been bullied at school one day and returned home feeling upset, sad and hurt. Her father failed to notice that anything was wrong, despite the fact that her body language and sullen demeanour clearly conveyed the message. Instead, he carried on with his day. Mary went to her bedroom alone to cope with her emotions herself, a pattern that repeated itself throughout her childhood.

Over time Mary becomes avoidant of sharing her feelings and withdraws, she experiences severe anxiety as she internalizes her worries and, later struggles to hold down relationships. People tell her she is distant and lacks empathy.

## Unfair treatment

Seven year-old Paul tripped and fell over a display rack in a busy department store. He began to cry and a few of the other shoppers stopped to watch the commotion. Instead of soothing her son, Paul's mother yanked him by the arm and scolded him for causing a scene in public. Paul felt shame for having an accident.

As on many similar occasions, he had no opportunity to express his emotions and, over time, he develops anxiety along with a deep feeling that no matter what he does, he is always to blame.

## Conditional love

Jack played football for his school team with the support and encouragement of his father, who showered him with love and compliments when he performed well on the football field, but was distant and emotionally absent when they were away from the game. Jack feared that if he decided he no longer wanted to play football he would face a severe negative reaction from his father. The love and praise he received had become conditional on him doing well on the football field.

As he grows, Jack starts to believe that love comes with strings attached. This affects his adult relationships and causes him to struggle with intimacy, trust and emotional connection. Jack feels he is not good enough and that nobody can love him simply for who he is. He struggles with low self-esteem and over-work as he strives to be the best at everything he does in an attempt to gain the approval he never received in childhood.

## Never good enough

Catherine brought home her school report card with seven A and two B grades. Most parents would be delighted at such a wonderful performance, but Catherine's were clear that the results were simply not good enough and that they believed she could do better. Some of Catherine's friends achieved much worse results than her and later she heard them talking about how their parents celebrated their success; one friend was taken out for dinner as a reward.

In adulthood Catherine never feels 'good enough'. She finds herself constantly seeking approval and acknowledgement. This causes problems with friendships and relationships and Catherine often feels lonely and empty inside.

## Bringing herself up

Annie's parents were mostly absent from her life when she was growing up, due to their busy careers. She became self-sufficient at a young age and prepared her own meals, while babysitting her younger sister and taking care of the household chores. She learned that if she was to survive then she had to parent herself most of the time, because nobody else was going to do it.

Annie becomes an adult well before her time and later in life becomes incredibly self-sufficient. While this can be a useful trait it also causes her to struggle with emotional connection and intimacy. Annie also finds it hard to trust and keeps herself guarded around other people.

## Abandoned

Andy went to the cinema in the evening with his friends. The movie finished late and he asked his father to pick him up for a ride home. After saying goodbye to his friends, Andy waited for his father in the dark, empty car park, but his father didn't come. He stood alone in the car park, scared in the darkness. His father had forgotten. He would have to find his own way home.

These types of episodes can seem minor to parents, and perhaps if they only happen once, then they are, but when they recur throughout childhood they can cause real abandonment issues for the child who has been forgotten.

In later life Andy faces challenges in situations where he senses that he has been abandoned or forgotten.

## Rejected

A couple divorced when their daughter Kimberley was still a toddler. She stayed with her mother and her father left the family home. As the years passed, Kimberley rarely saw her father, and on the handful of occasions he did arrange to pay her a visit, he showed up late or didn't bother to turn up at all. This left her feeling let down and upset, yet Kimberley's mother spoke highly of this man who seems totally disinterested in her. She continued to paint a picture of him as the perfect father.

Kimberley's mother didn't recognize the harm of these infrequent and erratic visits. She failed to put any boundaries in place to protect her daughter from the damage this man was causing by coming and going as and when he pleased.

In later life Kimberley struggles to form healthy, balanced relationships with men and experiences issues with her sense of worth. She always expects disappointment, which leaves her with a negative outlook on life and low moods.

## Other examples

Emotional neglect comes in many forms and these are just some of the most common examples. The following list provides further parenting styles that are likely to cause issues with CEN.

- Absent boundaries – failure to set and enforce appropriate rules
- Favouritism – towards siblings or other family members
- Fear of anger – discomfort and disapproval around a child who expresses anger
- Avoidance – of uncomfortable topics that could cause conflict or heightened emotions

- Ignoring – a child's mistake and allowing them to work life out for themselves
- Casting a shadow – over a child so they believe their parent is more important and that their needs take priority over their son or daughter's.

## CEN is subtle

These scenarios should provide you with some common examples of CEN. However, they don't come anywhere close to covering the vast range of behaviours that can cause a child serious issues later in life. CEN can be even more subtle than the examples given here, and parents can unknowingly project their own stress or negative emotions on to their children in ways that even an outside observer may struggle to notice.

For example, a father who has a busy career may return home from work with thoughts of business weighing heavily on his mind; when his daughter attempts to speak to him, she finds that he is not giving her any attention and is instead talking to her mother about his work worries. She feels ignored, unheard and unwanted. This behaviour is repeated and reinforced, in later life it could translate into her developing a strong desire to feel noticed and accepted by other people, alongside issues with her sense of worthiness and self-esteem.

Another example might be a busy mother with three young children who is feeling stressed after looking after them all day without having a moment to herself. When she finally gets a chance to relax for a few minutes her five-year-old son comes into the room and asks her to play a game with him. Instead of responding in a clear, calm and appropriate manner she rolls her eyes, sighs and snaps at him out of frustration. 'Can't you see I'm trying to relax?' she snaps. Her young son is unable to make sense of her reaction and feels that he must be to blame in some way. Continued over time, this behaviour can translate into feelings of him not being 'good enough' in adulthood, along with a strong desire to gain approval from other people. It may also cause issues with expressing emotions and feelings, and problems in relationships.

You may be a parent yourself and might have found yourself feeling concerned about your relationship with your own children as you read some of these examples. If so, don't panic, as your own understanding and awareness expands, so will your ability to accept any flaws and make changes to the way you parent. You can use everything you learn in this book to help you become the very best parent you can be.

I also think it is important to make it clear that an isolated incident along the lines of the behaviour I have described in these examples is unlikely to be enough to cause severe CEN. It is a pattern of parental behaviour repeated over an extended period of time that causes the real problems.

Now you understand what Childhood Emotional Neglect looks like, let's take a look at trauma and abuse before we explore how to tell if you have been affected.

# Trauma and abuse

Trauma and abuse are far more obvious than the invisible poison of CEN, involving actions that may be carried out with intent, unlike emotional neglect, which is usually unintentional. Many of the people I work with in my role as a sobriety coach have experienced a combination of CEN and trauma. In some cases overt trauma or abuse was inflicted by someone other than parents, and in others it was one or both of the parents who left their child traumatized.

Research has shown that trauma, abuse and neglect of children under the age of six can have the most profound impact in later life, stifling their ability to form secure attachments, express emotions and feelings, and cultivate a healthy sense of self-worth. Babies and toddlers discover emotions and feelings which develop through early exploration of communication. Babies start to express themselves and understand how others are feeling by beginning to interpret expressions, sounds, words, body language and, of course, behaviour.

At this early stage, a child's brain is like a computer that is being programmed with core values and beliefs. The impact of neglect, abuse and trauma at this stage can be profound, and prevent the formation of healthy and logical beliefs. Instead, defensive beliefs based around an inbuilt need to self-soothe, self-protect and avoid pain associated with emotional discomfort become hardwired. This is not to say that the impact of neglect, trauma and abuse in later life are not profound, but the older the child, the more ability they have to process and understand a situation. In many cases, the damage is done by the age of six and the toxic behaviour continues for many years beyond, often until the child becomes an adult or until such time as they learn how to address the problems and set suitable boundaries.

Children who have suffered CEN at an early age are more susceptible to physical abuse, with the effects of the neglect making them more vulnerable to an abusive person.

Here are the most common types of trauma and abuse.

## Early childhood trauma

Early childhood trauma refers to traumatic experiences that happen to infants and toddlers under the age of six. Young children are generally unable to express their feelings in a threatening or stressful dangerous situation, and adults mistakenly believe that their age prevents them being impacted by a traumatic episode happening around them.

Evidence shows that young children are severely affected by trauma and the threat of danger, either to themselves, their parents or carers. These symptoms of trauma are obviously displayed in later life, and they have been well-researched and documented.

Early childhood trauma covers a broad range of events that might have occurred before the age of six. These could include sexual abuse, violence, the loss of a parent, natural disasters or any other episodes that might lead to the child feeling a sense of threat to their safety, or exceptionally heightened stress levels.

# Bullying

Bullying often takes place in a school or educational environment and involves the use of violence, aggression, threats, coercion or abuse to intimidate, dominate and exert control over someone.

The perpetrator will often repeat the behaviour. Sometimes the bullying is carried out by one person, sometimes by a group. It is incredibly traumatic for the person being bullied; they feel helpless, believing they are weak for this to be happening to them.

Those who have been bullied often experience social, emotional and behavioural problems in later life. In some cases they may become bullies themselves as a defence strategy against any future episodes of the same nature and to feel a sense of safety, importance and self-worth.

# Physical abuse

Physical abuse can come in many different forms and is one of the most common types of childhood trauma. Not all physical abuse is intentional, but it is almost always traumatic for the victim.

Any act that results in someone committing physical injury to a child can be broadly defined as physical abuse or potentially traumatic, this can range from injuries that leave marks or bruises through to broken bones. Regardless of whether it is intentional or not, the impact of physical abuse on a child is devastating, especially when the perpetrator is a trusted and loved parent or caregiver. In later life the child may become emotionally detached and struggle with problems around anger, self-esteem and depression.

# Domestic violence

Domestic violence trauma happens when children witness their parents or caregivers inflicting or threatening violence on each other. Children are often a silent casualty of this type of trauma and older children may cope by hiding when these episodes occur. They find themselves living in a state of fear and may end up directly or indirectly injured as a result of domestic violence. They are also more likely to experience emotional neglect. The resulting trauma of witnessing this distressing behaviour can lead to a range of mental health related issues in later life.

If you are reading this and fear you are in an abusive or violent relationship, or your domestic circumstances are unsafe, please refer to the resources at the back of this book for sources of help and support.

# Medical trauma

Medical trauma relates to the responses that children have to medical procedures, frightening experiences of treatment, or the pain of a severe illness or injury. This type of trauma can be specific to one episode, or related to multiple medical events. Medical trauma is often tied to the child's own subjective experience of the event, as opposed to the severity of a procedure or treatment, and can cause significant stress and anxiety that can remain with the child as they move into adulthood.

If you have your own children who fear medical treatment, please refer to the resources at the back of this book for recommendations of how to help them.

# Sexual abuse

Sexual abuse happens when an adult, or another child obtains sexual gratification by using a child. Sexual abuse can take the form of physical or non-physical behaviour (such as voyeurism) and it may also include grooming and coercion to make the child believe that the abuse is normal and acceptable behaviour.

Children who have suffered sexual abuse can be affected in many different ways and display a range of behavioural and emotional characteristics that are common in many types of trauma. One of the most common impacts of sexual abuse in adulthood is that individuals find themselves struggling to form intimate relationships, and have problems trusting people enough to allow them to get close.

# Grief-related trauma

Children are resilient and will often cope well and adjust after the death of a loved one. However, a sudden unexpected loss or a death that had been expected for some time, for example due to a long illness, can leave a child severely traumatized.

Children who have been affected by grief-related trauma can experience a wide range of symptoms from withdrawal and feelings of numbness, through to behavioural, social and emotional problems.

# Disasters and catastrophes

The fear of a disaster or the experience of being caught up in one can cause a child serious trauma. Natural disasters might include earthquakes, tornados, pandemics, tsunamis, wildfires or droughts. Non-natural disasters, such as being involved in a car accident or experiencing a long period trapped in a lift or on an underground train, can cause similar feelings of fear and panic to those that would be experienced in a natural disaster.

Thankfully these types of events are rare. However the trauma can cause a wide range of problems, especially if there has also been damage or loss caused to the family due to the event – losing a family home, for example, or a loved one being injured.

You may have identified with some of the above from your own experiences. Regardless of the type of neglect, trauma or abuse you might have experienced, I want you to know that you can move through this, and you can heal. So continue reading and keep learning. In the next chapter we will look at the key signs to help you identify whether neglect and trauma are impacting you in adulthood.

# 2 | How do you know if you have been affected?

One of the biggest challenges faced by adults who have suffered trauma, neglect or abuse in childhood is that we often don't understand what is wrong with us. We feel somehow different to other people, or empty inside, but we are unable to understand or identify exactly where the feelings are coming from, or what is causing them.

I went to doctors, hypnotherapists and counsellors to try and address my problems, because I believed I was suffering from depression and anxiety. The doctors were quick to offer me medication and the counsellors nodded their heads, mirrored my words and empathized with me. Nobody had the answers I needed, perhaps because I didn't know what was wrong.

## The signs of trauma, abuse and neglect

So, what are the signs that an adult has been affected by childhood emotional neglect, trauma or abuse?

The list of 50 questions that follows are common traits displayed in adulthood where there has been CEN, trauma or abuse in childhood. It is by no means a comprehensive list and it has been designed to provide you with a guide rather than any kind of diagnosis. Keep a note of how many apply to you as you read through the list.

1. You have a sense that something is wrong, but you don't know what it is.
2. You have a feeling that you are hollow inside, that you are empty or have a void within you.
3. People tell you that you have a lack of empathy.
4. You react badly to rejection.
5. You often feel sad, unhappy or down for no obvious reason.
6. You have trouble understanding or feeling your emotions.
7. You would describe yourself as highly sensitive.
8. You struggle to understand people's expectations of you and your own expectations of yourself.
9. You find it hard to motivate yourself.
10. You struggle with self-discipline.
11. You mostly hide how you really feel.

12. You are a people-pleaser and have difficulty saying 'no'.
13. You struggle to maintain meaningful friendships.
14. You feel that your happiness is dependent on other people.
15. You experience unpredictable moods or mood-swings.
16. You experience a feeling of helplessness.
17. You have been told you are needy, possessive or clingy.
18. You feel like a fake or a fraud.
19. You feel uncomfortable when someone pays you a sincere compliment.
20. You experience regular negative internal self-talk.
21. You often judge yourself more harshly than you judge other people.
22. You prefer the company of animals to the company of other people.
23. You find it hard to deal with people in authority positions.
24. You have had problems with relationships and intimacy.
25. You constantly feel that your life could be much better.
26. You are rarely fully 'present' in the current moment.
27. You are mostly negative, even when you try not to be.
28. You can have aggressive or angry outbursts.
29. You have irrational emotional responses to certain situations, people or events.
30. You engage in addictive behaviour – alcohol, drugs, gambling, online shopping, food, sex, porn, work, exercise.
31. You develop attractions to, or obsessions with, people who are unavailable.
32. You have a hyperactive or restless nature that feels like you are always 'on the go'.
33. You react badly to any form of criticism.
34. Small talk makes you feel uncomfortable or awkward.
35. You are much more comfortable in the company of one gender, for example males only or females only.
36. You have low self-esteem or self-worth – this can include a feeling of not being 'good enough'.
37. You have a sense of being numb to your feelings.
38. You talk over people or interrupt them before they have finished speaking.
39. Being touched can make you uncomfortable, for example being hugged.
40. You have an expectation of perfectionism.
41. You have a sense that you are more important and entitled than other people, or you feel that you are inferior to other people.
42. You are easily emotionally overwhelmed.
43. You can easily become angry with yourself.

44. You feel that things mostly go wrong for you and expect disappointment.
45. You have difficulty interpreting the emotions and expectations of other people, as well as your own.
46. You struggle to express your emotions and feelings.
47. You rarely experience true joy and happiness.
48. You have trouble being able to relax.
49. You find it difficult to become still, reflective, calm and silent.
50. You struggle reaching out for help when you need it.

If you identified with any of the symptoms, characteristics or behaviour traits in the list then I strongly recommend that you continue reading through this book – there is a likelihood you have some work to do in order to heal the issues from your childhood that have affected you as an adult.

We will look at the specifics of trauma in more detail later, but the following questions will allow you to gain further understanding as to whether you have symptoms of past trauma:

- Can you recall past events or experiences that caused you severe stress or fear?
- Have you experienced disturbing nightmares, flashbacks or daydreams about the events?
- Do you have trouble getting a good night's sleep?
- Are you aware that you have a lot of uncomfortable feelings about past events that you have never dealt with?
- Do you feel strong emotions when something reminds you of past events?
- Do you avoid people, places, objects or situations that remind you of past events?
- Do you feel distant or isolated from other people?
- Are you easily irritated or do you experience angry outbursts?
- Do you struggle with negative thoughts about yourself and your life?
- Do you struggle to concentrate?
- Do you feel numbness about past events?
- Do you avoid talking about past events?
- Do you sometimes feel as though past events didn't really happen?
- Do you struggle with strong negative emotions such as shame, anger, guilt, hopelessness?
- Do you experience physical discomfort such as tension, increased heart rate, sweating, or upset stomach?
- Do you scare easily and have a heightened sense that danger is always close by?

These questions are designed as a simple guide only and should not be taken as any kind of formal assessment for trauma. However, if you found yourself answering mostly 'yes', there is a good chance that you have been experiencing symptoms of past trauma and I am pleased that you have picked up this book and are doing something proactive about it. Well done.

Don't be dismayed if you have identified a number of the traits on these lists. Try to see this instead as a wonderful gift. You have uncovered something incredibly important and you can begin to take the necessary steps to heal. Imagine if you had never explored what was going on, and continued living in a world of pain and suffering for the rest of your life.

Research has shown that the way our parents treat us in childhood shapes the way that we treat ourselves in adulthood. Now you have clarity and awareness you are in a position to reclaim the power, and learn what steps you need to take in order to heal.

Throughout the book I will provide you with the support, tools and clear strategies that will enable you to overcome emotional neglect and trauma once and for all. Soon you will be learning how to get rid of these invisible demons in order to reconnect with the true and authentic version of yourself. If you can adopt a positive mindset about this experience and approach it with a sense of excitement and curiosity, you may well find that you enjoy the process.

What we expect is very often what we get; try and maintain an open mind and a positive outlook. It will set you up for long-term success. On my journey to sobriety I discovered that it was very similar to learning a new skill, and it took practice, commitment and discipline. There were bumps in the road and a few setbacks along the way, but I stuck with it, learning and growing until I achieved my goal. Healing from CEN is very similar, don't criticize yourself if you experience setbacks, use them to learn and grow stronger, explore what the experience is telling you and what you can do differently in the future.

I mentioned the importance of keeping a journal as you go forward. An important part of the healing process involves becoming more aware and paying attention to your behaviour, feelings, emotions and thoughts. You can use your journal to gather data about yourself. Try to avoid becoming judgemental or self-critical, and instead approach the whole process with an observational and inquisitive eye. Imagine that you are an outsider looking at your life from a distance. Observe what you see without emotion, judgement or fear. Notice what is going on and begin paying attention as you start to explore who you really are.

Write an entry in your journal right now to describe what feelings you noticed as you answered the 50 questions about the adult traits of trauma and neglect.

The key to finding complete freedom from CEN, trauma and abuse is learning to love yourself just the way you are, working on becoming authentic, managing your emotions and feeling your feelings without suppressing them, judging yourself or reacting in a negative manner. When I embarked on this process I had no idea how to start 'feeling a feeling' or 'being authentic', but over time and with practice – just like learning a new skill – it began to happen.

Let's continue moving down the road to recovery with an open-hearted presence and awareness. In the next chapter we will look at some examples of how different types of CEN, trauma and abuse influence our behaviour in adulthood.

# 3 | How do neglect and trauma impact our adult lives?

The impact of Childhood Emotional Neglect and trauma can influence almost every area of our adult lives. I experienced issues with relationships, parenting, friendships, socializing and work. On top of this, I had horrendous anxiety and felt depressed most of the time. There were even occasions where I had thoughts about whether ending my life would be the best option to stop the excruciating pain I was feeling.

*If you ever experience thoughts about suicide please reach out for help.* No matter how tough it may seem in that moment, things will get better. You may not believe it, or be able to see it now, but please take it from me, don't waste a beautiful life – especially as you haven't yet experienced what it is like to become happy and at peace by moving through issues from the past. There is a wealth of support available for anyone experiencing thoughts about suicide, and you can find more details in the Resources section at the back of this book.

## Emotional shutdown

One of the biggest issues to impact adults who have experienced CEN or trauma is 'emotional shutdown'. It caused me to become disconnected from my feelings as I repressed my emotions instead of expressing them in a healthy way.

Throughout my childhood my mother was critical of me; on occasion she would also shame me in front of other people, traits that she still possesses. I can see myself as a child, sitting at the kitchen table, having only eaten a few mouthfuls of the dinner she cooked for me – I am full and I don't want the rest. 'For God's sake, child! I don't know why I bother giving you food, it is wasted on you. The dog would be more grateful than you are,' my mother snarls at me through gritted teeth. She snatches the plate away as food slides over the edge and spills on to the floor. I can see rage in her eyes. I don't want her to be angry with me so I stay quiet and leave the table. I head back to my bedroom and spend the rest of the evening on my own.

I was angry and scared, but I didn't express my feelings because I feared the consequences. Instead I pushed them away so I didn't have to feel them and, over time, I became numb and unconscious to the emotions. As a child, this strategy might be the only option available when we are faced with angry, critical, overbearing, untrustworthy or unreasonable adults. In many cases we have no choice but to keep our mouths shut and to numb ourselves to any negative emotions we are feeling.

The problem with repressing our emotions is that over time, as we continue to avoid what we are feeling, we end up accumulating more and more trauma. Because we have failed to express our feelings, the trauma silently grows within our minds and bodies. As we continue to push down our emotions we learn and adapt to the environment we have found ourselves in. We often create an invisible safety forcefield to protect ourselves from further emotional pain. This defensive barrier hampers us as we become older as it prevents us from being able to release our feelings in a healthy manner. It can also stop us forming authentic emotional connections with other people.

The most commonly repressed emotions are anger, sadness, shame, fear and envy. Let's imagine each of those individual repressed emotions as if it were a house brick. Every time an emotion is pushed down deep within us we add another brick to our wall of defences. Over time the wall grows higher and heavier, and eventually it grows so big that nobody can get through it, nothing can get in and nothing can get out.

The defence strategy that we were forced to use in childhood can cause numerous problems as we become adults, for example, as it causes us to become emotionally unavailable in intimate relationships. The system that protected us as children ends up working against us as we remain stuck behind a wall of suffering.

We expend huge amounts of energy fighting our emotions, doing all we can to avoid experiencing our feelings. It is common for adults who have repressed their emotions to seek out unhealthy coping mechanisms to distract and keep themselves busy. The following is a list of behaviours that adults may adopt in an attempt to avoid their emotions:

- Acting compulsively
- Tendency to develop addictions
- Struggling to feel joy and happiness
- Having an expectation that things will go wrong
- Being overly trusting and missing obvious warning signs
- Feeling a strong need to be in control
- Feeling as though people take advantage of them
- Becoming easily embarrassed or humiliated
- Feeling superior (or inferior) to other people
- Struggling to say 'no', even when they want to
- Having a need for perfectionism
- Thinking about feelings instead of fully feeling them

- Struggling to express their anger, or experience angry outbursts
- Being afraid of confrontation or conflict
- Struggling to accept or believe compliments from others
- Feeling like they are constantly 'on the go'
- Struggling in situations where they need to be silent or sit still for long periods
- Finding themselves very distressed by rejection
- Becoming overwhelmed by worry over minor problems
- Experiencing problems with intimacy
- Becoming isolated and withdrawn, especially after conflict or rejection
- Behaving in similar ways to their parents
- Becoming involved in co-dependent relationships
- Avoiding speaking about their wants and needs
- Feeling depressed and anxious
- Having low self-esteem and a lack of true-self-worth
- Finding it difficult to be vulnerable
- Feeling numb inside, without understanding why.

These behaviours can threaten relationships, impact social lives and damage careers. They can also trigger depression and anxiety along with a number of other serious mental and physical health problems.

Can you identify with any of the traits described above? If you are using a journal, take some time to notice how your own childhood experiences have shaped you as an adult. Can you think of specific examples or recurring patterns of behaviour that link back to events from your past? Writing out a list of any behaviours that link back to your past is incredibly useful – by getting them down in your journal you will be able to explore each of them in more depth.

As always in this process, please approach this task with a sense of curiosity, without judgement of yourself or others, and with nothing more than a perspective of observation. If you experience any uncomfortable emotions or feelings as you write, take 10 to 15 minutes' 'time out' before returning and investigating the feelings you experienced, as well as the original behaviours you are looking at in more detail.

This process will allow you to begin to tune in to yourself and start taking down the emotional brick wall that you have erected as a defence mechanism. The wall probably served you well as a child, but as an adult it is holding you back from being the true version of yourself. As you continue working through this book you might notice that your wall is starting to come down, brick by brick. Be gentle with yourself, don't rush the process and come back to any chapters where you feel like the information may not have stuck and you need a refresher.

Be proactive. Start to notice what is going on inside yourself, whether negative or positive feelings, or even a sense of rage, fear or pain. Paying attention to your emotions and feelings is fundamental to removing the bricks in your emotional wall and moving towards a place of healing.

If you don't feel comfortable looking at events from your past, return to this exercise when you feel ready. There is no rush, and it is important that you feel strong enough to cope with whatever comes up as you start to explore.

# Label your feelings

An excellent strategy is to begin labelling your feelings and emotions as soon as you notice them. An 'emotion wheel' can make it easier to identify exactly what you are feeling – for one example of an emotion wheel, visit <www.healthline. com/health/emotion-wheel#plutchik-wheel>. Draw or print out a copy of the wheel and keep it somewhere that you can easily get to it, or save it to your smartphone. Get used to applying a single label or name to each and every feeling you experience as it arises. This will help you to cultivate your internal awareness and, over time, to fully reconnect with your feelings.

An alternative to the emotion wheel are 'feelings cards', which look like a deck of playing cards with each one having the name of a feeling on it. You can use them to clearly label whatever you feel in any given moment.

From here onwards, if you find yourself experiencing strong or overwhelming emotions at any point, take some time out if you need it and make a note of the exact feelings that are with you. For example, if you are feeling extreme anger, there is no benefit or positive outcome in shouting or becoming confrontational. Instead, practise calmly verbalizing how you feel by simply naming the emotion. Do this alone to start with. Try practising in a mirror. Then, as you go forward, try to express yourself to others in the same calm manner.

You don't need to do anything more than to calmly say 'that made me feel really angry'. Say it slowly, notice your tone, savour the words as they come out of your mouth, and know that this is enough to express the emotion within. Pay attention to how you feel before, during and after expressing yourself.

In some cases, you may need to take specific action to put certain situations right. If you feel that some form of positive action is necessary, such as putting a boundary in place or apologizing to someone, then do this at a time that feels right to you. Don't rush into it. Ensure you take the time to think carefully before you act and consider the consequences of any action that you might be thinking of taking.

The more you get used to the practice of naming and labelling your feelings and emotions as you experience them, the more your internal brick wall of emotional defence will start to come down. Maybe you could start practising this right now? How do you feel at this moment? Can you express it calmly by labelling the feeling?

Later, we will look in more depth at how to express your feelings to other people, along with specific strategies that you can use for dealing with uncomfortable emotions. For now, simply try and create a new habit of naming and labelling every feeling you experience and start noticing the difference it makes to your level of self-awareness.

Be aware that everything passes. Begin to notice that nothing, including the emotions you feel, lasts forever. Our very existence, everything we experience and everything we know is ever-changing and impermanent. Allow the knowledge of impermanence to see you through any challenging periods. If you can find the strength to sit with discomfort and notice that it always weakens before passing, it will allow you to become stronger when another episode arises.

# Handling uncomfortable thoughts

We have between 60,000 and 80,000 thoughts every single day; our minds are incredibly busy places. Most are transient and we do not pay attention to them. However, when you have experienced CEN or suffered past trauma, you can find yourself triggered by certain thoughts which send you spiralling into the discomfort of emotional overwhelm.

It is almost impossible to control our thoughts. They are similar to a fast-flowing river of chatter in our minds and there is no way of hitting pause and stopping the powerful current. We have no choice but to observe the river, but we can do this from the safety of the riverbank instead of getting into the water and being washed away. Just because we have a thought, we do not have to act on it, or react to it. We can learn to observe it with a sense of curiosity and allow it to pass if we feel that it isn't going to serve us.

As well as visualizing your thoughts as a fast-flowing river, you can view them as trains passing through a busy station: thousands come through each day, some are noisy, some are quiet, others are elegant and some are downright ugly. Your job, as the manager of the station, is to simply sit in your control room, to observe the trains as they come and go and allow them to pass through without judgement or reaction. Don't board any of the trains or get actively involved with anything that will cause you suffering, simply watch them arrive and watch them leave . . . they always leave.

# A quick mindfulness exercise

Here is a mindfulness technique to handle challenging thoughts that refuse to leave quickly.

**Sit with your eyes closed and breathe slowly in and out through your nose. As you breathe, anchor your attention to your breath and follow it as it flows in,**

**and then out. Once you are settled and begin to feel a sense of calm, start to visualize any challenging thoughts as clouds floating across a clear blue sky.**

**Know that all things pass, just like clouds in the sky. As you sit calmly in stillness, observe the clouds as they move across the sky and watch them fade away into the distance.**

If you attempt this exercise and find that your mind is full of chatter or you struggle to concentrate, simply acknowledge the thoughts that have come to mind, pull your attention back to your breath and observe your 'thought clouds' in the sky. Sometimes I am pulled away by thoughts and have to return to the anchor of my breath over and over. I don't allow myself to become frustrated and I accept whatever comes up exactly as it is.

I usually spend around ten minutes on this exercise and find that it helps to significantly weaken uncomfortable thoughts. It can also help to say the word 'thought' as and when each one arises. This allows you to acknowledge any thoughts without judgement, before allowing them to pass.

Later, we will look at more techniques for dealing with uncomfortable thoughts, feelings and emotions as well as strategies for expressing them in a healthy way. For now, practise noticing and naming your feelings and paying attention to what is going on within you. If you struggle with unwelcome thoughts, try experimenting with these tactics to help yourself get back in control.

# 4 | Unpackaging trauma

Healing from traumatic events that happened during our childhood can feel like a real challenge. It can be easy to convince ourselves that we have been damaged beyond repair and that there is no possibility of ever being happy.

Instead of dwelling on negative thoughts, begin to consider how your life might look without the suffering, and focus on becoming unstuck as a goal towards which you are steadily working. The extent of your trauma will often depend on the amount of time and work required to experience positive changes. It doesn't matter how long it takes to heal, the important thing is to keep moving forward.

Take things slowly, pace yourself and avoid the urge to rush in as you may find that things you have read don't stick. Try to gently unpackage your trauma, take the time to reflect on what you read in this book and what you write in your accompanying journal. Ensure you refresh yourself on any chapters that don't provide you with a breakthrough the first time you read them. You might want to consider working methodically on one chapter each day and, when you reach the end of the book, you can revisit anything that you feel needs more exploration.

Your goal, ultimately, is to become free from trauma. If that seems like an overwhelming or impossible task, try breaking this down into smaller, more achievable objectives.

Picture, for example, the seemingly huge goal of buying a new house. Breaking the process down into smaller goals might work as follows:

*First goal*: Work out how much you can afford and create a savings plan, then start saving.

*Second goal*: Research the areas you may want to live in and make a shortlist.

*Third goal*: Find out what finance is available and make enquiries.

*Fourth goal*: Finalize an area and specific neighbourhood.

*Fifth goal*: Research properties and make a shortlist, then organize viewings.

*Sixth goal*: Make a decision on a suitable property and begin negotiating the best deal.

*Seventh goal*: Once the offer is agreed, complete legal process and purchase.

*Eighth goal*: Finalize the purchase and move in.

Breaking down goals that feel like a big challenge into several smaller ones helps us to feel more motivated, and to notice progress on our path to healing. You can create your own set of goals based on the chapters you have already read in the book and you can add to them as you continue to read more.

Use your journal to set goals, stay on track, make notes and reflect on your progress.

# So what exactly is trauma?

We experience trauma in childhood when we believe that we are in severe danger, feel threatened, are extremely frightened or emotionally overwhelmed by a situation we are in. As we saw in Chapter 1, trauma can come in many different forms including physical violence, verbal abuse, sexual abuse, natural disasters, accidents, bullying, witnessing domestic violence, psychological abuse, the loss of a loved one and serious illnesses or injuries.

Trauma can be a one-off episode or it can be repeated over time, as is common with violence, verbal and sexual abuse. Our individual makeup determines our reaction to a traumatic event and different people will respond to the same event in different ways. Two children of the same age who encountered the same kind of trauma might respond very differently, despite living through the same experience.

There are three main types of trauma:

- **Acute trauma:** From a one-off, stressful, scary or dangerous event.
- **Chronic trauma:** From repeated exposure to highly stressful events, such as physical abuse, bullying or sexual abuse. These episodes are often carried out over a prolonged period of time.
- **Complex trauma:** from being exposed to multiple traumatic events.

You may not know for certain whether you have experienced past trauma; you might find that episodes that seemed innocuous at the time have left you with deep wounds that have held you back later in life.

Keep an open mind as you continue reading and try not to become hung up on labelling yourself. Labels can serve a purpose, but I have found them to become restrictive – if we begin labelling ourselves as 'victims' or 'survivors' it can point us towards a particular kind of mindset. Finish the book before you make any decisions that could define your perspective.

This process needs you to treat yourself with compassion, to be gentle with yourself as you learn to acknowledge and accept what happened. 'Acceptance' does not make what happened right, or okay, but it will allow you to move forward and let go of any desire to argue with the reality of the past.

You may have identified that you have traits associated with trauma or neglect when you answered the questions in Chapter 2. Keep in mind that without this awareness you would never be able to heal.

Some people can go on to develop symptoms of PTSD (Post-Traumatic Stress Disorder). This happens when trauma symptoms worsen over time and people find themselves avoiding thinking about the event, experiencing vivid flashbacks and nightmares and intentionally staying away from places, people or situations that might trigger painful memories.

It is estimated that 3 to 15 per cent of girls and 1 to 6 per cent of boys develop PTSD after a traumatic event. The majority of these children return to a normal state within a fairly short amount of time, whereas a minority may experience symptoms over the medium to longer term.

Traumatic events can impact children both mentally and physically, and studies have shown that trauma can affect brain development. Research has also found that the more extreme the trauma a child has been exposed to, the higher the risk of developing serious physical and mental health problems in later life. This is another reason not to avoid facing up to any past issues. We owe it to ourselves to work on our healing.

We all have unique stories from our past and they are part of who we are. We can't rewrite history and we can't argue with the reality of 'what is'. However, trauma does not have to define us. Now is your time to write a new and powerful story. Turn your 'victim' mentality into a 'victory' mindset that will change your life. Stop surviving – I want you to put the work in and thrive instead.

My past trauma and neglect left me feeling as though I could never be normal, whatever that means, and that I was very different from everyone else. If you have felt this way then I want you to know that you are good enough as you are, you are worthy, and you can find a happier, brighter and more peaceful life.

# Beginning to face trauma

Healing childhood trauma is tough. The trauma we experienced when we were young ends up shaping our adult life in many different ways. Our beliefs, behaviours, emotions and feelings are all affected and some people can also experience severe psychological disorders and physical health problems.

One of the biggest challenges to overcome with trauma is finding the strength to face up to it and making a personal commitment to continue our work. This means processing challenging emotions that can be attached to the trauma. For some people it is this fear of looking at the past which causes them to stay stuck.

Before you begin looking closer at past traumas, I want you to be mindful of 'retraumatizing' yourself. This can happen when we re-experience past traumatic events, either by recalling them in detail or by partaking in behaviours that are similar to the original trauma. There can be a risk of opening up old wounds from the past and reinforcing your inner child's emotional responses as a way of coping.

There are a number of ways that you can protect yourself from becoming retraumatized. Create a personal recovery plan that feels comfortable and manageable to you by incorporating any of the following suggestions that you find useful.

# How to avoid becoming retraumatized

## 1 Work at your own pace

It is important to work at a pace that feels comfortable to you. If you don't feel ready to look closer at past trauma right now, you can come back to it later when you are confident that you are equipped to do so. However, there is no avoiding the fact that we have to look into the past events at some point in order to make sense of them and break free.

I wrote this book in a way that will guide you through the six stages on the path to freedom. My belief is that if you follow all of the advice and put in the work you will notice some big positive changes. However, if anything makes you feel uncomfortable or upset, you can come back to it when you feel ready.

You hold the power of choice about how deeply you wish to go into your past and you can choose when and if you would like to do it. Only begin to explore your trauma when you feel ready – it might take you hours, days, weeks or even months to feel able to mentally return to your past and you should know that this is absolutely fine.

## 2 Stick to the facts

When you explore your past trauma it is crucial that you keep to the facts, instead of creating stories and casting judgements. You are simply looking to acknowledge what happened and accept it as reality, there is no need to go any further.

## 3 Avoid too much detail

As well as sticking to the facts, it is important to avoid retelling your story with gory details or vivid descriptive accounts of what happened. This can activate your brain and nervous system and impact the areas that have been affected already by deepening the traumatic wounds.

When I recalled the sexual abuse I suffered as a teenager I didn't go into the detail of what happened; it would serve no positive purpose. Instead, I became able to accept that it had happened, and understand how it had shaped me later in life.

## 4 Understand your triggers

If you can identify behaviours, thoughts, feelings, people, places, situations and environments that trigger an overwhelming emotional response in you, it is possible to take steps to protect yourself from becoming retraumatized. You can put healthy boundaries in place to keep yourself safe and gain a clear understanding of what makes you feel threatened. We will look closer at setting boundaries later in the book.

## 5 Relax yourself

When our nervous system becomes activated through triggers or retraumatization, the rational adult is replaced by the troubled child within. You can use techniques like mindfulness, breathing exercises and meditation to bring the adult back, and calm yourself down.

When we have experienced trauma, we often spend much of our time living in our heads and not enough time using the power of our body to relax or calm down. I will share some powerful techniques for managing difficult thoughts, feelings and emotions later in the book.

## 6 Put it somewhere safe

If you find yourself dwelling on your past trauma, try to put the trauma somewhere safe. Find somewhere suitable that would serve as a container for the trauma – a cabinet, shoebox, drawer or locked container, for example – then visualize an image that represents what you have been replaying in your mind. Once you have the image held in your mind, picture yourself putting it in the safe place you have chosen, so it is safely stored away.

Say out loud to yourself:

**'I give myself permission not to dwell on traumatic experiences unless I am actively working on healing them. I know where to find them.'**

## 7 Have help on hand

If you become overwhelmed with emotion you may find it helpful to have someone supportive on hand who you can contact to talk things through. This might be a trusted close friend, a family member, a therapist or a trauma support helpline (see Resources section).

Make sure you know who you would feel most comfortable speaking to if you felt that you needed to talk to someone at any point during your exploration of the past.

# 8 Don't discount medication

People who have experienced trauma often perceive threats with much more sensitivity than someone who has lived a trauma-free life. When we experience trauma it affects the chemical neurotransmitters in our brain and we can feel constantly on edge and become easily triggered into a 'fight, flight or freeze' response.

Medication can reduce the amount of time we spend dwelling on the past and also lessen the triggering episodes. It can be especially useful for people who experience vivid flashbacks and nightmares about their past and can move them from a place of feeling hopeless to one where they have a much more positive and hopeful outlook.

Medication also minimizes the chances of depressive and anxious episodes and allows people to be in a much more stable place when it comes to revisiting anything from their past. Most people, however, can heal without the need for a prescription and I would prefer you to explore this route first.

# 9 Be patient

There is no getting away from the fact that healing from trauma is not an overnight process. It impacts our minds, bodies and lives in every possible way and there can be a lot to work through and unpackage. While you may be keen to see progress it is important not to rush, regardless of how long ago the trauma occurred, or how insignificant you might think it was.

As we go through the process of dealing with trauma, it is normal to experience feelings of loss, anger, grief, sadness, despair, fear and anxiety. Allow these emotions to be with you and learn how to acknowledge them, don't push them away.

You may find that once one strong feeling fades, another arises to take its place. Don't be tempted to wrestle with it. Just allow it to be what it is and notice it with a calm sense of curiosity before allowing it to pass.

My own grieving process lasted for several months as I came to terms with the feeling of loss that came with understanding that my mother and father did not give me what most other children had on an emotional level. There were occasions where I felt extreme anger and had hateful thoughts about my parents, and other times when I felt sadness for both myself and them, as I understood how their own upbringing had caused them to be emotionally absent when I needed them.

Trauma is hard to deal with. If we attempt to rush the process or push away feelings to avoid discomfort, or get to our goal faster, we will end up setting ourselves back.

## 10 We have to look into the darkness

When we feel ready and find the strength to acknowledge and explore the traumatic episodes from our lives, we bring them out of the darkness and into the light. This is the point when something incredible happens and we begin to notice how much 'mentally lighter' we become. In my own experience, it felt like a weight that I had carried on my back for over thirty years had started to lift as I looked closer at what had happened and became comfortable with accepting and sharing my experiences around 'safe' people.

To get to this lighter place, we have to look into the darkness. The freedom we seek is there on the other side of the dark, waiting for you. All you have to do is look, accept, and feel the feelings and the light will come to you. If you refuse to look, you will continue to repeat the same damaging behaviour patterns and your trauma will fester in your soul until you get to a point where you feel as though you can't handle the pain any longer.

If you feel comfortable, you can begin dealing with this right now. You have nothing to fear. The short-term pain is nothing compared to a lifetime of suffering, and in many cases it begins to lift quickly. However, if you don't yet feel ready, simply continue to work through the book and come back to this part when you feel mentally equipped to take a closer look.

## 11 Celebrate your work

I lived as an ego-driven false version of myself for over three decades. I bragged about my 'perfect' life on social media in an effort to gain approval and feel validated, but all the while I endured daily pain from anxiety, depression and triggering episodes that caused emotional meltdowns. My mind was racing all the time. I was also drinking heavily. Honestly, I wish I had dealt with my issues 20 or 30 years ago – it was the best thing I have ever done. Celebrate the fact that you are taking positive action now, and you won't stop until you reach the place that you want to get to.

You should already be forming a structure that will help you begin to change and the remaining chapters will cover what you need to ensure you are fully equipped to continue moving down the right path. But trauma can often be more complex than CEN, especially in extreme cases, so I have created a roadmap to help you navigate through the essential steps that you will need to take in order to break free.

# A roadmap to healing trauma

## 1 Understand your story

In order to get to the root of why you have been suffering, you need to understand the story of your life and make sense of what might have happened in the past to discover what has shaped you in adulthood. This doesn't just mean understanding the trauma you have experienced, but taking the time to create a visual timeline of your life and creating a very clear picture of the pivotal moments that may have influenced you.

As well as understanding your story it is important to accept that it is reality and it happened. That does not mean that you have to forgive or forget specific episodes or traumatic events. You are not giving up or giving in and this is not a sign of weakness. In fact, acceptance is often harder to achieve than taking the path of least resistance and staying stuck. Just because you consciously choose to accept that something happened, it does not mean that you agree with it or support it. It simply means learning to accept the situation for what it was – a reality.

This process will also help you maintain a rational and realistic viewpoint on your past. By taking the time to fully understand your own story and getting in touch with the reality of things exactly as they were, you will find it much easier to accept the past. This acceptance will form a solid foundation on which to build the rest of your life.

## 2 Become your 'true-self'

Most of us who have been impacted by trauma in childhood end up projecting a false version of ourselves. I used to be a party animal when I socialized because I believed that this was the version of me that people liked the most. When I was in a work environment I became confident, sensible, reliable and hard-working: the first one in the office each morning, doing all I could in order to achieve promotion before my colleagues, even if it meant stepping on people on my way up the career ladder. I had a huge desire to impress. This was another false version of me – I wasn't being my true-self. I was never aware of this behaviour, and it wasn't until I woke up and shone a light on it that I was able to make a positive change that put the real version of me first in my life.

One of the effects of trauma is that we can believe that the real version of who we are is somehow not good enough, and in most cases we don't even know who the real version of us is. Low self-esteem and lack of self-worth can compel us to adapt our behaviour so we feel that we will fit in with specific people and situations.

This behaviour is self-defeating and it holds many people back. How can we know if the real version of us is not good enough if we have never even looked? We cast judgements and form limiting beliefs about the one person in our lives that we need to look after without ever getting to know them.

Living my false-self kept me well and truly stuck for years. When I eventually discovered who I really was, I actually liked that person. In fact, I didn't just like them, I began slowly to love them, and that feeling has stayed with me.

# 3 Identify your values

Our personal values act like a guidance system for a happy life. If we consciously and mindfully live in line with our values, we will find that we have our needs and desires met, and are able to invite peace, calm and joy into our lives.

If we don't know our values we end up getting lost, finding ourselves in places we don't want to be and wondering how we ended up there. Your values are your internal map and compass, they will guide you towards a life of contentment.

When you know what your values are you can also find a sense of true purpose in your life because they will signpost you towards what is important to you and what really matters. Over time, as we live in accordance with our values, we tend to become really clear about our purpose in life and we might even dedicate our time, career and resources to a cause, mission or purpose that we believe in.

Identifying your values will also help you become more confident and make difficult decisions much more easily. They give you stability and comfort because you know who you really are and what you really want, you have a set of rules by which to live your life.

Above all, knowing what your values are will help you uncover the true version of you. It will shift you away from behaviours you might only engage in to feel accepted or impress other people. The new insights will move you to a place where you begin to do what you want based on what you truly desire; living in line with your values will provide an honest foundation to help you enjoy an authentic, happy life.

# 4 Express, name and feel your emotions and feelings, even grief

It can take time and practise tuning in to your emotions and feelings. By making a habit of noticing everything that arises within you it is possible to accelerate the process. The best strategy is to pause when you experience a new feeling, then put a single word label on what you feel – for example, 'anger', 'grief', 'guilt', 'shame', 'rage' or 'sadness'.

Learn how to allow the feeling to be with you without any judgement. Be curious, ask yourself what it is attempting to tell you. Maybe something in your life needs to change? Perhaps you need to put a boundary in place to protect yourself from someone toxic? Pay attention to the fact that feelings always pass and teach yourself to welcome all feelings in, before you observe them moving away.

It is important to express your feelings in a safe and healthy way in order to stop them causing you long-term suffering. You will find strategies for doing this effectively later in the book. Healing from trauma can cause us to experience strong emotions as we begin the process of grieving what we have lost or what we never had when we were younger. Although this can feel painful, it is important to allow yourself to go through the stages of grieving in order to come out on the other side. Grieving does not mean you have to relive the events, but you may find that you experience a range of uncomfortable feelings as you work through the process. Recognizing this is a sure sign that you are healing.

## 5 Become authentic and speak your truth

Most people who suffer trauma have a strong desire to be liked, so tend to avoid conflict at all costs, even if it goes against our values.

If you want to break free, this has to stop.

Once you become aware of your values, you will understand what the authentic version of you needs, and you will have a roadmap that allows you to become the truest version of yourself. There will be times when people will try and pull you towards actions or behaviours that directly go against your values, and it is in these moments that you need to speak your truth, to say 'no', and express your feelings honestly. You will also need to set clear boundaries to prevent a similar situation occurring in the future.

Although it can feel hard at first when you find your 'NO', it is incredibly empowering. We are more able to look after ourselves when we remove toxic and emotionally triggering situations and people from our lives.

## 6 Accept that you will still experience discomfort

There is nobody on earth who doesn't experience emotional discomfort. Even His Holiness the 14th Dalai Lama, regarded by many as the happiest person alive, speaks of times when loss, trauma and disaster has caused him emotional pain. The Dalai Lama has attained happiness because he accepts things for what they are and he understands that he cannot change the reality of what is. He knows there is no point exhausting himself by fighting against a truth he cannot change.

Like him, we should accept that part of being human is acknowledging that life does not bring us happiness at all times – it is not a right. Life will bring us suffering, loss, grief and misfortune at times, just as it does to everyone. Just like clouds in the sky, people, experiences, feelings, sadness and joy come and go. Sometimes the sky will be full of dark, evil-looking thunderclouds but they soon move on as the wind pushes them away to be replaced by sunny skies.

## 7 Make sure you have suitable support on hand

Some people describe overcoming challenges in their life, such as healing trauma, as like climbing a huge mountain. It can feel like a tough uphill struggle with moments where you need to hang in there and avoid jagged rocks that have fallen from above. There may be moments on the climb when you take a tumble and end up back at one of the basecamps. This doesn't mean you won't make it to the top, it simply tells you that you have more work to do and invites you to look closer at the setback to discover what you can learn from it.

You wouldn't climb a mountain alone, and this is why making sure you have the right support around you is essential. This book will give you all the equipment you need in order to navigate the rocky mountain face, but you need to surround yourself with a supportive team of people that you can trust and rely on if the going gets tough.

Having such people around you not only gives you strength in the knowledge that help is close at hand, it also ensures you have safe people with whom you can share your innermost thoughts and feelings. It is important to become open and vulnerable by sharing anything negative we encounter, especially anything that makes us feel a sense of guilt or shame, such as behaviour, lies or secrets we have held on to.

Make sure you find suitable, safe people. This might be a therapist, a therapy group, an online community or trusted friends and family members. I recommend a therapy group as it will give you the opportunity to practise saying what you really feel, sharing your truth and being authentic in a judgement-free safe space.

## 8 Become connected to other people

When we have suffered trauma in the past we can shut down emotionally. This shutdown often results in us becoming frozen as we try to protect ourselves. What we don't tend to realize is that this does more harm than good.

When we shut ourselves down in this way, not only do we become numb, we also lose the ability to connect emotionally with others. I have worked with many people in long-term relationships who have suffered trauma as children, and their partners often talk of an internal emotional brick wall which they can't get over, and have been blocked from seeing the true version of the person they love. Over the longer term this can lead to an emotional disconnect between two people and may even cause relationships to fail unless something changes fundamentally.

Part of this process is about learning to love yourself. When you do this, you begin to learn how to love others in a healthy, respectful and safe way. You will find that love starts to flow out of you and, in return, you will begin to open yourself up to receiving the love of which you are worthy.

## 9 Gather the data

It is important to track your progress and I recommend making daily journal entries and using a mood tracking app to keep a close eye on changes in your emotions. This data will allow you to access an analytical assessment of how you are progressing. You will also be able to notice patterns and specific situations that might cause an emotional reaction and take steps to keep yourself safe. Paying attention to your moods and emotions will also enable you to become more aware and mindful as and when things come up.

The data you gather will give you an honest reflection of your life and, as time passes, you will be able to easily identify if you need to increase the amount of work you are putting into your recovery or whether what you are doing is yielding results.

Try and view the data you gather without emotion – look at the facts and make an objective decision about what you need to do for the best outcome.

## 10 Seek specialist help if necessary

The effects of trauma vary greatly from person to person and in some cases we have to accept that we need specialist help. Allow your feelings, the data you gather and your journal entries to guide you on this.

If you decide that you need to work with a specialist, make sure you do your research and find someone who has experience of working with similar issues to your own. Don't be afraid to ask direct questions or obtain references; after all, you are the one who will be paying for the service.

Don't rush into working with the first therapist you find and, if they don't feel like a good fit, move on to the next one. Always ask for a no-obligation initial session or video call to find out if they are someone you think you could work with. Make sure you understand their process and expectations in terms of results. Equally, if you are experiencing any kind of physical symptoms make sure you seek out medical help rather than living in pain.

It can feel hard to become unstuck from trauma, and there is no doubt that it is painful at times, but living in a state of lifelong suffering is far more painful than doing the work and experiencing the relatively short period of discomfort required to break free.

This book has everything you need to set you up for long-lasting success. Take one step at a time, avoid pushing yourself too hard and try to make a true commitment to putting in the work that will allow you to experience the change you want.

# 5 | Getting to know your inner child

Each and every one of us has an inner child. How well do you know yours?

'Inner Child' or 'The Child Within' are terms used in psychology to describe a person's child-like traits and behaviours, positive and negative. Our inner child is best described as a child-like sub-personality that exists within us all. It is a beautiful part of your psyche, it retains all the innocence, joy, wonder, passion, awe and creativity towards life that you had when you were young. Your inner child is the child that lives within you. It allows you to be playful, carefree, creative and joyful. But your child needs to feel safe and loved in order to express positivity. You need to be connected with it by meeting your own needs, noticing how you feel and becoming authentic.

Our inner child is often revealed through our outward behaviours, reactions and emotions. It is particularly apparent when we are faced with certain life challenges or when we have been left feeling hurt or are suffering. Adult children of emotionally neglectful parents usually carry a wounded inner child that has been heavily influenced by what we were taught when we were young, and the behaviours we witnessed before we entered puberty. When our inner child is wounded we can experience overwhelming and extreme reactions to things that don't bother most people.

Our inner child can be one of the biggest actors when it comes to identifying CEN or trauma. When faced with a triggering situation, it can have hysterical, overwhelming or irrational reactions. We express these reactions as an adult, but if we were to pause and ask ourselves how old we feel in that moment, we would likely place ourselves at around seven years old.

Your inner child's reactions will provide you with a huge signpost towards what might be triggering you. Take some time to think about occasions when you have had an irrational reaction in the past that might have resembled a childish response. Does this sound familiar? How old did you feel when you were experiencing the overwhelming emotions?

These reactions are usually triggered when we run into behaviours, situations, feelings and emotions that subconsciously remind us of our past trauma and neglect. For example, if you had parents who were too busy to listen to you as a child, and you felt constantly ignored when you were young, you might find that you now have an overwhelming emotional reaction as an adult when you feel unheard, or that you shut down when people appear to be ignoring you.

When you have a *hysterical* reaction it is almost always tied to something *historical*.

My hope is that, as you grow, you will experience fewer of these kinds of reactions, but they may still occur and it is important that you take steps to allow your inner child to feel safe. Stop allowing it to take the driving seat with your emotions, behaviour and feelings whenever you encounter a reminder of a negative experience from your childhood.

Working with this book will enable you to allow your child within to feel truly free and at peace.

# How to heal your inner child

If you have suffered CEN or childhood trauma, your inner child is wounded, and it is important that you take appropriate steps to heal. This can involve a process of grieving, which at times can feel emotional and uncomfortable. Stick with the process. As you practise the strategies outlined in this book, you will notice that you are becoming stronger, breaking free from being stuck in discomfort and negativity.

Our child within reflects the child that we once were. It holds all the positive and negative feelings and emotions that were within us when we were young. As adults, all those emotions remain inside us, but the positive feelings have usually become locked away. Healing your inner child unlocks them and releases joy, creativity, awe, enthusiasm and excitement back into your life, just like the childhood version of you.

Suppressing our feelings and emotions may have been necessary when we were young, as we probably had no other way of getting our needs met. But in adulthood, this behaviour no longer serves us in a positive way and it needs to change in order for us to become unstuck.

We often feel a strong sense of pain when we experience specific types of emotions as adults, and these feelings are directly linked to episodes and behaviours from our childhood. Rejection, abandonment, shame and anger are among the most common, because our upbringing has taught us to expect to feel and behave this way in certain situations. We may also have become used to disappointment and have an underlying belief that things never work out the way we want, or that we are simply not 'good enough'.

As emotionally neglected children, we learned to obtain love and approval by:

- always trying to make our parents happy;
- not saying what we really feel;
- accepting disappointment and rejection;
- believing that we aren't good enough;

- suppressing strong emotions such as anger, fear and sadness;
- not answering back or challenging our parents even when we believed they were wrong;
- accepting unreasonable behaviour.

Healing your inner child involves you directing your conscious mind towards the feelings you have within you. This will enable you to bring them out of the darkness and into the light so you can unearth the root causes and understand the challenges that they have created for you in adulthood.

From here you can take steps to reconnect with your inner child and ensure you keep them safe. This often means setting healthy personal boundaries to avoid any people or situations that might trigger you. These are 'toxic' people or situations and it is important that you begin to notice what, where and who negatively triggers your inner child. It is these difficult and painful moments that will enable you to create a safe environment for yourself.

Use the following steps as a roadmap to healing your inner child, and please ensure you are gentle with yourself. The process of looking inwards and facing up to uncomfortable memories can be challenging and upsetting. If you find yourself overwhelmed at any point, take a timeout and return when you feel ready.

# Steps to healing your wounded inner child

## 1 Acknowledge your child exists within you

When we are resistant to, or have doubts about, the existence of our inner child, or hold reservations about the process of healing, we end up putting roadblocks in our own way. Essentially, that which we resist, will persist.

A simple but important step towards your healing is acknowledging that your inner child exists and that episodes from your childhood are causing you pain in adulthood.

Look at the evidence you have available. Think of the times when you have experienced an overwhelming reaction, occasions when friends or family pointed out that you were being oversensitive, times when you've asked yourself why other people aren't triggered by the things that cause you to have a childish meltdown. Remember – a *hysterical* reaction in the present is almost always related to a *historical* event.

These triggering episodes are a gift, even though they don't feel like it at the time. They allow you to see the existence of your inner child, and acknowledge that they are present within you. As you reflect on occasions where you have had an inner child reaction, be really clear about the age you felt yourself to be in those situations. Most people will feel like a child when they are in the midst of these overwhelming responses that happen when they have been triggered.

Identifying the specific age that you feel during a triggering episode can also provide you with clues to the period in your life that may have shaped your emotional responses in adulthood. If it feels uncomfortable, look closer. This process will enable the uncomfortable to become comfortable, but it won't happen if you don't look.

The first step in the process of healing is to accept and believe that you have an inner child, and that your pain is coming from events that happened in your childhood. Simply gather the evidence, then acknowledge that your inner child is present within you through your entire life.

## 2 Speak to the child within

Your inner child is a great communicator. It talks to you using feelings. Treat every feeling you experience as a message, it is trying to tell you something in order to keep you safe and help you to feel comforted.

Use your journal to name each feeling that arises, and work on tracing anything negative back to specific events from your childhood. It is fairly easy to find clues because the events that cause strong feelings in adulthood almost always bear a similarity to events that caused pain when we were young.

As you begin to pay attention to what you feel, and what your child is communicating to you, it is common to notice:

- Shame or guilt
- Pain of rejection
- Anger or rage
- A sense of being abandoned
- Feelings of not being worthy or good enough
- Anxiety
- Sadness and depression
- Uncertainty or feelings of insecurity.

I was regularly triggered in situations where I felt rejected. This was linked to my biological father abandoning me when I was young, and my mother being emotionally absent when I needed her most. For example, when my son was young he used to want hugs and cuddles all the time, and I mean *all* the freaking time! I loved that warmth and closeness as I squeezed him tightly while he giggled in my arms. But as he grew up and became a teenager the cuddles didn't seem to come as often as they once had.

I still find myself longing for those magical moments and, on occasion, I can't hold back from asking him for a hug. My request is usually met with a firm 15-year-old 'NO', swiftly followed by a bedroom door being slammed in my face as he returns to the sanctuary of his headphones and death metal music.

I am now denied those beautiful, love-filled moments when I felt his heart beating against me, those few seconds of connection that made me feel so tightly connected to him. He has gone, he has grown (but I bet he will return one day and hug me again).

Of course, when I am denied, I am rejected; when I am rejected I become emotional. It is overwhelming and it envelops me like a fog. I try and fight my way out, but the more I fight, the more lost I become in the mist that is causing my emotional blindness.

It is when we find ourselves lost in the fog that we need to hear our inner child. So I will speak to my inner child and ask:

'How do you feel at the moment?'

'What is this feeling trying to tell me?'

'Where is it coming from?'

'What can I do to support you?'

'What is it you need right now?'

You can use these questions to speak to your inner child. You will likely find they enable you to experience some incredible breakthroughs, especially after you have created a new habit of connecting with your child when you encounter uncomfortable emotions and feelings.

Over time, I have come to understand that there was no chance of me getting those hugs. I accepted that – I couldn't control it, I couldn't change it and I knew I would cause myself suffering if I tried. Instead of attempting to control the situation, I took the time to understand what it was that I wanted in those moments, and then worked out how I could get my needs met.

It was clear that I needed to feel loved and desired, rather than rejected. Knowing that my wife Michelle never turns down a hug, I put a healthy boundary in place: *'When I need a hug, I will ask Michelle'*.

At the same time, I formed a healthy belief statement that: *'If my son wants a hug, he'll ask for one'.*

And occasionally, he does.

## 3 Write to your child

Using your journal to express your emotions and feelings is a powerful process. It allows you to move confusion out of your mind and on to paper, and this is often where you will begin to find yourself making much more sense of what is going on within.

An excellent strategy for moving your healing process forward is to write a letter to your inner child. This helps you to acknowledge the negative memories that have shaped you as an adult, as well as offering your adult wisdom and insights to provide rational explanations for episodes that you may not have been able to understand or fully process at the time.

Before writing a letter, it can help to look at photographs of yourself from when you were a child. Spend some time reflecting on them and imagining yourself being the young person in the images. If you can, try and visualize yourself in the moments that you see in the photographs, can you reconnect with the younger you and experience how you felt at the time? If so, use what you feel to help with what you write in your letter.

The goal of writing a letter to your inner child is to allow them to make sense of the experiences that may have left them hurt and confused at the time. The adult version of you can make much more sense of what might have happened and will be able to give your child a new perspective, as well as letting them know that they are safe now, and that there is no need to continue feeling distressed.

Don't expect to write one letter and for your inner child to instantly feel safe and secure. I recommend you write as often as possible until you feel a sense of warmth towards, and reconnection with, your child. You might want to write a letter each week and address different episodes you experienced in each one. Over time, you will begin to ease your own pain. As with much of this process, it takes work, it takes time, and it needs your commitment to change.

## 4 Calm your mind and reconnect

I found that acknowledging, speaking and writing to my inner child were all a huge help and they enabled me to begin to feel as though I was reconnecting. I also felt the internal hostility and the anger I held for myself starting to soften as I spent more time focusing on the process of healing.

When I realized that the actions I was taking were working, I decided that I wanted to go further, I wanted to tune into my inner child on a different level and find out if I could actually make him feel safe, happy and loved.

I decided to use meditation to create the connection. I already meditated daily as part of my self-care routine, usually ten minutes each morning and evening. I treat it like a prescription from the doctor and do it religiously because it has such a noticeably calming effect on me.

It was my wife who suggested that I commit to meditating regularly when she noticed the difference in my stress and anxiety levels when I stopped doing it for a few weeks. She couldn't believe how much of an impact it had made to my sense of wellbeing and she made it clear that she much prefers the version of me who is relaxed and at peace, because I am using this fantastic practice regularly.

I use an app on my smartphone called Calm. Many of the meditations are guided and the instructor talks you through what to do. They are perfect for anyone – beginners or more advanced – and the fact that you only need 10 to 20 minutes out of your day means that there really isn't an excuse for failing to show up.

## Seven apps to feel calmer fast

- Calm: for meditation
- Day One: for journaling
- Colorfy: relaxing colouring app
- iBreathe: breathing and anxiety exercises
- Dark Noise: ambient noise to sleep or focus
- Headspace: for meditation and mindfulness
- Insight Timer: free meditation.

Connecting to your inner child requires the ability to look within. When you meditate it can help to scan your body and tune into where you are feeling tension or stress, before breathing in and out of the area to release any discomfort.

My advice is to create a routine that you will stick to, and ideally have at least two sessions of meditation per day lasting ten minutes or more each. As you practise, you will find that you will be able to look inwards, find peace and become calm more easily. It can take a few sessions to begin to feel an improvement, and you might find your head is buzzing with thoughts when you start out. Don't fight the thoughts, simply allow them to pass without judgement like clouds floating across the sky.

What these meditation apps don't usually provide are practices specific to healing your inner child, and I recommend that you do one of these two to three times a week. The point of an inner-child meditation is for you to visualize your child within and to make them feel safe, loved and supported. You can also ask them the questions I listed above (*'What is it you need right now?'* or *'How can I make you feel safe and loved?'*) and as you meditate and visualize, you will find the answers come to you.

In most cases the process involves closing your eyes, focusing on your breath until you feel relaxed, then beginning to observe the child within. I prefer to use a guided meditation whenever possible, and it is common for instructors to not only have us speak to our inner child, but to visualize holding or hugging them. It can be an incredibly powerful process and you can find many excellent free inner-child-specific meditation practices by searching on YouTube or Google.

As well as sending feelings of love to the child inside of us, meditation will also enable us to become fully present and accept and notice our emotions and feelings as they arise. It can help us learn to express them in a healthy way and understand the impermanence of all things when we observe them weaken and fade away.

# 5 Become the child you are

Another great way to connect with your inner child is to become them. I'm sure you can identify moments in your adult life when you have been playful, full of joy and had a feeling of being totally carefree, just like a big kid. In those moments you are very likely connected to the wonderful positivity that lives inside your child.

Those powerful moments, when you play like a child and feel truly free, offer you a gateway to your inner child. However, it can be a challenge when CEN or past trauma is stifling us, because these moments tend to be few and far between. However, we can practise becoming more connected and spending more time in a playful and happy place.

It can help to have an intention of becoming your inner child for a short period of time each day. Maybe you could paint, draw or play music just like the smaller version of you used to do. Allow yourself to really connect with your child within, don't overthink it, and let whatever flows from within happen naturally.

During my own experience of healing, I recognized that I felt much happier when I became playful and made a conscious effort to be in that place as often as I could manage. This took time and practice, and sometimes I had to 'fake it until I made it'. Sometimes I would sink back into a dark mood, and beat myself up with negative self-talk, labelling myself as stupid for thinking I could just snap out of my sadness and become playful.

But I knew that my behaviour was driven by beliefs that had been formed from past negative experiences. They were no longer serving me in a positive way. Beliefs can be changed, I knew this from having given up drinking. I used to believe that drinking enabled me to relax, de-stress and have fun – all completely untrue. In order to stop drinking I needed to form new, positive beliefs that no longer prevented me from being the person I wanted to be.

The best way to do this was by educating myself and working on my mindset. Over time, and with persistence and practice, it worked. My beliefs transformed and I found myself passionately sober with no further need for willpower.

It was this approach – persistence and patience, and the knowledge that beliefs aren't fixed – that enabled me to let go of my darkness and become mindfully playful. I made it my intention to become a big kid at least once a day, and I would write that intention in big letters in my journal each morning.

Initially it felt wooden, as though I was acting. But the more I stuck with it, the more natural it became and the more carefree I felt. Over time, I found myself feeling naturally more playful without the need to consciously make an effort. It became a new normal, and it felt good.

Make an effort to practise being childlike and playful as often as possible. At first it will feel awkward, but stick with it and it will begin to feel more natural, and you will find yourself in a much happier state of mind. It can also help to reconnect with the activities, hobbies and pastimes that you loved as a child. Take some time to think about what really lights you up, about the activities that caused you to lose track of time because you became so immersed in them. If you can identify what they might be, it is a great place to go to in order to reconnect with your inner child.

It can take time and practice to begin to feel truly reconnected. Avoid the urge to give up, keep working on it and note down the progress in your journal in order to collect data that proves you are moving forward and growing.

You may find that, as you connect to your inner child, you start listening to them much more closely. Not only will this help you find the guidance you need to go forward, it may also allow you to uncover issues from the past that you had long since forgotten about. Listen to what they have to say without judgement or emotional reaction, in the knowledge that anything you discover will help you grow stronger.

# 6 | Emotions and feelings explained

I use the terms 'emotions' and 'feelings' many times in this book, and I am sure you have a pretty good idea of what they are. The next step is for you to develop a level of insight so you can notice what you are experiencing within yourself at any given moment.

It is common for people to avoid speaking about their feelings, and as you become more aware of your own, you will probably notice how much people talk about superficial topics like their work and their relationships, sharing gossip and news while avoiding being honest about how they are really feeling.

Our upbringing plays a big part in determining how comfortable we feel sharing our innermost emotions. Some people can express themselves easily, while others feel a sense of fear at the prospect of showing what is inside to the outside world, because they were never taught how to do it.

The good news is that noticing, naming and expressing your feelings is a skill and, just like any new skill, it simply takes practice in order to make it a healthy and powerful habit. As you become accustomed to the new technique you will also learn how to label and best describe your feelings in order to articulate them effectively, and express exactly what you are experiencing.

When scientists study human emotions, they measure them by asking people what they are 'feeling' at the time. There is no way of recording or measuring the level of emotion or feeling that a person is experiencing and a word like 'sad' or 'angry' could mean different things to different people. Someone who uses the word 'sad' as a throwaway term and says it at the slightest hint of any negativity may not experience the same impact or intensity as other people do when they use the same word. I like to imagine each emotion as being on a spectrum, with each person having their own thresholds.

Having clarity around what your feelings actually mean to you is important, as is being able to express them in a healthy way.

## Emotions and feelings – the difference

An emotion is described most simply as a conscious reaction or state which we experience as a strong feeling. The emotion is usually directed towards a specific person, object or situation.

A feeling is the reaction we have to an emotion. For example, if we watch a movie with a tragic ending, we may experience a strong emotion as the closing credits roll up the screen. The feeling associated with this would likely be sadness and we may express it physically by crying, or internally by feeling down.

Psychologists mostly agree that there are six basic types of emotions that we can feel. These are:

- Happiness
- Fear
- Anger
- Disgust
- Sadness
- Surprise

These six form the foundations of all emotions and feelings we experience. Consider them as category headings, under which sit many other more specific types of emotions. For example, under the 'anger' category you will find humiliation, criticism and betrayal as some of the more precise subheadings. Be mindful that it is possible to experience a mixture of more than one emotion at the same time.

Our emotions are created by our brain as a way of allowing us to make sense of bodily sensations based on past experiences. Our brain is constantly monitoring the sensations happening in our body, such as the beating of our heart, the rate of our breathing and any pain we might be experiencing. When the brain notices a new sensation it will do its best to work out what it means based on all the information it has available. The data our brain uses to make these decisions includes our past experiences and external stimuli.

Our brain wants to keep us alive and will distribute energy to specific areas of the body based on what it believes is needed in any given moment or situation. Much of what the brain does is based on a prediction of what it thinks will happen, which is why our past experiences play such an enormous part in our present-day emotional wellbeing. Simply put, our brain allows us to make sense of what we experience by providing us with emotions.

Because of this, we are able to take a level of control over our own emotions by using our body. Try intentionally smiling while you hold your head high and your shoulders back, with a little practice your brain will get the message that this represents happiness and will provide you with exactly that. Avoid positions that deliver a message of misery or sadness, like slouching, or putting your head in your hands, as this will bring up emotions you probably don't want.

# Past trauma informs present emotions

When our son Robin was around five years old, Michelle and I decided it would be nice to take him on holiday to the Spanish island of Menorca for a week of sun and family time. We were all looking forward to the holiday – Robin was so excited he had his bucket and spade packed in the suitcase several weeks before we were due to leave.

When the day of our trip finally arrived, we headed to the airport, checked in and before long we were on board, crammed in with 250 other passengers, all desperately trying to escape the grey, rainy English skies. The flight was scheduled to take just over two hours – easy.

Around halfway into the flight, it felt like the plane was experiencing turbulence, which has happened on most flights I have taken. The bumping and jolting sensation went on for a few more minutes before the plane settled down into a smooth flight. I felt mild anxiety, but my brain used my past experience of flying to indicate that there was no need to feel anything more than this, and to regulate my emotions.

Not long afterwards, the plane shuddered violently and dropped like a stone. Hopefully, you have never been on a packed passenger plane falling from the sky – the only way to describe it is like what I would imagine it would feel to be in a lift dropping down a shaft with no cable to slow it down.

The plane fell for what seemed like an eternity, but in reality was probably less than a minute. Eventually the awful sensation stopped and it seemed like the pilot was regaining control. None of the passengers knew what had happened and I assumed it was severe turbulence – but it felt more serious. My heart was thumping in my chest.

Moments later, one of the crew rushed along the aisle in between the passengers. He had a look of terror on his face as he shouted: 'Don't panic!' Of course, panic instantly erupted. Oxygen masks dropped from above our heads – we put them on immediately as the plane had lost cabin pressure and no longer had any oxygen to keep the passengers alive and breathing. My hands were shaking so much I could barely hold the mask as I remembered all the occasions in the past that I had ignored the safety instructions. I fumbled around my son's face trying to attach his mask, but my hands were shaking so badly that I couldn't do it. Desperate to help him, I hadn't put my own mask on first, as we're always told to do.

Eventually Michelle – calm oasis in the sandstorm desert of my life – took control. She put Robin's mask on and then she did mine. We could breathe again. What followed were among the strangest few minutes I have ever encountered. None of the passengers had any idea what was happening and everyone was in a state of panic. Once our masks were in place, throughout the plane there was absolute silence. Everyone sat quietly, wondering what would happen. The silence was heightened by a lack of noise from the plane's engines. It felt as though we were gliding, rather than being powered by two enormous Rolls Royce jet engines.

The silence continued. Everyone, including me, contemplated the possibility that these might be their last moments alive. I had never experienced fear like it. Eventually a member of the crew spoke, voice trembling, over the intercom – to tell us that we had lost cabin pressure and some power and would be making an emergency landing in Paris.

'If we make it that far,' I whispered to Michelle, who faked a smile, tears in her eyes. The three of us held hands and squeezed them tightly. We were still holding hands as we saw Paris come into view below us. We started to make out the lights of the airport through the dusky night and broken cloud cover. The pilot was making small adjustments to our direction and our altitude was much lower now.

The silence was broken as someone sobbed loudly.

The tannoy sounded again: 'We will shortly be making an emergency landing. When you hear the words "brace, brace, brace", please adopt the brace position for your own safety.'

Now we could see the brightly illuminated airport and the lights of the runway. I saw flashing red and blue lights twinkling along either side of the landing strip and as we prepared to land, Michelle turned to me and said, 'Those lights are rows of ambulances and fire engines.'

Moments later we were instructed to take up the brace position. As I sat with my hands on my head, a montage of memories, key life moments, flashed through my mind. There was a huge bump as the tyres hit the tarmac. The plane wobbled and juddered as it shot down the runway, the lights of the emergency services a blur of blues and reds through the window as we rushed past.

Finally, the plane did stop and of course we made it out alive. We later found out that part of the tail had come away and struck the fuselage causing a partial power loss and failure of the cabin pressure. The huge drop was a decision made by the captain to bring the plane quickly down to a level where it would destabilize naturally.

Since that day Robin and Michelle have both been absolutely terrified of flying. Michelle has been on a 'fear of flying' course, and Robin experiences panic attacks before taking a flight. We were on a flight earlier this year and encountered a lot of turbulence on the way – they were both in pieces and crying uncontrollably. Strangely, I was unaffected.

When we have experienced CEN or trauma, we are often left with heightened reactions to situations. Our brain uses the data it has stored about our past experiences to create a template of how it should react. Both Robin and Michelle now receive messages from their brain which tell them that flying represents serious danger, and they both experience heightened emotions and strong feelings of fear and anxiety, even when there is nothing to fear. Their brains use the data available to make sense of the situation, and the trauma they both experienced had made flying now an almost-debilitating experience for them both.

The same types of past traumatic events can affect different people in different ways. It may be that, unlike Michelle and Robin, who had only taken a handful of flights, I had always been a confident flyer and had taken enough flights in the past for my brain to conclude that this was a once in a lifetime episode.

Thankfully, we can retrain our brains by bringing mindful awareness to our responses and learning techniques that will allow us to deal with discomfort in a healthy way.

# Feeling your feelings

You may have heard therapists talk about 'feeling your feelings' and you might have wondered how to actually do so. I was the same, I wanted to feel my feelings but I only ever seemed to experience mood swings, meltdowns, panic attacks and depressive episodes.

I knew I had been feeling something for decades – an internal pain. But this isn't what therapists are referring to when they talk about 'feeling our feelings'. I was simply experiencing inner child reactions to my past. I never paused, reflected or dug deeper to understand my feelings at any given time.

Instead of responding in a healthy way to what I was feeling, I would either refuse to feel them or I would judge my emotions with negative internal self-talk. Neither of these strategies helped me, in fact they were adding to my problems. Our emotions don't come from nowhere, they are an important signpost that points us to an area of our life that we need to look at more closely. By ignoring or judging them we avoid the helpful information and lessons they are trying to teach us.

Repressed emotions stay within us and, over time, they build up and weigh us down, both mentally and physically. When we are able to fully experience our feelings, negative and positive, we can process them completely and release them. We feel free and lighter, we are true to ourselves and mentally healthier.

If you were to take only one piece of advice away from this book, I would want you to learn how to *feel your feelings*. Feeling your feelings is the equivalent of pushing over the first domino in a long row that leads to a place of healing. Once you push the first one down, the rest will naturally topple and fall. By learning to feel your feelings you start a chain reaction and everything else slowly begins to fall into place. If you fail to acknowledge what you feel, you will remain firmly stuck. I began to feel my own feelings while watching a TV documentary where a child's mother died. I sobbed for almost 15 minutes, having never cried at a television programme or film before.

Our repressed emotions and past experiences are triggers that negatively impact our wellbeing and happiness. If you can increase your awareness of what you're feeling, you will begin to make real progress towards breaking free from suffering.

# ANTS

I have created a process called ANTS to help you start feeling your feelings. It relates specifically to challenging emotions and will allow you to work through them in a healthy way. Bear in mind that there is a big difference between being aware of an emotion and actually *feeling* it fully.

A – Acknowledge when an uncomfortable emotion has arisen. Become conscious that it is with you and avoid any urge to push it away.

N – Name the feeling that you experience by labelling it with a single word. It might be 'ashamed', 'unloved', 'lonely', 'jealous', 'sad', 'worthless' or 'disappointed', for example.

T – Think about what caused the painful feeling, can you pinpoint a trigger? If so, you can take steps to prevent the same situation from happening again. Take the time to explore your past and see if you can make a link to any episodes from childhood.

S – Story: consider whether you are telling yourself a story about what it means to feel what you are feeling. Our past experiences can cause us to believe specific stories when we feel a certain way. These can be damaging to our self-esteem and cause us to detach from the reality of what the feeling is trying to tell us.

When I experienced uncomfortable feelings I believed that:

- If I was hurt – I was a victim, unmanly and making a fuss.
- If I was afraid – I was weak and had no courage.
- If I was angry – I had no control of a situation and I was being unreasonable.
- If I was anxious – I wasn't good enough and incapable of handling a situation.

As I practised self-awareness, it became easier to notice when I was telling myself a false story that would damage my self-esteem. I was then able to look at my feelings objectively, like an observer looking from a distance, and view what I was feeling with non-judgemental curiosity in order to find the truth.

I also used a reframing technique which helped me move my focus from self-judgement to a belief that served me in a more positive way. I wrote down a handful of positive belief statements in my journal and repeated them to myself if I ever struggled to accept a feeling.

Some of the reframe statements I used were:

- Experiencing emotions means I am alive, they are opportunities to improve and grow by exploring what they mean.
- Emotions are always with me and they are constantly changing, it is normal, and I owe it to myself to accept and feel them.
- By accepting my feelings and searching for their meaning I am becoming the best version of myself.

In order to have complete freedom from painful feelings, it is vital that we are able to accept them for what they are without any self-blaming or story-telling. If you can become conscious of the episodes that happened in your life which are causing painful feelings within you, it will help you to weaken the power they hold.

Use this simple seven-step practice to connect fully to your feelings:

1. Close your eyes and sit in stillness. Breathe steadily in and out through your nose. Avoid snatching your breath and keep the flow of air as natural as possible. Focus your attention on being grounded: imagine you are a strong oak tree with roots extending out of you into the ground so nothing can topple you over. Lock your attention on to the areas of your body that have contact with the ground and imagine the roots holding you firmly into the surface beneath you.

2. If any thoughts come to mind, allow them to be, without judgement. It can help to say out loud 'thought' as they pop up. Don't fight them, it is perfectly normal for this to happen, especially when you first start to practice this process. Once you have acknowledged a thought, return your attention to the areas of your body that have contact with the floor.

3. Begin to scan your body, starting at the very top of your head and slowly moving to every other area as you shift your attention all the way down, eventually ending at your feet. Cover every inch of your body as you slowly scan, including your eyes, tongue, fingers, naval and toes.

4. Notice how your body feels, can you locate any tension? Is a specific area holding uncomfortable feelings? Continue scanning your body until you tune into an area you are drawn towards. When you locate it ask yourself how it feels, try to be specific and label it, for example, 'warm', 'cool', 'heavy', 'tingly', 'tense' or 'soft'.

5. Simply observe the feeling with complete awareness, accept that it is with you at this moment. You might find it helpful to welcome it in and speak to it

with a gentle 'hello, anger, welcome to my body'. Continue to simply sit with whatever it is you are feeling.

6. Begin to visualize your breath coming into the area of your body that is holding the feeling, inhale directly into this area and allow the pure, clean energy to flow into you. As you exhale, visualize the feeling leaving the same area and allow any negative energy to leave your body. Continue the process and pay attention to the emotion as you notice it softening. Be careful not to try and force anything or become frustrated if it doesn't instantly weaken, take your time and notice how it slowly softens.

7. As the emotion fades, you will have successfully released the energy attached to it. You have allowed it to be free without repressing it. You may now find that you experience other negative feelings, sitting behind the initial emotion you encountered. If this happens, simply repeat the process until you feel at peace, and free from discomfort.

Invest your time into practising the process of learning to fully experience your feelings and you will notice positive changes. Before long you will master the technique and have a new tool for addressing the pain of uncomfortable emotions.

Be kind to yourself. As with any new skill, there will be setbacks and times when you feel like you can't do it. If you stumble, try to avoid criticizing yourself and instead take steps to learn what you could do differently as you go forward.

# 7 | Is it possible to heal?

I was a big baby, weighing over nine pounds when I was born by caesarean section in 1973, and subsequently suffering from jaundice. I was immediately placed in an incubator without feeling the touch of my mother. Caesarean sections were a major procedure in those days and she would be unable to hold me for several weeks while she healed.

Early bonding with a baby is critical in order to begin forming an attachment and, these days, mothers are encouraged to hold their newborn as quickly and often as possible, especially with skin-to-skin contact, to begin forming a healthy relationship. This unspoken nurturing helps to create a secure-attachment bond which allows the baby to trust the mother and to communicate their feelings safely.

Babies who develop a secure attachment bond through physical contact and positive early communication are better able to:

- maintain a healthy emotional balance;
- develop and maintain fulfilling emotional relationships;
- have a strong sense of self-worth and feel confident about themselves;
- express and share their feelings;
- ask for help and seek suitable support;
- enjoy the company of other people;
- accept and rebound from loss and disappointment.

This bond stems from an unspoken exchange between the mother and her baby that pulls the two of them together to create a strong connection of unconditional love and care. It helps to form the way the child develops emotionally, socially, physically and intellectually.

I got off to a bad start and things didn't get much better as the years went by. My biological father left when I was only two years old, and my mother then married my step-father. It was a marriage of convenience and they lived separate lives under the same roof. I knew none of this, and grew up in a home that was devoid of love and full of toxic secrets.

On top of this, my mother was emotionally absent. She was critical of me and rarely expressed an interest in my world, or my feelings. As I grew older I struggled to handle any type of rejection and felt drawn to situations and people where I felt in control.

As time went by my insecurities seemed to worsen, and, in my thirties, I believed myself to be depressed, anxious, and to have problems with addiction. It was a miserable existence with only two types of mood: dark, and darker.

I ran my own business, a busy marketing company with twenty or so staff. My work was draining and I was being emotionally triggered on an almost daily basis. If a client complained I felt rejected; if a client cancelled their service with us I felt abandoned; if there was an issue with a member of staff I became anxious and afraid of conflict. I began to drink more and more in the evenings in a subconscious attempt to escape from the worries the business was bringing into my life.

Eventually I experienced a moment of clarity while reading a book which talked about the importance of doing what we love rather than staying in roles that we hate. I realized I hated the role and, in that moment, I decided I needed to get out.

My wife – and business partner – hired a manager who could take care of my day-to-day responsibilities, and finally I was free. My intention was to use my time to understand why I felt so empty, and to somehow heal. I also wanted to try and discover what it was that I really enjoyed doing and to make that my career instead.

To begin with I was at a complete loss. I didn't know where to start; progress was slow, and answers eluded me. It was around this time that I decided to quit drinking. I wanted to see what an alcohol-free life felt like and I jumped in with both feet. As I said earlier, I'm not suggesting you quit alcohol if you don't want to do so. But I must share with you that stopping drinking had a huge impact on my levels of anxiety and improved my ability to handle challenging situations calmly and rationally.

Alcohol pours fuel on the fire of anxiety and depression and it dramatically affects our physical and mental health. The best place to heal CEN and trauma is from a place of stability, and the most stable I have ever felt is after I kicked alcohol for good.

# Addictions

You might find you have addictions or compulsive behaviours that you use as a coping mechanism: you may not realize that you use them for this purpose, but you cannot resist them. A good measure is to consider whether you feel in control of a particular behaviour, or whether you feel that it is in control of you.

## Most common addictions

- **Substance misuse:** alcohol, smoking, vaping and drugs (prescription or illegal)
- **Sex:** acting out, affairs, porn, sex workers, fetishes or masturbating

- **Food:** binge eating, dieting or eating certain types of food
- **Gambling:** online or in-person
- **Internet:** online chat, gaming, social media, smartphones and use of computers
- **Self-harm:** seeking pain, cutting or causing injury
- **Exercise:** over-exercising
- **Shopping:** online or in-person
- **Working:** obsessive and always plugged in to work
- **Religion:** obsession as opposed to devotion

It is important to be clear that some of these common addictions are perfectly healthy in moderation. The problems happen when we are unable to resist the urge to repeat the behaviour regularly, and when we put it ahead of other important areas of our lives. If you believe that you have an unhealthy addiction, consider taking a break from it as you work through the process of healing. Refer to the Resources section at the back of this book for recommendations to address addictive behaviour.

We believe our addictions serve us because they provide us with an escape and a feeling of being soothed. However, the reality is that indulging in behaviours for short-term gratification leaves us with a happiness deficiency that causes us to crave more of the damaging behaviour. We end up in a painful cycle where we believe unhealthy behaviour is the only way to comfort ourselves, and if we don't find a way to break free we can damage many areas of our lives.

# Steps towards healing

This process is a journey, not an overnight or instant change. It takes time, it requires commitment and you will almost certainly experience a few setbacks as you move forward. There is no specific destination, either. We are simply moving forward and noticing what we experience as we travel down a new path. A sense of curiosity and open-mindedness is critical; and don't rush your journey. Take a break, admire the view at any time you like before continuing.

As a unique experience for each individual, overcoming CEN and trauma is not a process of erasing memories or learning to forget about past events. Instead we need to learn how to prevent our past controlling our present-day emotions. It is essential not to try and force the process. Take time to digest the information you uncover, and reflect on what you learn. Work through the journey in stages, taking time out whenever you feel it is needed, and refreshing your understanding of any elements of your work when you feel that it hasn't sunk in fully.

For most people the journey to healing CEN and trauma has six stages. In my own experience I went through each of the stages and, in most cases, people who have become aware of the root cause of their issues will travel through the same steps. Some might move through them in a different order and, depending on the severity of events from the past, others may find themselves at the latter steps very quickly. Remember, it isn't a race; there is a huge benefit to working slowly and mindfully.

# The stages to healing

## Stage 1: Unawareness

This is possibly the most painful stage of CEN and trauma. You're living with severe internal discomfort, experiencing negative emotions and often being impacted on a social, emotional and behavioural level.

Worst of all, you're unaware of what is happening. You have no idea why you feel this way. You might believe that you have mental health problems and that you will be stuck with this sense of hopelessness forever.

## Stage 2: Awareness

Awareness is a gift. When we become aware that our issues relate to past trauma or emotional neglect, we instantly move out of the first stage with a sense of relief that we have an understanding of what is happening, and why we feel the way we do.

That said, the awareness stage can also feel overwhelming. We have identified the root cause of our problems but we may not have a clear understanding of how to heal our troubled inner child and hold on to a fear of looking more closely at the past.

When we become aware, it is essential we have a sense of momentum and a desire to bring the suffering to the end. Healing happens when we begin immersing ourselves in learning all we can about the best methods of recovery from CEN and trauma.

## Stage 3: Education, exploration and learning

It is vital that we immerse ourselves in exploring and learning about the causes, effects and treatments of CEN and trauma. The more we understand, the more sense we make of the way we feel inside.

This new understanding provides us with a logical framework for healing, we begin to understand the root causes and we can work on educating ourselves to discover the best strategies for changing and healing.

Don't underestimate the power of committing yourself to working hard on exploring your issues, you are putting together a huge puzzle piece by piece and with each new discovery, you take one step closer to solving the entire thing.

## Stage 4: Practising, integrating and implementing

As we learn, we grow and become stronger. We discover new ways of behaving along with strategies and tactics for handling any uncomfortable feelings and emotions we experience.

We become able to bring these new skills into our daily lives and gently take steps to implement them and notice what changes they allow us to experience. As we become more confident in the new skills, we will grow stronger, become more resilient and heal faster.

## Stage 5: Transforming and becoming

After a period of adjustment, as we bring our newfound behaviours and skills into our lives, we start to transform and this is where lasting change happens.

We begin to master our new life and start to feel happier and unaffected by the issues that may have triggered us in the past. We learn how to keep ourselves safe, express our feelings, speak our truth and put boundaries in place to prevent toxicity entering our lives.

We become new, we become whole and we become happy.

## Stage 6: Spiritual awakening

The final stage of healing happens when we become fully 'awake'. We are conscious and connected to our inner-self. We fully experience our feelings and emotions and live in the present moment.

We are rarely triggered or driven by our ego and have no desire for the approval of others. We no longer focus on the past or the future and we feel a true sense of emotional connection with the people we care about.

We find inner peace.

Throughout the rest of the book, we will explore each element of healing in much more detail. I will provide you with specific strategies that worked for me and have worked for many other people that I have worked with.

# 8 | Let's talk about our parents

In order to understand our own story we need to take a closer look at that of our parents. There are few parents who do not love their children, and you should try not to blame them; doing so can cause you more trauma and pain. If you notice that you are blaming one, or both, of your parents, simply acknowledge the feelings – label them and write them down in your journal, and explore them in more depth with curiosity.

In some cases of serious trauma it may be difficult to let go of blame. If you are struggling, consider seeking out specialist therapy to allow you to move through the emotional block.

Often, our parents will have suffered very similar experiences to us as children. Thus they believe that the way they parent is the right way. They are products of learned behaviour, of which they are usually completely unaware. The behaviours that cause CEN and trauma are passed down from generation to generation. You can bring an end to the pain, and stop future generations suffering in the same way. Keep in mind that it won't just be your life that is changed by healing, but those of your children, grandchildren and each future generation beyond.

My mother was brought up in a strict household. Her father was an aggressive, controlling, angry and violent man. My grandmother often stood by while he let rip at my mother for breaking his unreasonable and draconian rules. My grandmother's fear of her husband left her scared to get involved, which left my mother feeling completely alone in these stressful moments.

When I learned about my mother's childhood experiences, it weakened my desire to blame her for the issues that arose from her emotional absence. She had an equally challenging time as a child as I did, and I understood how her father's behaviour had shaped her and passed through each generation. No doubt my grandfather had experienced an equally difficult time when he was younger.

The fact that these behaviour traits are passed from one generation to the next made me think about my own son. I had no doubt already projected my own negativity onto him, and I knew I needed to do whatever it took to change myself for the better and end the toxicity that ran through each generation. Although I worried that maybe the damage was already done, I knew I couldn't change the past, so I decided to change the future instead.

When I finally opened up to my mother about the challenges I had been facing and explained the impact of her emotional neglect on me, she began sharing more about her own childhood and it helped me make sense of things. It was another big piece of the jigsaw puzzle.

My mother and step-father were mostly permissive parents – they allowed me to do pretty much whatever I wanted and failed to set clear or healthy boundaries. As a result of this, I got into trouble and was forced to find my own way in life. At other times my mother was controlling and critical, particularly when she risked incurring disapproval from other people, and I now see how this is linked to her own lack of self-worth, linked directly to the actions of her father.

It can help to understand the different types of parents that commonly cause CEN and trauma in their children and I have outlined these in the following section. There is no 'one size fits all', and some parents cross over with a mixture of different traits. They might have some tendencies from one style and some from another. Keep an open mind as you read these.

By gaining a better understanding of the most common parenting styles that generate CEN, you will be able to obtain more clarity about your own parents and make more sense of your own behaviour traits.

## The authoritarian

Authoritarian parenting is the strictest style of parenting. A common attitude of these types of parents is that children should be seen and not heard. These parents are often considered 'old school' or 'traditional' in their style.

They place a heavy emphasis on the rules that they set and will often fail to explain the reasons for these rules being in place. They expect their children to obey all rules without question or argument. They may express anger or even use physical punishment if their children step over the strict boundaries they have imposed.

Children often find themselves on the wrong end of harsh punishment if they dare to speak up, challenge the parent or break the rules. The authoritarian parent views this as 'answering back', which is discouraged, causing children to suppress feelings and emotions through fear of the consequences.

These parents usually lack a loving nature, they are not intimate or warm and children often find themselves scared in their presence. They rule by fear and can sometimes be best described as a bully, especially if their punishment transitions from verbal to physical.

Authoritarian parents can also have incredibly high expectations of their children and often become angry if they feel that their standards have not been met.

Some of the most common effects on adult children of an authoritarian parent are:

- Issues with self-esteem and self-worth
- Problems with confidence

- Overachieving and seeking approval
- A deep sense that something is missing
- Normalizing of aggressive or violent behaviour
- A tendency towards depression and anxiety
- Issues with social skills.

# The 'me-first' parent

These types of parents tend to put their own needs ahead of those of their children. They are self-involved and self-important. The damage they can cause to their children through their egocentric behaviour is often quite extreme.

'Me-first' parents often display narcissistic and sociopathic traits along with an authoritarian nature. It is not uncommon for them to have double standards and to engage in addictive behaviours and abuse substances like alcohol and drugs.

These parents might use their children to make themselves feel special, playing games or controlling situations to ensure they feel loved, or basking in their child's reflected glory at any given opportunity. They may become angry if the child doesn't meet their expectations, fails to deliver the anticipated response or deflects the attention away from the parent.

'Me-first' parents can cause serious damage to their children and it might be difficult to accept that your parents fall into this category. However, because it is the easiest type of parenting to identify it allows people to clearly see that their parents have likely neglected them emotionally.

Some of the most common negative effects on adult children of a 'me-first' parent include:

- Issues with self-worth
- A tendency towards depression and anxiety
- Narcissistic and sociopathic traits
- Problems forming intimate relationships
- Difficulty expressing feelings and emotions
- Easily triggered by similar behaviour
- Feelings of insecurity
- Problems trusting others
- A tendency to form co-dependent relationships.

# The permissive parent

Permissive parents are not at all strict, and they avoid having many rules in place for their children. Their expectations are low and they don't set healthy boundaries, thus exposing their children to dangerous situations.

The children of these parents feel that they, not the adult, are in charge and rarely find themselves having to face the consequences of any negative behaviour, as their parents prefer to avoid confrontation and conflict.

As children mature, they need to experience freedom and responsibility, but permissive parents are overly lenient and their low expectations are usually apparent from an early age. They might allow their children to hang out with unsuitable friends or they may not know where their kids are outside school hours. They might fail to set sensible times for their children to study or go to bed, and allow them to play computer games late into the night instead.

Permissive parents struggle to say 'no' to their children because they don't want to upset them, or can't face the stress of conflict. They might give in quickly when their child asks for sweets or treats in a supermarket, for example, and will put certain aspects of the child's needs ahead of their own in order to have the easiest life possible.

These parents follow the path of least resistance, but in doing so they are simply causing problems that will surface as their children get older. Children are left with poor self-discipline as well as feelings of insecurity and confusion due to the lack of guidance, boundaries and support.

Some of the most common negative effects on children of a permissive parent include:

- Insecurity from a lack of boundary setting
- Selfish nature and dislike of sharing
- Irresponsible and reckless behaviour
- Unable to take responsibility for their behaviour
- Poor self-control and self-regulation
- Poor social skills and anti-social behaviour
- Issues with authority figures
- Lack of self-discipline.

## The absent or uninvolved parent

Absent or uninvolved parents are not present in their children's lives as much as they should be. They have other priorities, such as work, or other important commitments that leave little time for parenting.

These parents are emotionally absent without leave in the lives of their children. They believe they are doing the best for their family, especially if they are working hard to earn more money and better themselves. In fact, they are causing more damage than they realize by allowing their other commitments to take priority over their children.

In some cases, the parent might be physically absent due to a career that sends them away for extended periods, but relationship breakdowns and divorce can also cause a parent to be much less involved than they should be.

Even when an uninvolved parent is around their kids, they can be preoccupied with their own priorities and appear uninterested in talking about anything other than what is important to them. Instead of spending quality time playing, connecting and engaging with their children, they are too wrapped up in their own world to give them the attention they need.

These parents are also prone to substance abuse and addiction, which they may use as a coping mechanism for stress and anxiety. Problems with addiction will cause further neglect to their children and deepen the wounds that have already been caused by their parent's absence.

Children of absent or uninvolved parents feel left on their own to get on with their lives and to deal with any challenges. They may blame themselves and suffer problems relating to their self-worth by believing that their uninvolved parent does not love them.

Some of the most common effects on children of an absent or uninvolved parent include:

- Difficulty expressing feelings and emotions
- Low self-esteem and issues with self-worth
- Struggle to handle rejection
- Emotional neediness
- Tendency to seek love, attention and approval from others
- Difficulty sustaining healthy relationships
- Difficulty with social interaction
- Problems with decision making
- Lack of healthy coping skills.

## The struggling parent

Struggling parents end up emotionally neglecting their children because they are weighed down by the other challenges they are facing in their lives.

Struggling parents have often been dealt a tough hand. They may have to care for another member of the family who is unwell or has special needs, they might be experiencing depression or illness themselves or have been recently divorced or bereaved.

The struggling parent would be present, connected and fully engaged with their children if they weren't hurt, caring for others, depressed, ill or grieving. They simply don't have the emotional capacity or mental bandwidth to be attentive to their kids. They are struggling so much with their own challenges that they feel like they have nothing left to give.

Children of struggling parents can find themselves taking care of them, as though the roles have reversed and the child becomes the parent. Children can feel great empathy towards their parent, and in some cases will feel obligated to look after them throughout their life. Anger and resentment build as children are forced to grow up quickly, missing out on a proper childhood at the same time as feeling restricted and trapped due to the needs of the person who is meant to be their own caregiver.

Some of the most common effects on adult children of a struggling parent include:

- Becoming self-sufficient
- Issues with blaming and shame
- An over-sensitive sense of fairness
- A guarded approach to expressing feelings and emotions
- A strong sense of empathy and a desire to help others
- Putting other people's needs way ahead of their own
- Relationship and intimacy problems.

# Becoming your parents

Parenting styles tend to be passed from generation to generation. For example, if you had a permissive parent then the chances are that your parents learned their behaviour through their own experiences as children.

Do bear in mind that parents can adapt their styles as their children change and get older, and there are many different styles of parenting. My mother adopted several different styles, but at her core was a permissive nature intertwined with a 'me-first' attitude. She allowed me to do pretty much what I wanted. When I started senior school she experienced a mental breakdown and a depressive episode, becoming totally unavailable to me as she struggled with her own mental health challenges.

I also experienced traits of the authoritarian parent in my mother, where she would implement unreasonable rules, usually because she wanted to put herself first. I was often left confused by the contradictions between her permissiveness and her restrictions.

My step-father was mostly absent, working long hours – I rarely saw him. On the occasions he was around he was preoccupied with the challenges and stresses that came with running his own business. The time I was able to spend with him was good, he was an excellent listener and always offered helpful and sensible advice. In fact, he would have been the perfect father, had he only been available more often.

My parents' permissive approach made it easy for me to get involved with the wrong people and when I was 13, a much older boy who lived in the same street befriended me. I looked up to him, he was good looking, clever and cool – everything I wanted to be. We started to hang out together – I have since considered whether a more emotionally connected parent would have examined this new friendship closer.

This boy manipulated and sexually abused me. I was confused and upset, wondering if it meant I was gay, although I had always felt attracted to girls. I blamed myself, I hadn't said 'no' and I had gone along with what he suggested with very little resistance. I didn't speak a word about what had happened and carried a huge sense of shame within me until I was 40 years old.

When I shared this episode with my wife, it felt incredible to bring such a deeply held thing out into the light. As soon as I realized she wasn't judging me and that she cared, and wanted to help, I began to feel lighter. I have since spoken openly about this episode and have found that the more I share, the less power it holds over me. Now I feel as though I have claimed the power back and turned a negative experience into something that can help other people.

It would be easy to blame my parents for not being aware of where I was or what I was doing. It was their responsibility to ensure that I was safe. However, blaming them solves nothing. Instead, I have learned to accept that my parents were doing the best they could with what they had at the time.

Later in my journey to recovery I found it helpful to use my journal to notice how my own behaviour as an adult compared with that of both my mother and my father. I liked to believe I was totally different, but when I looked closely, the comparisons were startling and this motivated me to change, to become an independent adult who lived as the authentic and true version of himself.

- I am anxious, worry all the time and constantly feel like I have a 'fight or flight' response within me – *my mother is the same.*
- I judge and criticize myself and others – *my mother is the same.*
- I don't express my emotions – *my mother is the same.*
- I have struggled to maintain healthy relationships in the past – *my mother is the same.*
- People say I have no empathy – *my mother is the same.*
- I experience childish reactions when emotions overwhelm me – *my mother is the same.*
- I avoid conflict at all costs – *my mother is the same.*
- I do things I don't want to do in order to please people – *my mother is the same.*

- I experience regular low moods and episodes of depression – *my mother is the same.*
- I constantly seek the approval of other people – *my mother is the same.*
- I don't have many friends – *my mother is the same.*
- I never feel 'good enough' – *my mother is the same.*

Writing out this list helped me move away from any urge to blame my mother and also gave me much more clarity around some of the negative traits that were holding me back. Take the time to write a similar list in your journal; what traits do you share with your parents?

# Is it your mother, father, or both?

In most cases of CEN or past trauma, we find that there is one parent who we consider more responsible for our wounds than the other. Remember that this is not about pointing the finger of blame. However, it is common for men to find that their issues often relate to their mothers and for women to find that their fathers were the major contributor to the challenges they encounter in adult life, although this isn't always the case.

The issues are compounded when one parent has been a dominant force in any neglectful or abusive behaviour while the other has turned a blind eye and failed to provide appropriate support or protection when it was so badly needed. Equally, two abusive parents can cause significant trauma by carrying out similar behaviours. In each of these scenarios the child can be left feeling helpless with nobody to turn to for comfort, love and support.

Take a moment to consider whether one, or both, of your parents were:

- treating the other parent badly;
- not loving, caring or supportive of you or each other;
- struggling with addictive behaviour;
- overbearing, controlling or failing to respect your personal boundaries;
- emotionally absent;
- physically absent for most of the time, maybe they left the family when you were young or worked away much of the time;
- critical, or shaming, of you – do you feel 'good enough' for them?;
- more interested in their own problems than yours;
- always too busy for you;
- displaying narcissistic or sociopathic tendencies.

One major area of our lives that is impacted by toxic parenting are the intimate relationships we form as adults. Commonly, certain patterns of behaviour will play out that can place a strain on a romantic partnership. For example, heterosexual men might take out their 'mother issues' on their female partners, and women may do the same to their male partner with their 'father issues'.

Mother and father wounds can impact men and women alike, there are no hard and fast rules. The wounds that are left from a deficit of mothering or fathering in childhood can dramatically influence our adult relationships and, in many cases, they can cause co-dependent or avoidant behaviours to develop, due to the lack of adequate parenting.

If you can begin to notice your own behaviour as you become more self-aware, then you will be able to take steps to start improving the close relationships that matter to you the most. We will look more closely at relationships later in the book.

## Mother wounds

Wounds from our mothers can take the form of hurtful comments in times of need, such as like 'don't be such a baby', 'man up', 'stop making such a fuss' or 'big girls shouldn't cry'. Such emotionally cold messages can cause significant issues with mental wellbeing and emotional stability, especially when they are repeated over and over.

Mothers who cause CEN may be distant, critical, absent, cold or incredibly over-bearing. Some might go so far as to involve themselves in every area of their son or daughters' lives, casting judgements, invading privacy and offering opinions at every opportunity on their choice of partners, clothes, careers and friends, causing their child to either rebel, or adjust their behaviour to keep their mother happy.

People who suffer 'mother wounds' often feel lost and unable to understand why they feel different to other people, but can't identify any reason for this.

When you look back at your childhood you might identify such issues as:

- Constantly striving to do better or achieve more to try and gain your mother's approval or attention
- Feeling that saying or doing the wrong thing could lead to a loss of your relationship with your mother
- Feeling that your mother has never truly accepted you, or approved of you just the way you are
- Having to support, care for, or protect your mother instead of her doing this for you
- Feeling that your mother may not care for you or love you
- Never talking deeply to your mother about the things that matter to you
- Never relating to your mother on an emotional level
- Feeling that your mother may love or care for your siblings more than you.

We can spend a lifetime ignoring these kinds of painful thoughts, and the reason it feels like we can't understand what is going on is because we have become detached from our emotions and feelings as a way of protecting ourselves from the hurt inflicted by an emotionally neglectful parent. In many cases a child learns that their mother is an unreliable source of emotional support and that the only way to soothe themselves is to detach from the thing that they long to be connected with the most – the love, touch, support and comfort of their mother. They will eventually learn to ignore the deep sense of sadness, anger and pain at having a mother who has failed to provide what they needed.

When a mother fails to provide her child with the reassurance that they are loveable exactly as they are, unconditionally 'good enough', the child develops low self-esteem. As an adult, they may not have a clear sense of what the true version of themselves actually looks like. Some may feel ashamed of who they think they are, or feel that they are to blame for their past, all the while remaining stuck and struggling to understand where the feelings are coming from.

Many people describe how they feel empty inside and emotionally lost. These people have had no mother available to soothe them or support them emotionally, and often seek out comfort from external sources. This might be drugs, alcohol, porn, gambling, food, exercise, work or by sexually acting out through affairs, one-night stands, chat or video services, or the use of sex workers.

Mother wounds commonly impact close intimate relationships, although most people don't see it until it is too late. Adults who have suffered emotional neglect or trauma may subconsciously seek out a partner who is more like a replacement mother than an equal. This is particularly common among men, who may find themselves subconsciously driven by their unmet mother-needs when they choose their female partner. An adult's expectations of their partner is often greatly influenced by past trauma and neglect. If their mother treated them like a small child and looked after their every need, even when they grow older they may expect the same treatment from a partner.

This can lead to an unequal balance of power within an intimate relationship. People might feel a need to be controlling or very submissive depending on the dynamic of the relationship and the nature of the past neglect or trauma.

Partners of people who have been affected by neglect or trauma may feel that their loved one is distant and lacking in empathy during difficult moments. This can put long-term relationships under strain as the partners feel disconnected and distant from each other. Without action the partnership may fail and the relationship end. Until the mother wound is healed, the wounded adult will continue to repeat the same patterns and behaviours over and over without ever understanding why they get involved in self-defeating and damaging behaviours, or why they seem unable to maintain healthy, loving relationships.

# Father wounds

Father wounds are caused by the absence of love, comfort, support and nurturing from a birth father or an older male role model, such as a step-father. All children have a deep desire to feel protected and loved by their father, they also need a strong male role model who validates them and shows them that he is proud of who they are, exactly as they are.

These painful wounds can be caused by fathers who are:

- Absent – due to divorce, careers and death
- Abusive – physically, sexually, verbally or mentally
- Addicted – to alcohol, drugs, gambling or work, for example
- Controlling – authoritarian, dominating and overbearing
- Holding back – failing to verbalize emotions or feelings of love, support and care
- Neglectful – making their child feel unimportant and unworthy.

Many people who experience father wounds find themselves with issues relating to their self-esteem and overall sense of worth, but it can touch almost every area of life from marriage, career and friendships to unhealthy and even illegal behaviour. Children who lacked a loving and caring relationship with their father can also experience anger issues, anxiety, inability to trust, tendencies to isolate, emotional detachment, and a propensity to selfishness.

If you feel that your lack of strong parental relationships has left you with emotional baggage, you are not alone. At the same time, always remember that those who realize that there is work to be done in order to heal can reclaim control. Regardless of whether you grew up in a home that lacked love and emotional connection or not, you *can* nurture healthy relationships and provide a loving and supportive environment for your own children.

Single parents are able to provide a wonderful, loving and stable environment for their children if they are able to overcome any issues that might have been holding them back.

The majority of relationships don't break down, and some couples stay together because of their children. Wounded adults can misdirect their anger and hurt towards their partner and, unless they are able to become self-aware and work on healing, it is unlikely the cycle of suffering will end or the relationship will improve. Even if an intimate relationship fails, the adult will still carry the wound and it will be taken into all future partnerships until they become conscious about what is happening and choose to change.

Our fathers are a huge influence on our lives and the quality of our relationship with them has a huge bearing on how we end up relating to ourselves as adults.

When we can start to notice our unhealed wounds and understand them better, then we can move towards healing them.

As you explore the story of your past, you might find that it seems obvious that one of your parents is more responsible than the other. Bear in mind that our parents will likely both have had their part to play in our neglect and trauma, even if the impact is subtle – look closely and you will probably see it.

I initially believed that my own issues were caused as a result of my father abandoning my mother and me. For my entire life, I had idolized my mother and wouldn't hear a bad word said against her. It was only when I started to explore my past in more depth that I realized she had been emotionally absent and failed to provide the love, support, comfort and protection I needed.

I make no apology for repeating myself here: please try and avoid blaming your parents. This is not about them, it is about you and your healing. You are bound to have feelings of anger, sadness, rage, shame and disappointment. This is perfectly normal and it simply means that you are human. It is for you to work through the negative emotions that you experience as part of your healing process, but hanging on to them and blaming others will not help.

Learning to accept the past for what it was and forgive your parents is the ideal place to reach in order to find long-lasting peace. Don't expect this to happen overnight though, it could take months or even years to feel ready to completely let go and forgive. Don't try and force anything or rush the process, it needs to be natural and you should simply learn to allow the feelings you encounter to be with you, and pay close attention to whatever comes up.

By following the techniques and processes outlined throughout this book, you will be able to move towards a place where you can become connected with the real version of you, so you can learn how to start loving yourself, accept the past and soften the pain and discomfort that you have been experiencing.

# 9 | Friends, siblings and heartbreak

Emotional neglect and trauma are not exclusive to our parents and you may have found that when you look back to your childhood, your parents were supportive, comforted you, made you feel safe and met all your emotional needs.

While in many cases the roots of neglect come from the primary caregiver, we may also find that the behaviour of people in our wider family and circle of friends, peers, and authority figures can have an equally damaging impact on the way we are shaped in later life.

You may have identified obvious examples of abusive behaviour in your life already, such as bullying, violence or sexual abuse. But it can be hard to notice when we have become involved in a toxic relationship when we are young, and these can be just as harmful as parental neglect.

## Toxic friendships

One of the most common covert behaviours comes in the form of toxic friendships while we are at school. These relationships are characterized by close friends who might become emotionally unsupportive or they may begin to exclude us, shame us or break our trust.

When we are friends with toxic people we can end up feeling confused, as if walking on eggshells. Unhealthy friendships often feature controlling and narcissistic behaviour and the neglected party may find themselves people-pleasing or becoming involved in behaviour they don't want to participate in, just to keep their toxic friend happy and on-side.

These kinds of friends will often momentarily change their behaviour and can quickly switch from feeling like a trusted ally to our worst enemy. This has a detrimental effect on our self-esteem while it can be mentally draining trying to navigate our way around their emotional instability.

Toxic friendships almost always cause us increased stress and anxiety, yet the whole purpose of true friendships is to feel less stressed and more happy. Toxic friends leave us feeling isolated and unsupported as they fail to show up when we really need them, and they usually lack the ability to be empathetic or emotionally available for us.

One of the biggest challenges with any form of toxic relationship is that we may begin to believe that we are to blame. When we feel flawed due to constant put downs, or constantly ignored and abandoned when we need help, we may begin to believe that we are responsible when a relationship becomes toxic.

Some of the warning signs that a friendship (or other relationship) may be toxic include:

- You give way more than you get in return
- You know they gossip about you
- They are egotistical; they come first, always
- You often question why you are friends with this person
- You have lost trust in them
- You feel anxious or nervous around them
- They have shamed you or put you down
- You find yourself making excuses on their behalf
- If they don't like something about you they try to make you change
- It feels like they sometimes use you and take advantage
- They sometimes apologize but don't mean it
- They fail to keep their promises
- Their behaviour embarrasses you.

At school, I was friends with a boy called Steven. We were the same age and had known each other since we were young. Sometimes I would hang out at his house and occasionally he would come to mine; we played video games on the Atari console together and we enjoyed each other's company.

However, he became part of a gang of older boys and one evening I made the mistake of taking a shortcut through a dimly lit alleyway that backs on to the street I lived in. I had used the cut-through hundreds of times in the past on my way to school and even in the dark I had no fear, despite it being the perfect place for a predator to conceal themselves.

As I walked alone in the dark I was approached by three hooded boys who refused to allow me to pass. I couldn't make out their faces until one of them, who had been fumbling in his pocket, looked directly at me. It was Steven! He had a knife in his hand and was pointing it straight at me. He acted as though we had never met and seemed intent on causing me serious harm, I didn't hang around to find out and bolted like a startled deer – fortunately the trio didn't catch me. After this episode I occasionally saw Steven at school, but stayed out of his way and we never spoke again; he had become a toxic friend.

One of the best methods for dealing with toxic people is to take action that gives you back the power in any given situation. Try talking to the source of the toxicity, expressing clearly and calmly how their behaviour makes you feel and what your expectation is of them in the future in order to enjoy a healthy friendship.

You might find this wake-up call causes their behaviour to change. However, if it persists then you owe it to yourself to put clear boundaries in place and impose whatever sanctions you need to ensure you feel safe. In some cases that may even mean distancing yourself from the friendship or cutting contact.

# Siblings

Bullying and abuse from siblings is another common type of harmful behaviour within family units. It often remains underreported and has become a silent epidemic in many societies.

The impact of being abused by a sibling can result in similar symptoms to those generated by parental trauma or neglect. I often encounter people who believe they had a perfect childhood and felt that their parents met all their emotional needs, but when I probe deeper I discover that hurtful and abusive behaviour by a brother or sister had caused them to live in a state of constant fear and anxiety.

It is important to be clear that sibling squabbles and rivalry are totally different to abuse. It is common for brothers and sisters to argue, fight and become competitive on occasion, often competing for the attention or approval of their parents. But it is another matter when the goal is to cause harm or suffering to another person.

Abuse from a sibling is compounded when parents turn a blind eye and fail to provide the support required to keep the affected child safe. This is a double blow when the child finds themselves abused by their brother or sister and emotionally abandoned by their parents when they most need them.

Dealing with an abusive sibling can be a challenge, especially when we continue to live with them. But expressing how they make us feel, no matter what the consequences, is essential. If it feels uncomfortable to do this one-to-one, then it makes sense to have the conversation in the presence of either a non-judgemental third-party such as a therapist, teacher or a friend, or consider having a parent present with whom you feel safe to be open and honest.

Being open, authentic and honest is critical. Regardless of how the bully reacts, we end up stronger in the knowledge that we have shared our true feelings and will most likely have cleared the air to create an opportunity for further dialogue. This isn't about how they react, it is about us being authentic and truthful about how we have been made to feel.

If you no longer live with a sibling then the best plan is to approach the situation in the same way as you would with a toxic friendship, by expressing your feelings and putting clear boundaries in place.

If you find the prospect of confronting a bullying sibling overwhelming, it is essential that you avoid keeping the issue to yourself. You might find it easier to write them a letter or send an email. If you are unsure of the best approach, take the time to talk to someone supportive about what has been happening. As soon as you share you will no longer be alone, and will begin to feel lighter.

# Authority figures and older people

When we are young we trust adults by default, especially those in a position of responsibility. This might be a group leader, manager, sports coach or anyone older who you respect, such as a family friend, or someone in a formal position of trust like a doctor or teacher.

The fact is that almost any adult will be in a 'position of trust' by default when they are working with, or befriending, children and young adults. Unfortunately a minority of them will break that trust. Any abusive behaviour can be incredibly harmful and damaging and has the potential to cause similar long-lasting traits to those that we have previously explored.

When I was a teenager, my step-father was the manager of Bejam, a local frozen food store. Occasionally he would allow me to go into work with him on a Saturday morning to earn some extra pocket money. One of my jobs was to unpack boxes of frozen vegetables by the delivery bay, which was buried deep in the bowels of the vast building. There were several men in their early twenties who worked in and around the same area and, on the surface, they appeared friendly. But, rather like the toxic friendship that we looked at earlier in the chapter, their behaviour had another side to it.

The pranks started out small, with comments and items being thrown around, but on one occasion they locked me in a metal food cage. I laughed along and after what seemed like forever, they finally let me out. At this point I was starting to feel really scared, but I didn't say anything, even though my step-father was in an office no more than 50 metres away. My overwhelming urge to be liked and accepted overrode my need to protect myself.

On my next Saturday morning visit, I was working by the delivery bay when the same thing happened. As the cage rolled towards me I felt sick, knowing that I had no way of fighting back. This time the abuse went further. At the far end of the delivery bay was a huge walk-in freezer the size of two double garages where the frozen products were kept before going on to the shop floor. The temperature gauge outside the freezer read –20 °C. My heart was pounding as they wheeled the cage closer, right into the freezing dark heart of the icy cold room.

As they left me in the cold trapped in the cage, I could see their silhouettes through the icy fog. They were pulling the shutter across and then... *slam*. It was closed. I was in the darkness, and I was beginning to freeze.

I am unsure how traumatized this event left me – I have no doubt it caused an emotional scar of some description. If you can clearly recollect a painful memory with good detail and see it like a movie in your mind's eye, then the chances are you suffered some form of trauma from it. I can picture these episodes of bullying as though they happened yesterday. My pain was multiplied because my step-father was the manager and, although he had no clue what was happening, I believed he should somehow have protected me and reprimanded the aggressors.

Clearly I didn't freeze to death and they let me out sometime later – I'm not sure when, but it was long enough. But instead of telling the men who had wheeled me into the freezer that their behaviour had gone too far and then letting my step-father (and their manager) know about it, I laughed it off. I wanted them to like me and I played along. Of course, their behaviour continued and I eventually found a Saturday job at a local carpet store instead, where the older men were respectful and had a healthy influence on me, treating me like an equal.

# Heartbreak and rejection

When we are young and experience a breakup, it can hurt badly, especially if it is the first time we have experienced love. The feelings of loss, sadness and suffering feel akin to grieving a death and it seems the intensity of the emotion will never fade. In our teenage years we are still developing physically, mentally and emotionally and the impact of having our heart broken feels all the more raw because we have never experienced such powerful emotions and feelings in our lives before.

As adults, we develop the ability to handle the ending of relationships better, as we have more of an acceptance that this is an inherent risk of being involved with someone on an intimate level. But for younger people it can come like an enormous, gut-wrenching bolt out of the blue. Some teenagers don't talk about what has happened when their relationship ends and compound their pain by not sharing it. It can be common for them to blame themselves and begin to believe that they must have something wrong with them.

Research has shown that teenagers and young adults can experience symptoms of trauma following a breakup, with some developing flashbacks, nightmares, a sense of hopelessness and feeling emotionally overwhelmed. While there is no conclusive evidence that PTSD can be attributed to teenage heartbreak, there is a strong argument for it and it is important that anyone affected seeks the appropriate support.

Being rejected by a boyfriend or girlfriend as a teenager can become far more intense when we already have issues around neglect or trauma. It can reinforce our subconscious belief that we are not worthy and unknowingly shape our future actions. Sometimes this takes the form of 'jump before I am pushed' behaviour, where people will act out or sabotage specific areas of their life in the belief that they will be rejected at some point anyway, so they may as well feel as though they are in control.

If you have experienced the pain of a relationship breakup during your life you can take comfort in the fact that it will help you on your journey to healing. The process of overcoming trauma and CEN can feel similar to the end of a toxic relationship and the grieving process that follows, before reaching a place where we feel free and no longer think about the ex who brought drama and negativity into our lives.

# 10 | The path to recovery

By now you may have started to form a clear understanding of what sits at the heart of the challenges you have been experiencing. You may have also been able to link specific behaviours, events or situations that you encountered around your parents to emotional episodes that you have experienced in your own adult life. If so, well done, this is a breakthrough and a clear sign that you are making progress.

The episodes that cause us to have an overwhelming emotional reaction in adulthood are called triggers, and throughout the book I will ensure that you know exactly how to overcome them in a healthy way.

Have you started to notice what it is that triggers you? How old do you feel when you are triggered? Can you identify specific traits or behaviours from your parents in situations that cause an intense emotional reaction? Start to gather the data and you will quickly cultivate a heightened awareness and a desire to overcome these debilitating episodes.

Here are two examples of triggering episodes:

**Ruth shared a post about her expensive new laptop on social media. One of her online friends made a comment that criticized her for showing off. The comment caused Ruth to spiral into a powerful emotional response; she was triggered. Ruth allowed herself a time out and, when the adult was back in control, she explored the episode, rather like a detective would investigate a crime scene. She realized that her reaction stemmed from her father, who would often be critical of her, and she noticed how any form of criticism could make her feel overwhelming emotion.**

**Mark sent an email message to a friend who was usually supportive, asking them for their advice about some relationship challenges he was facing. Two days later he had not received a reply and began to feel overwhelmed by emotion. He felt like he was being ignored and his anger began to boil. When the adult-Mark was back in control, he felt ready to explore what happened closer and he realized that what he really felt was a fear of being rejected, concluding that it was related to his father abandoning him when he was five years old.**

Keep an open mind. Any triggers that you experience will act as a signpost towards the underlying cause. Instead of beating yourself up or becoming frustrated, treat your triggers as a gift that will point you towards the information you need to help you heal. Explore each and every one of them with judgement-free curiosity.

The process of recovering and healing will see you moving through the ten stages that I outlined in Chapter 4. I hope you feel like you are progressing steadily down the right path and developing a clear understanding of why you feel the way you do at times. You may even have noticed that some of your emotions and feelings have started to soften or weaken since you began naming them when they arise in you, keep working on this, it is important.

In order to heal fully, we need to reconnect with the true version of ourselves and learn to love them just as they are. Over the years, we have avoided interacting with (or as) our 'true-self' through a deep rooted fear that they will not be accepted and a worry about what we might discover if we dare to look.

# Connecting with your true-self

To heal, the mask we wear to convince the world we are a good person needs to come off. Start to drop ego-driven behaviours and any unhelpful traits and become consciously 'naked'. When you are able to do this, you are free to become authentic and start to experience peace in your life.

Use your journal to work through these five actions to begin connecting with the true version of yourself. This will guide you towards healing your childhood wounds and bringing your suffering to an end for good.

**Action 1**: Discover and practice being your 'true-self'. You can do this by creating a clear picture of who you really are:

- Identify what makes you feel good, what helps you grow and what makes you experience joy.
- Identify what makes you feel down. This could be people, places, behaviours or situations.
- Get clear on what you admire about yourself. Identify your strengths and talents, and recognize the qualities that make you a good person.

**Action 2**: Accept all parts of yourself, including the darker side. All humans are made up of good and bad parts. We all have darker aspects of our personality that we fail to notice (commonly known as our shadow). To become whole we can nurture an awareness of what we keep in our shadow and begin to accept these parts of the rich tapestry of who we really are.

While this may sound negative, the goal in this step is to create a conscious awareness of what we hide in our shadow by bringing it out into the light, so it no longer causes suffering and enables us to live as our 'true-self'.

A therapist once said to me, 'If you spot it, you've got it'. He was explaining how to find the parts of my personality that I had failed to see in myself. These examples will help you become more shadow-conscious:

Dev would become extremely angry when he saw greedy people; he would rage if he spotted someone overeating and his blood would boil when he saw people who he perceived as extravagant on a material level. Drivers of supercars pushed his emotional buttons in a big way. His hatred of greed was a protection mechanism that covered up the shame he held about his own greedy behaviour. Instead of 'owning' this part of his personality, he projected it on to others.

Mary had felt for some time that her boss hated her; she couldn't put her finger on why, but deep down she had become convinced that he disliked her for no good reason. She would rant to her co-workers about how unfair it was that he held her in such a negative light, while they comforted her and pointed out her positive qualities. The reality was that Mary did not 'own' the part of her that disliked her boss, instead she protected herself by projecting on to him.

Whenever Nita saw a sex scene on the television she become angry and would quickly reach for the remote control and switch it off, before venting to her husband about how unnecessary and inappropriate it was to show these scenes. Nita was projecting her own insecurity and shame around sex, instead of accepting that it is part of her individual make-up.

Harry would often make jokes to his friends about people who were overweight, he would also point out strangers while he was socializing and comment about their physical appearance to his companions. Harry's projection covered his own deep insecurities about his body, he hated the way he looked but had never owned it, instead he projected his disgust outwards on to others.

Action 3: Understand what your needs are and learn how to meet them in a healthy and safe manner. Our needs are a combination of emotional, physical and spiritual, we can often identify them when we become clear on our core values.

Action 4: We must accept and share the experiences that have caused us pain in a safe space and grieve the hurt that they have caused us.

Action 5: We must learn how to express our emotions and feelings in a healthy way and use our values as a compass to guide us through life.

These five actions, combined with the six stages of healing I previously shared, are fundamental to you reconnecting with the authentic version of yourself and moving through any pain and suffering.

This book is structured to guide you through the entire process. Take the time to ensure that you have fully explored and understood each section before you move on to the next one and if anything doesn't sink in, make sure you read it again or conduct further research about the specific topic online. It is also important to allow yourself time to digest and reflect on the work you are doing. I found the process of healing stirred up many uncomfortable memories and I would often have to spend time quietly reflecting or obtaining a healthy perspective on past events using my journal.

There were times when exploring my past would emotionally overwhelm me to the point that I felt in a worse place than before I began the process. However, I knew that the only way to overcome what I was facing would be to continue working through it. As soon as I had composed myself, I would note down my experience in my journal, name the specific emotions that had been with me and explore them all in more depth with a calm, curious and rational approach.

Above all, be gentle with yourself. It is common to have neglected our own needs when we have experienced CEN or trauma, and we can leave ourselves sorely lacking the self-love that we so desperately need. Try not to force anything, keep reading, thinking, reflecting and learning. As you do, you should feel yourself becoming free and noticing a sense of having more personal power as a feeling of peace begins to emerge.

Consistency is important when it comes to making a long-lasting life change and comedian Jerry Seinfeld uses an excellent technique that will serve you well if you adopt it on your personal journey to healing. His strategy ensures he avoids procrastination and produces a solid standard of work, which has made him one of the highest earning, top-rated comedians of all time.

Some years ago in a small comedy club, a young performer was lucky enough to run into Seinfeld backstage after he had appeared in front of the tightly packed audience in the venue. He caught Seinfeld's attention and said, 'Any tips for a young comic to write better material?'

Seinfeld replied, 'The way to be a better comic is to create better jokes, and the way to create better jokes is to write every day.' He went on to explain that the young comic should invest in a 12-month wall planner and place it somewhere prominent. He told the comic to get himself a red marker pen and for each day he completed the task of writing, he was to put a big X over that day on the chart. He explained how the red X's would create a streak which would grow each day and that the chain would become a motivator because the longer it became, the more the comedian would enjoy looking at it.

He finished up by telling the young comic, 'Your only job is to not break the chain.'

This simple, but highly effective method became known as 'The Seinfeld Strategy' and it is a great tool to ensure we don't get demotivated, especially after a tough day or a setback. The strategy takes the emphasis away from specific episodes, events or outcomes and, instead, focuses us on the process of not breaking the chain by showing up and putting in the work consistently.

You can bring this technique into your own life. All you need is a wallchart and a marker pen. Make sure you pick a task that is meaningful enough to allow you to notice results over time, but balance this with a realistic understanding of what you can actually achieve on a daily basis. Keep the tasks you give yourself simple; for example, you might choose to spend one hour each day working on your recovery from neglect and trauma. But if an hour is too much of a stretch, reduce the time to ensure you can keep your chain going.

The process of recovery took me around six to eight months from when I originally became aware that I had suffered emotional neglect and trauma. However, I didn't have this book and had to find my own way using the limited range of tools and resources that were available to me at the time. I also worked with a therapist who had suffered similar experiences in his own childhood. This was incredibly helpful, and if you feel that a level of face-to-face support would be beneficial, then I would encourage you to seek it out.

The reason my sobriety coaching delivers such excellent results is because I have lived through the experience and I have come out the other side, having turned my life around. This means that people who are struggling with alcohol abuse are able to relate to me much better than they would to someone who has never dealt with their own struggle. The fact that I have been on my own sobriety journey also means that I have learned many of the lessons through first-hand experience, I fully understand what my clients are going through and I will usually know the best way of handling it.

If you decide that working with a therapist will be beneficial, my advice is that you do your research. Find someone who has a proven track record, specializes in CEN and trauma and has, ideally, overcome their own similar issues.

# 11 | Expressing our emotions and feelings in a healthy way

It is important that we learn to express our feelings and emotions in order to become the real version of ourselves. When we have suffered past trauma or CEN, we are susceptible to being emotionally triggered by people, situations and behaviours that remind us of the past. But we can also experience painful feelings for no apparent reason.

We experience discomfort when we feel:

- Angry
- Fearful
- Worried
- Hurt
- Depressed
- Jealous
- Anxious
- Sad
- Lonely
- Annoyed

We experience happiness, contentment and peace when we feel:

- Joyful
- Acknowledged
- Hopeful
- Excited
- Satisfied
- Content
- Amused
- Serene
- Relaxed
- Loved

Throughout this book, I mostly explore negative feelings and emotions because I want to help you experience them less. However, it is important to stay mindful of when you feel positivity, even if it seems like a rare occurrence in your life right now. Expressing your positive feelings is also a healthy habit to learn. If someone has made you feel happy, let them know – light up their day. Don't get caught in the trap of believing that you should only pay attention to uncomfortable feelings.

Pay attention to speaking your positive feelings out loud. It can take a bit of practice but, once you have developed the skill and the courage to verbalize them, you will gain back some of your personal power and control over your mood. If we can learn to express how we feel in a safe and healthy way, we will avoid repressing emotions and remain free from the burden this creates.

Imagine each unexpressed feeling as emotional baggage we have to carry around, getting heavier over the years.

Expressing your feelings will help you to become whole, truthful and authentic, and to behave in line with your values. I make it my goal to use this approach every single day as I know that it allows me to live my best life. I made a non-negotiable promise to myself that I will keep my baggage to a minimum and I stay mindful about keeping it that way, even when the odd thought I don't like slips under my radar.

After you have explored your shadow, and have understood and accepted all parts of yourself, you will no longer have any fear about showing your inside on the outside. When you can do this you will stop limiting yourself and will be on the path to freedom.

Having feelings and emotions is part of being human. A huge amount of growth comes with allowing yourself to feel everything and simply 'experiencing it' for what it is. While we are awake, we will always be in some kind of emotional state. We are never without a feeling or an emotion, so instead of ignoring them or attempting to fight them, begin to allow 'what is' to be with you in that moment through a sense of knowing acceptance.

Notice when you ignore or suppress emotions and feelings. I fostered a new habit of naming everything I felt as soon as I experienced it. Ensure you continue to build this new habit: when you notice a feeling or emotion, name it, label it, explore it, consider what is underneath it, then find out what might be driving it. Catch yourself if you push it away, hide from it or attempt to ignore it.

I put a lot of work into learning the healthiest ways of expressing my emotions and feelings. Sometimes this involved verbalizing them in a safe space or writing them down in my journal, on other occasions it meant allowing myself to simply sit and observe them without judgement until I felt like they had softened. There were times when I experienced intense anger or sadness to the point that I would cry, or punch a pillow. All of these are healthy ways to express feelings, there is nothing wrong with a good cry, or a physical release.

I have created a process that will allow you to express and release your feelings and emotions in a healthy and safe way, use this method and practice the new skill of noticing, acknowledging and expressing what you experience as it arises.

Instead of being afraid of your negative feelings and emotions, treat them as the gift that is helping you heal. Give yourself permission to feel pleased when a feeling or emotion arises, as it gives you an opportunity to practice your healthy new habits. Each and every feeling you experience will be with you for a reason - it is inviting you to explore, it wants you to find out why it arrived and to discover what you need to do in order to release it.

# The process of expressing emotions and feelings in a healthy way

**Step 1**: When you notice any sense of discomfort or unease you should pause for a moment. Take a few long, slow breaths in and out through your nose in order to become present and grounded.

**Step 2**: Either in your mind or using your journal, answer the following questions:

- How do I feel at this moment?
- What is it that I need right now?

Take some time to think about what you really need, maybe it is a hug, a connection, a sleep, or a walk in nature, for example.

- What is making me feel this way?

Consider where the feeling is coming from, begin to understand why it is with you and make sense of it.

**Step 3**: Name and label your emotion or feeling. If you are unsure of what you are experiencing, use an emotion wheel.

**Step 4**: Accept that this emotion or feeling is with you in this moment. Avoid any judgement, criticism, negative self-talk or temptation to suppress or fight what you are experiencing. Welcome the feelings in, no matter how negative. Give yourself full permission to feel them and be safe in the knowledge that you know how to express and release them.

Remember that no feeling is permanent, they always pass.

**Step 5**: Write. Use your journal and spill everything out onto the blank pages. You don't need to think or plan what you intend to write, just allow it to flow, this is your private space.

Make a commitment to yourself that you will journal. It might feel like hard work at times but it really is your best friend when it comes to helping you heal. If you find yourself skipping entries or missing days, remind yourself why you are doing this and why you want to change your life. Then refocus and reset with a new sense of motivation.

# Verbalize how you feel where appropriate

Once I had created a habit of expressing my feelings in my journal, I began to work on verbalizing them whenever I believed it was appropriate. Initially I shared my feelings with my wife, my 'safe person'. She is non-judgemental, incredibly supportive and a brilliant listener (which is lucky because she has a husband who rarely stops talking).

As I made progress, I realized that there were, and are, times when I needed to express how I felt to a specific person, usually when their behaviour triggered a negative reaction. This felt daunting to me at first, and it will feel daunting to you – it might mean speaking your truth to a friend, work colleague or somebody you don't get along with. However, it is your commitment to making these changes and doing the work which will allow you to find the strength to push through any discomfort.

It took time, but now I am able to express my feelings to anyone. I practiced in order to feel confident before I started to slowly share with others, and I still take the time to consider whether I am 'projecting' and need to look more closely at myself and the potential consequences of my actions.

There were many dummy runs talking to myself in the mirror before I felt confident enough to tell someone face to face how they had made me feel. But when for the first time I was able to do it, I felt an enormous amount of personal power which drove me on with this liberating new habit.

There have been a couple of occasions where someone has triggered me, I have spoken the truth and explained calmly how they have made me feel, and my honesty resulted in them becoming triggered in turn. This can happen, and when it does, I ensure that I stay in my lane. I can't control the other person and I know that I have been honest and authentic.

It is important that you consider carefully exactly what you want to say before you express yourself. Avoid being critical and making brutal or hurtful statements. State the facts calmly and with empathy for the other person.

When my mother confessed to me recently that she had left me with a family friend for two weeks when I was 11 months old so she could head off on a cruise with my biological father, I felt a swelling of anger building inside of me. The conversation was via text message, so I wrote my feelings down in my journal. A few days later I arranged to meet her; I knew that I needed to tell her how her revelation had made me feel.

As we sat together I told her how sad I felt about having been left behind at such a young age, but how I respected her honesty. I spoke calmly, I didn't raise my voice and I kept empathy in my words, gently stating the facts – *this was how your actions made me feel, and I am letting you know.*

As soon as the words 'angry' and 'sad' left my lips, the emotion I was holding faded. I had spoken it out loud, I had expressed it in a healthy way and been totally authentic about how I felt.

My mother agreed she should have stayed with me, confessed it was a difficult time, and apologized. As she took ownership, I no longer had any logical reason to hang on to the negativity. I had handed my negative feelings back to her and by accepting her mistake, she had taken them from me.

Of course, we won't always get an apology when we express our feelings. But on the occasions that we do, it allows us to transfer any negativity we hold on to the person who has accepted responsibility. It is one of the most powerful feelings we will experience in the process of healing.

# Owning your feelings and setting boundaries

Before you head out into the world to tell everyone how you feel, practise expressing your feelings and emotions verbally in a calm and empathetic way on your own. Try speaking to yourself in a mirror. Depending how you feel, you might say:

**'When I am ignored it makes me feel really sad'** or **'When people don't return my calls I feel really anxious.'**

Make the statement about you, not about the person you are talking to. If you were to say:

**'When *YOU* ignore me *YOU* make me feel really sad',** you are blaming the individual for *your* negative feelings and can create conflict.

When you are able to say:

**'When *I* think I am being ignored, it makes *ME* feel really sad',** you are placing the emphasis on *you* and *your* feelings, as opposed to pointing the finger of blame.

Perfect the skill of speaking in a calm and soft tone and avoid accusations. You will soon find that you are able to calmly express your feelings to almost anyone.

It can also help to set boundaries at the same time as expressing how you feel, here is an example:

**Charlie forgets to call his wife at lunchtime while he is at work. He usually calls her every day without fail, in fact, it is a daily ritual. But on this occasion he had become caught up resolving a problem at work and it completely slipped his mind.**

**His wife Sarah, who is at home awaiting the call, starts to become anxious, worried that something is wrong. She tries to call Charlie, but his phone is in his locker and there is no answer. Before long she has convinced herself that something awful has happened and spends the afternoon becoming more agitated, creating horrendous stories in her mind with awful dramatic outcomes.**

**Later that evening, Charlie walks through the door. Sarah feels a sense of relief, but it is overshadowed by anger because he seems to have totally forgotten about her. He apologizes as soon as it dawns on him that today's call had slipped his mind, but she can't dispel her feelings so easily.**

**Sarah could express how she feels and set expectations and boundaries at the same time by using the following three-step approach, which builds on the previous strategy. I use this method and it works perfectly.**

Adopting a compassionate tone, and once she feels ready and confident, Sarah should calmly express herself using these three steps:

1. State the issue and make it about you. In Sarah's case: 'When people don't call *me* when *I* think they will. . . '.
2. Express the feeling: '. . . it makes *me* feel anxious and angry. . . '.
3. Explain how you would like to be treated: '. . . and I would rather people ensured they called me when they promised, or let me know if it's not possible'.

With these words, Sarah will have expressed how she feels, explained what behaviour caused the feeling and made it clear how she expects to be treated in future. Use this process as a template whenever you need to express your feelings or set clear boundaries for what you expect in future.

**'When people [*insert the behaviour that has triggered you*] it makes me feel [*insert how you feel*] and I would rather they [*insert the behaviour you would like instead*].'**

Try to practise this by yourself. Stand in front of the mirror and visualize yourself talking to the other person. Before long, you will feel ready to speak your true feelings and state your expectations out loud to the people who need to hear them.

I learned this three-step process like a script and I have used it repeatedly to calmly express myself and clearly state how I expect to be treated in specific situations. Take the time to perfect it and then discover how empowering it feels to offload without becoming emotional, at the same time as clearly setting your expectations. It is incredibly simple to learn and, when you find the courage to speak up, you will unlock a new power from within.

I also found that people began to respect and trust me more because I was being authentic. I had become one of those people who 'always speaks the truth' and people respect that. There have been occasions where I have expressed my feelings and people have thanked me and then told me that they wished they had the ability to be so honest.

Because we become totally authentic through this process, we also become incredibly honest. Honest people attract other honest people and I have had many occasions where I have been open, vulnerable and authentic as I shared my feelings and this, in turn, has enabled someone else to open up to me about something deeply personal.

Recently, as I talked to a friend about my experience of sexual abuse, she told me that she had also been abused. She had never told anyone, she said, and had carried it as an emotional weight for decades. Straight after she told me she said that she felt better already, as though something within had lightened.

I realized that speaking my truth invited other people to do the same. I instantly felt more connected to those who allowed me in, and shared their deep personal experiences. In every case the relationship has become stronger and moved to a level where we can comfortably talk about almost anything without fear.

Practise expressing your feelings. It is a strategy that will set you up for long lasting success in this process and, if you can find the courage to speak the truth when you know it is what you need to do, you will claim back an enormous amount of personal power in your life.

# 12 | Discovering and practising being your 'true-self'

As we have explored, at the core of healing from CEN and trauma is the process of discovering and reconnecting with your 'true-self'. This involves getting to know exactly who you are, without seeking any approval or permission from other people.

When you are able to know your true-self, you will immediately remove many obstacles as you stop wasting your energy and time in the wrong areas and instead become fully present, aware and confident.

When I began the process of discovering my true-self, I used my journal and asked myself the following question:

'Who am I, exactly?'

My first answer saw me talking about my achievements, my career, my material possessions, how much money I have and my hobbies. But this was not the answer I needed. I had to imagine myself without any ego, possessions, achievements, money, hobbies or career and then look at what exactly was left when all of this was stripped away. What did the 'naked' Simon really look like?

Don't mistake the process of self-understanding for self-indulgence. While you might think that asking questions about 'finding yourself' is fundamentally a self-indulgent process, it is actually one of the most unselfish processes you can undertake.

This process can enable you to become a better person, partner and parent. We owe it to ourselves to look right into the mirror and ask the uncomfortable questions so we can see who is behind the noise.

So I asked myself again:

'Who am I, exactly?'

This time I began to find some answers and I started to build a picture of what the true Simon really looked like. I started to understand that there was no way of ever finding my true-self unless I could see every facet of my life and evaluate myself in a completely honest and truthful way, good and bad.

I have created a process to help you answer this question, but I would also encourage you to use your journal and write down whatever comes up without too much planning or thinking. The process of simply free-writing can be incredibly insightful and you will often find some important nuggets of wisdom in the words that flow.

You might want to think of this process a little bit like a personality test. Your goal is to uncover exactly what the raw and real version of you looks like to create a clearer picture of who the true you really is. When you have this insight you will be in a great position to avoid triggering episodes, set healthy boundaries and engage in meaningful relationships and activities.

Another excellent practice is to start talking more about who you are than what you do.

# The steps to finding your true-self

## 1 Understand your story

You would think that we all know our own story, but you will be surprised how many memories are hidden away deep in the vault of our minds, and until we switch the light on and begin rummaging around, it can be hard to make sense of everything. If we can make the story of our own life available to see visually, it gives us a new perspective and we can make more sense of many aspects of how we are.

I created a timeline of my life. I found a free online 'timeline creator' tool that allowed me to draw everything out and, on there, I detailed everything that I had encountered on my life journey, from episodes of bullying at school to having my heart broken by the girl I had fallen in love with when I was 14. I added each and every memory and the more I added, the more I seemed to recollect. Before long the data was spilling out onto the timeline as wave after wave of memories flooded me.

As quickly as I entered one memory on my timeline another would come to mind. I added information about the period when I dabbled with hard drugs, episodes of bullying at school, accidents and injuries, sexual encounters, drinking behaviour, happy memories, fights with my parents, sexual abuse and plenty of behaviour that I still felt shame and guilt about. By the end, my timeline was crammed full of information and it was providing answers for me before I even began the next step.

Once I had created a timeline, I wrote out the story of my life in my journal. I ensured that what I wrote did not have too much emotion attached to it, trying to simply stick to the facts and nothing more.

I spent a lot of time on these activities, and as I reflected on what I had written, I made adjustments and additions and kept a flexible approach, rather than being rigid with what I had written the first time around.

In order for you to break your current patterns of behaviour, it is essential that you acknowledge and understand what is causing your suffering. That is your goal as you create your timeline and write your story.

Be brave. Stop hiding from those stories that cause you to feel shame, guilt, pain or hurt. Get them all out, turn yourself inside out in the knowledge that this is what will help to set you free. I wrote out my deepest and darkest secrets in that journal, things about which I felt extreme shame that I had never shared with anyone. I knew I had to be completely honest. I left absolutely nothing out and I would urge you to do the same.

Keep reflecting on what you write, this is a process of understanding and discovery. Your goal is to stop turning away from the moments in your life that feel too painful and, instead, begin to use them to create new and powerful insights into your life. Use the most challenging episodes of your life to your advantage, they will help you deepen the understanding of yourself and guide you towards connecting with the real version of you.

The more painful a memory feels, the closer you should look, sit with the memory and look right at it. Gaze into the eyes of those memories that have caused you pain with no fear, notice what comes up and how it makes you feel, and get everything down on your timeline and in your life story.

By facing up to any discomfort in this process you will gain invaluable insights into your true-self. From here you can begin to make healthy choices about how you want to show up in the world going forward.

You may find that the insights and breakthroughs you experience in this process will enable you to begin distancing yourself from any harmful influences or toxic people that are causing you suffering. You might also recognize certain behaviours that have caused you harm and you will be able to make a conscious choice about whether this is serving you in a healthy way or not, and whether you need to make any changes to eliminate negative tendencies as you go forward.

Don't underestimate the power of creating your timeline and writing your story. Take some time over it. The more you can understand who you really are and get to know yourself, the more you will find yourself becoming free.

If you don't feel ready to look at your past yet, come back to this when you feel strong enough to begin exploring things more closely. There is no rush.

## 2 Know your core values

Our values reflect what really matters to us. They can act as moral guard-rails ensuring we remain aligned with our true-self. If we have a clear understanding of them, they will also enable us to move towards our goals and find a sense of purpose in life.

Many people are unaware of their values. It is essential that you develop a clear understanding of yours in order to learn more about yourself and what drives your beliefs and behaviours. This will help you create true meaning in your life.

Our values form an internal blueprint for the way we want to live. For example, someone who has 'trust' and 'honesty' as important core values is likely to experience extreme discomfort if they find themselves in a high pressure sales job that involves them exaggerating to customers or being dishonest in order to seal a deal. It directly opposes their core values and will cause them significant pain as a result. The same person will feel joy and fulfilment if they are in a role where they are surrounded by people who are honest and trustworthy. Our life blueprint will cause us to feel either suffering, joy, or something in between, based on whether we are meeting our own expectations or not.

If you can understand your values, you will have a clear picture of your own life blueprint. You can then take steps to ensure that everything you do in life aligns with them. When we live our life in line with our values, we nurture a sense of fulfilment, when we push against our values and carry out behaviour that opposes them, it causes us pain.

Over time, you will begin to understand yourself. You will learn exactly what brings you joy and happiness and what causes you pain. You will naturally begin to make positive decisions and choices while having a heightened awareness around whether any activity, behaviour or relationship is serving you in a helpful way or not.

I have detailed the most common personal values in a list for you to use. Refine the list down to around 10 to 15 values that you feel apply to you. Then refine it down again so you have no more than six to eight remaining. These will represent your core values. I suggest keeping a note of the values that didn't quite make it onto your final list as these will give you a deeper understanding of yourself.

Our values can change over time, it makes sense to revisit them and refresh your list every so often.

Once you have your list, I recommend assessing every single area of your life and checking it aligns with your values, and that nothing you do opposes them. Take the time to reflect on everything from your career, hobbies and relationships through to your behaviours and habits.

Your values are unique to you, and if you live your life in line with them they will act as a compass, keeping you on track for a happy life and ensuring that you spend your time engaging in the things that bring you joy and meet your needs.

| | | | |
|---|---|---|---|
| Abundance | Determination | Honour | Punctuality |
| Approachability | Decisiveness | Humility | Reflection |
| Approval | Dependability | Humour | Reliability |
| Awareness | Devotion | Impartiality | Resilience |
| Accessibility | Dignity | Independence | Respect |
| Accountability | Directness | Integrity | Security |
| Achievement | Discipline | Intelligence | Self-control |
| Action | Discretion | Intimacy | Self-reliance |
| Adventure | Drive | Inspiration | Significance |
| Agility | Duty | Joy | Simplicity |
| Altruism | Effectiveness | Justice | Sincerity |
| Ambition | Empathy | Kindness | Skill |
| Appreciation | Energy | Knowledge | Solidarity |
| Approachability | Enjoyment | Leadership | Spirituality |
| Approval | Enthusiasm | Learning | Spontaneity |
| Awareness | Equality | Liberty | Strength |
| Balance | Excellence | Liveliness | Stability |
| Beauty | Excitement | Logic | Structure |
| Being | Fairness | Love | Success |
| the Best | Faith | Loyalty | Status |
| Belonging | Fame | Mastery | Teamwork |
| Calmness | Family | Mindfulness | Thankfulness |
| Care | Fidelity | Modesty | Tolerance |
| Certainty | Flexibility | Money | Tradition |
| Cheerfulness | Frankness | Motivation | Tranquillity |
| Clarity | Freedom | Nature | Trust |
| Comfort | Freedom of | Open-mindedness | Trustworthiness |
| Commitment | Speech | Optimism | Truth |
| Compassion | Friendship | Order | Understanding |
| Competition | Frugality | Originality | Uniqueness |
| Confidence | Fulfilment | Passion | Unity |
| Connection | Fun | Patience | Valour |
| Consistency | Generosity | Peace | Variety |
| Continuity | Gratitude | Perfection | Vigour |
| Contribution | Growth | Persistence | Vitality |
| Control | Happiness | Philanthropy | Warmth |
| Courage | Harmony | Power | Wealth |
| Creativity | Health | Privacy | Wisdom |
| Curiosity | Honesty | Professionalism | Wonder |

A sensible process is for you to list out each of your six to eight core values and then identify which areas of your life meet the needs of that specific value. For example:

**Honesty:** I am almost always honest with others; my voluntary work allows me to be authentic and share the story of my past with the people I meet – I enjoy this work.

**Kindness:** I always try to be kind to others. My voluntary work reflects my kind approach and I also give to charity twice a month.

**Creativity:** I enjoy painting, knitting and crafts and make sure I do them at least twice a week.

Sometimes it isn't possible to align all areas of your life with your values. You may, for example, have a value of 'connection' – but one of your family members is unreliable and disconnected, she fails to reply to messages, doesn't answer your calls and sometimes forgets to turn up for lunch with you. This can be triggering and so it is through this process you discover what pushes against your core values.

This time, list your values and write next to each one what in your life might be opposing them, for example:

**Honesty:** My sales job involves me bending the truth. This is not honest.

**Kindness:** There are some people in my life who are unkind to me and ignore my messages and calls.

**Courage:** I know the importance of courage, but often find myself giving in to fear instead of stepping up when courage is required. This is especially true in relation to my parents to whom I can never say 'no', even when I want to.

Once you have become aware of the things that go against your values, consider what action you need to take. This may involve putting boundaries in place in order to protect yourself from having your values compromised by anyone, or anything, that you are unable to easily change or remove from your life.

Now, write down what actions you might need to take for each point that you have identified. For example:

**Honesty:** My job involves me bending the truth.

*Action*: I am keen to change career and I can now see why the role makes me unhappy. It is time to proactively change jobs or switch roles within my company.

**Kindness:** There are some people in my life who are unkind to me and ignore my messages and calls.

*Action*: My aunt and my brother are both unkind. They make comments about my weight and say hurtful things. Neither of them reply to my messages and I plan to make them both aware that I find this unacceptable, and that if they continue to do it, I will put boundaries in place to prevent myself being exposed to their behaviour.

**Courage**: I know the importance of courage, especially when it comes to self-growth. But I often find myself giving in to fear instead of stepping up when courage is required.

*Action*: I plan to learn more and will commit to finding the best methods of becoming courageous by educating myself with books and online resources.

When you reveal something that goes against your values, you need to give serious consideration to the impact it is having on your overall wellbeing. When I recognized behaviours, people, situations and habits that were clearly opposing some of my own values, I took appropriate steps so I could put my healing and happiness first.

You may have some areas of your life – hobbies, pastimes, jobs, relationships or other activities – that don't align with your core values, but they don't oppose them, either. In these instances it is important to take time to consider how these elements of your life serve you. Think about how much they matter to you, and whether your time and energy would be better spent on the things that bring you real joy.

This process will enable you to develop a true sense of purpose and understand what really matters to you. Studies have shown that the happiest people seek out meaning far more than they seek out pleasure.

It is important to learn how to let go of other people's expectations of us and become totally honest and truthful in our answers. This is about you - the process will give you the opportunity to discover your personal sense of meaning and purpose and you will have taken another step forward when it comes to healing from CEN and trauma.

# 13 | Identifying what is holding us back from being our 'true-self'

Has anyone ever told you to 'just be yourself'? It is possibly the most annoying advice anyone can offer. But it is also the most true. When we are truly 'being ourselves' we avoid the mental torment that comes with being false and we are able to drop the mask that covers the true, authentic and beautiful person we have been keeping hidden.

All this hiding and faking takes a lot of energy and, worst of all, we usually don't even realize we are doing it until we take the time to pause and look much more closely at ourselves. Wearing a mask is draining and causes us pain. We can find ourselves subconsciously acting out roles that we believe people want to see, we project a phoney version of ourselves into the world.

It is common for adults who have suffered CEN or past trauma to tell lies, bend the truth and hide secrets, often from the most important people in their lives. This can cause us to live with feelings of guilt and worry and, over time, these can weigh heavily on us.

The need to hide ourselves, to bend the truth and keep secrets, is driven by our ego, anger, resentment, fear, guilt or shame, along with our need to be accepted and our desire to please others and avoid conflict. You didn't feel 'good enough' for your parents in childhood, but you have to get over this: it's a fact of life that some people will like you, some people won't, and others probably won't care either way – and you can't change that.

## The 20/60/20 rule

In the world of business, many leaders use the '20/60/20 rule' to improve their management skills. I use the same rule, but have adapted it to help me overcome any desire to try and make people accept and approve of me. You might find that using this same mindset assists you in letting go of approval-seeking behaviours.

- **Your Fanclub 20%:** This group represents around 20 per cent of everyone you know and will be made up of friends, family, acquaintances and colleagues. They are the people who will be there for you no matter what, and will support you in whatever you do. In this group you will find your closest friends and the people who love and admire you exactly the way you are. You don't need to be false around these people, you bring happiness into their lives already and the relationships come without terms and conditions.

- **The Middle Ground 60%:** This is the largest group of people in your life and will mostly be made up of acquaintances, colleagues and friends in your wider circle, along with family members you may not be close to. The best way to describe this group is 'indifferent'. They generally don't care either way and usually have a 'take you or leave you' viewpoint. It is possible for people in this group to move into your 'Fanclub' as you spend more time with them and they become able to connect with the authentic version of you. It can be the case that approval seeking or ego-driven behaviour has caused people to stay on the fence and stay in the centre.

- **The Adverse Group 20%:** This group of people tend to be the judgemental types who have formed strong opinions, often before they have even spent any length of time getting to know someone. In many cases these people have their own insecurities and issues which they project by denigrating other people. This group of people are definitely not your fans, but if they had the opportunity to connect with you on a deeper level and see the real you, there is every chance they would be. However, it is also true that some of these people simply won't like you, and that is okay.

While the exact numbers may vary slightly from person to person, the concept almost always holds true and my hope is that, by reading this, you will begin to have an acceptance that there will always be people who love us, those who are indifferent and some who aren't too keen. The sooner you can accept this, the quicker you will be able to get to a place where you realize that adapting your behaviour to suit other people is pointless and draining.

Use your journal and write down any specific behaviours of your own that might have been driven by a desire to be accepted and approved by others and caused you to project a false version of yourself into the world.

I wrote down my own experiences when I answered this question and here are some of the responses I gave:

- I avoid conflict no matter what, because I want everyone to like me.
- I agree to things I would rather say 'no' to, because I fear being rejected.
- I behave in an extroverted manner as I believe that is what my friends want to see.
- I hold back from telling people how their words and actions make me feel.
- I believe that having more money makes me more popular and likeable.
- I believe that the nicer I am to others, the more they will like me.
- I have few personal boundaries and expose myself to suffering as a result.
- I put other people ahead of myself all the time.

- I keep secrets and tell lies.
- I often overshare information with the wrong people.
- I am too trusting of others and don't take enough time to ensure they are trustworthy.
- I am quick to judge other people and avoid judging myself.
- I believe that if I work hard, I will be more valuable to other people.

The only person that we have an obligation to in life is *ourselves*, and as you can see from my list, many of my own behaviours were directly influenced by the way I believed other people wanted to see me. When our own happiness and emotional wellbeing becomes contingent on the behaviour and actions of others, we have lost control of our lives and become disconnected with who we really are.

The false-self is a fake persona (or personas) that we create as children. It is a tool to protect us from trauma, hurt, neglect, suffering and the stresses that exist with our family and close relationships. The issues begin when we take this fake persona with us into adulthood and continue to use it by believing that it accurately reflects who we really are.

The problem for most adults is that we don't know any different; what we learned in childhood has formed the template for who we became as an adult and the false-self has taken up residence deep within our subconscious mind. We have no awareness and know no other way of being. We continue to carry this unhealthy imposter until we finally become aware that it is harming us and holding us back.

We have usually formed many of our beliefs and behaviours around this misguided version of ourselves and we then allow it, unwittingly, to run our lives. As adults we no longer need to be fake, we no longer need to think like a child and we no longer need to use a false persona as a tool to protect ourselves or to gain approval or acceptance from others.

Try to think of the 'false-self' as an ego-driven survival mechanism used to get by and to remain safe. We often use our ego to seek external validation and approval in order to soothe any insecurities or self-doubts we may have. Over the years, this fake persona forms a distorted view of who you think you really are and this is the only perspective that you are able to see. But you are safe now, you are no longer a child and you no longer need this survival mechanism; you are not under any threat.

When people use their false-self to seek validation from others in order to cover up their insecurities, I describe it as 'the big ego'. Some people have a small ego and, instead of seeking validation and approval from others, they will use their false-self as an inner critic and beat themselves up with negative self-talk and self-destructive thoughts.

By allowing the false-self to run the show, we are effectively handing over the reins of our emotional regulation, our behaviour and our sense of wellbeing to the five-year-old version of us. You wouldn't let a five-year-old drive your car, so why are you allowing one to drive your life?

The more I became aware of the traits of my masquerading 'false-self', the easier it was to catch myself when I stepped out of authenticity. Over time I was able to quickly notice, pause for a moment and step back into being my 'true-self'. Eventually this became a new and natural habit; I found that I was rarely being the false version any longer and whenever I had an urge towards ego-driven behaviour I would spot it and stop it.

If you feel that something is holding you back from uncovering your true-self, look closer. Maybe it's resistance and fear from your false-self desperately attempting to hang on to control. This imposter believes that it is keeping you safe and protecting you from harm and suffering. But it does the opposite. You need to remember that it thinks like the five-year-old version of you, not the rational, grown-up adult that you are now.

You are on a journey towards discovering your own truth and that is a wonderful thing, it will change your life. But knowing your own reality and uncovering who you really are may cause discomfort before you find yourself experiencing freedom and peace. It is this discomfort that is most likely holding you back if you have been finding it a challenge to understand what your true-self looks like. Your false-self doesn't want you to suffer or feel pain, and will try to turn you away from seeing the real version of you. Don't let it fool you, or it will keep you stuck and suffering forever; push through and make the uncomfortable become comfortable.

Break away from your limiting beliefs and explore your true-self with curiosity; make observations about yourself from a perspective of impartiality. Seek out your truth, and follow the path to becoming the authentic version of you. The path will lead you to a joyful life where you no longer seek approval, to please people or to beat yourself up with negative self-talk.

# The 'false-self' in action

## Steve

Steve was the youngest of three siblings and was in his late twenties when he began to have thoughts about ending his life that left him confused and frantic with worry. He had never had these kinds of thoughts before.

He enjoyed socializing, playing sports and partying with a large group of friends in his hometown. But this would be coming to an end soon as he'd recently been offered a new job with a prestigious law firm in a different city. The new position would open up the opportunity for him to become one of the youngest law firm partners in the country.

His new, high-paying job meant that he would have to relocate to another part of the country and would lose contact with the friends with whom he enjoyed socializing. His current job, in the same industry, was based in his hometown; there was no pressure in his role and he worked with a wonderful group of colleagues.

Steve had always felt intense pressure from his parents to achieve more in life, they would often say things like 'when you become a partner, we'll be so proud' or 'you'd make an amazing partner in a law firm'. He knew they were incredibly proud of him for landing the new role and he understood how important it was to them that he became a partner in a respected law firm. It felt like it was their dream come true, rather than his.

After one particularly heavy night out with his friends, Steve broke down when he returned home. In floods of tears, he began having serious thoughts about ending his life. He couldn't understand what was going on. He had it all – didn't he? Was he actually about to lose it all if he relocated and took the new job?

While he didn't attempt suicide, he described hearing an inner voice whispering about ending his life. The voice didn't leave him until he eventually fell asleep, the following morning he was still emotional, and his mind was swirling with questions and concerns. He decided to seek therapy to address the issues.

During therapy, it became clear that Steve's 'true-self' was the one who enjoyed living in his hometown, socializing and working in a job that he enjoyed without huge amounts of competition or pressure. Steve had never acknowledged or connected with the true version of who he was, or taken the time to identify what it was that he truly wanted and enjoyed in life.

'I understand that might be what I want, but I can't let my parents down. The new job means so much to them. I still don't understand why I had suicidal thoughts – it's never happened before,' Steve said to the therapist.

The therapist thought for a moment and replied, 'The suicidal voice you heard was coming from your true-self, a part of you that has been hidden since childhood. Since a young age you have been living as a false persona, projecting a fake version of who you really are into the world. The false version of you was formed by your beliefs about what your parents expected from you and I think you've reached a tipping point where the false-self was becoming such a huge part of who you actually are, that the true-self felt it was being destroyed.'

Steve looked stunned. 'Are you saying that the true version of me was suggesting I end my life?'

The therapist replied, 'Your true-self is the one that enjoys being with friends, socializing, working in a stress-free career and living in your hometown. The upcoming career move and relocating has probably made your true-self feel that you were heading down a path to future unhappiness, that you were allowing your false-self to take over and become the real you. It wouldn't allow that to happen and began to suggest destroying the false-self to protect the authentic version of you, even if it meant destroying itself in the process.'

Tears began to stream down Steve's face, 'What you are saying is so true, I have done so many things throughout my life that I didn't want to do, usually just to keep my parents happy. This career move is all about them, it has never been about me or what I want.'

It was all making sense to Steve. Over the coming weeks he continued his work in therapy and began to connect with the authentic version of who he really was. He started to become clear about what he wanted. He began to make choices and decisions that were about him and gradually learned to find his voice. This allowed him to be authentic and experience inner happiness and peace for the first time in a long time.

Steve turned down the new job and still works in his original role, he loves his friends and social life and, now he has become authentic, he feels more connection and joy from his close relationships than ever before. His parents were disappointed at first. Steve couldn't bring himself to say the words out loud so he wrote a letter to them and sat in front of them while they read it. He shared everything, including the suicidal thoughts he had experienced. After the initial shock, his parents could see their boy again, as he sat childlike in front of them. It was obvious how hard this had been for Steve and his parents felt guilt for the pressure they had applied over the years.

They showed compassion and empathy, and told Steve how much they respected and loved him for being so honest. They ended by explaining that his happiness and wellbeing was the most important thing to them, far more important than any job, and that was what they wanted him to focus on going forward.

## Claire

Claire had been an only child with a close connection to her mother and father up until she was five years old. At this point her parents decided to try for another baby through IVF treatment and, later that year, they welcomed three noisy triplets into the world.

Suddenly their hands were full, their attention was rarely on Claire any longer and she felt as though the triplets' needs had become far more important than her own. As a child, Claire reasoned that this was normal because the triplets were younger and their needs should be put ahead of her own. She had gone from having almost all of her emotional needs met by her parents, to a place where she suddenly felt as though she was alone.

One of the triplets also had a serious medical condition that required regular trips to the doctor and the hospital. There were often occasions where her parents didn't show up at important events during Claire's childhood because they were caught up with the day-to-day care of the triplets, or they had medical appointments that clashed. As the years went by they missed her score a goal for the school football team, her appearance in the school production of *Cats* and several parents' evenings.

Claire didn't give their lack of availability much thought while she was growing up. She formed a firm belief that the needs of the triplets were more important than hers and that thinking otherwise would be selfish. Without noticing it happen, she began to project a false version of herself into the world.

She became incredibly self-sufficient and fiercely independent. Almost two decades later she had developed a tough exterior and had carved out a brilliant career as a graphic designer, which she loved. People would often admire her strong nature, no-nonsense approach and ability to face and overcome challenging situations on her own, without letting emotion get in the way.

While she loved her career, she always had a sense that she was some kind of fraud and wasn't anywhere near as good at her job as some of her colleagues. She shut these thoughts down whenever they entered her head and instead focused on something positive, such as how lucky she was to have a career that she enjoyed.

Then she met Mark. He attended the same gym and she had tripped over his kit bag as she walked past a row of exercise bikes while texting a friend. Instead of becoming angry after a water bottle soaked his bag, he laughed. He seemed kind and he said that if she met him for a coffee it would more than make up for any damage her clumsiness had caused.

Over the next few weeks they met for many more coffees, they also met for dinners, trips to the theatre and a fun day of shopping in the city. As the weeks turned into months they became an item, and later that year they decided to move into their own home together.

The first few months together were wonderful, but after the initial euphoria of moving in as a couple began to fade, Mark found himself becoming increasingly frustrated. He would often become angry with Claire because he felt that she was unable to open up or connect on an emotional level, and he felt as though she was constantly holding back and guarded.

Claire didn't know what he was talking about and put his anger down to childish tantrums. But Mark was absolutely right. Claire had become so self-sufficient as a child after the triplets were born that she had created an emotional brick wall within herself. It acted as a defence that prevented anyone from getting in and hurting her, but it also stopped her from connecting on an emotional level with other people. It was a false version of her.

Two years later, the couple were experiencing a sense of disconnection. Mark was always very open about his feelings and emotions, but by now he had consciously stopped sharing with Claire because he received nothing in return.

Eventually Mark calmly expressed his fears for their relationship and explained how he felt the least connected on an emotional level than they had ever been. He was afraid that if things were to stay the same, he couldn't see them being an item in 12 months' time. He suggested to Claire that they undertake a course of relationship counselling.

Claire had been feeling it too, but she couldn't work out exactly where it was coming from or what was causing it. She knew that she and Mark seemed distant from each other and it wasn't how she wanted things to be. She was pleased when Mark suggested counselling and agreed to attend in the hope that they could get to the root of the problem; after all, she wanted to marry this man.

During counselling they were both encouraged to discover who they really were and what they really wanted in life. The process involved learning about the false and true versions of themselves. It was during this process that Claire began to realize why Mark had become so frustrated throughout their relationship.

She started to see how she had rarely been open, how she hardly ever shared how she was feeling or what emotions she was experiencing. As she learned more, she understood the importance of having a strong emotional connection and she could see how her guarded and self-protective traits had blocked this from happening.

Through the counselling process, Claire explored how her behaviour had changed and she soon realized that the tough exterior, guarded behaviour and emotionless persona was not who she actually was. In that moment, her emotional brick wall began to come down. Claire kept putting in the work with weekly therapy sessions, she also started to read self-help books, listened to podcasts and found online articles to accelerate her understanding. The more she educated herself, the quicker the bricks seemed to fall away.

Gradually she began to step out of her false-self and began to pay attention to her own feelings and emotions. It wasn't long before she started to share them with Mark. It felt challenging at first as it was completely alien to her, but she stuck with it and soon noticed how they were connecting on a much deeper level than ever before.

In one of their first sessions, the therapist had explained how he felt that they had a lack of true 'intimacy'. Claire initially thought that intimacy meant sex and she joked that 'there was no problem in that department'. The counsellor explained that intimacy is not only about sex, it is about allowing your partner to see inside of you. Claire didn't understand.

'In-To-Me-See' the counsellor said. 'Or, See In To Me,' said Claire, a lightbulb starting to glow deep in her mind. She was right – intimacy is about allowing people to see inside us by sharing feelings, speaking the truth and expressing emotions in a healthy way. Intimacy is emotional, as well as physical.

As Claire continued to work on letting go of the guarded, defensive false-self she had created, she became happier. She noticed how she felt lighter and carefree; she became authentic and accepted herself as she was. She also realized that, as a child, she had no choice but to become self-sufficient because it served her at the time, but it was limiting her in adulthood.

Claire worked on understanding why she felt like a fraud and realized that it was because she was exactly that, a fake version of herself. She also started to understand that some of her feelings of not being as good as her colleagues had stemmed from her never having gone to university, while everyone who worked alongside her had achieved degrees at some of the most prestigious educational institutions in the country.

She had recognized a form of imposter syndrome and was able to reframe her belief into a feeling of pride for achieving such a great career against the odds and accomplishing so much without going to university.

The more Claire connected with her true-self, the more authentic she became. In turn, she and Mark started to experience true intimacy and emotional connection in their relationship. Things between them were better than they had ever been, physically and emotionally.

On New Year's Eve they attended a fantastic ball at a five star hotel in the city. Just before midnight they were invited to a rooftop terrace to see the New Year in. The terrace on the twenty-fourth floor looked out across the river towards twinkly lights from skyscrapers, office blocks and homes in the distance. The city was vibrant, alive with activity as people excitedly prepared to countdown to a new year, with new beginnings and maybe even a new chapter of their lives just around the corner.

Mark squeezed Claire's hand as fireworks began to illuminate the inky city sky, huge bangs and streaks of colour ripping through the air above them as the cold December night caused them both to shiver. Claire was about to turn back and head inside to get her warm coat when Mark suddenly dropped to one knee.

His silhouette was bathed in greens, reds and yellows from the fireworks cracking and banging above their heads. Claire began to cry because she knew what he would say next:

'Will you marry me?'

# Exploring your limiting beliefs

If you have been convincing yourself that you are unable to change then I would like to invite you to start looking at the evidence and the truth in any beliefs that have been holding you back. I want to show you how to form new empowering beliefs that are completely true and will no longer limit you in life.

We often live with beliefs that hold us back and convince ourselves that they must be true just because we believe them. On occasion we might feel safer with our false beliefs rather than facing the truth, this is an illusion and it will keep you stuck. Just because you believe something, it doesn't mean it is true, keep an open mind as you begin to gently explore your reality.

Through my work as a sobriety coach, I work with many people who struggle to quit alcohol because they believe it adds something positive to their lives. They might think that it makes their life more fun, or helps them relax or eases their anxiety. These are all limiting beliefs. They are untrue and serve only to keep people stuck exactly where they are, in the tight grip of addiction.

As part of my coaching process I empower people to explore their beliefs about alcohol and understand how they are holding them back. Then I will work with them to form new and healthy beliefs based on the reality of a specific situation. The new beliefs are designed to allow them to become the best version of themselves.

Let's take the example of a heavy drinker who believes that they can only have fun if they drink alcohol. Their original belief statement might look something like this:

# Limiting belief

**'If I don't drink alcohol, I won't have fun. The only time I have fun is when I drink.'**

## Explore the evidence

Once we have identified the limiting belief (and most people have many different beliefs that need to be worked through in order to change), we will explore the evidence from a totally impartial perspective. A simple process is to write out the 'for' and 'against', rather like a defence and prosecution would do in a court case.

## Arguments FOR life only being fun when I drink

- Alcohol is a drug and numbs the senses (and pain) for a few hours after drinking. We lose our inhibitions and it can feel like we are having more fun for a short period of time.
- The first hour or two when we start drinking can seem like fun as we feel a sense of euphoria from the chemical reaction the alcohol causes.

## Arguments AGAINST life only being fun when I drink

- After the effects of alcohol have worn off, we are left with a hangover, feel tired, unmotivated, unproductive and have a strong urge to drink again as we experience cravings and withdrawal symptoms. None of this is fun.

- Alcohol causes a huge number of mental and physical health problems including cancer, heart problems and liver damage. None of these are fun.
- We have likely never had a period without drinking and have no evidence that life is more or less fun without alcohol. The belief is more likely to be an assumption.
- Have you ever seen a video of yourself drunk? We might feel like we are having fun but the people around us probably think we become rude, aggressive and obnoxious after drinking. This is no fun for our friends or our social life.
- There might have been occasions where we have carried out dangerous, regrettable, risky or reckless behaviour when we are drunk. Risking our health or our life is not fun.
- Alcohol is highly addictive and we often end up putting our relationship with drinking ahead of the important things in our life, such as our children, partners, careers and our all-round wellbeing. This is not fun.

I could easily make a list of arguments against life only being fun when someone drinks ten times longer, but I am sure you get the point. The evidence to support the limiting belief is far from black and white, in fact, the original belief is looking very shaky as we explore the reality in detail.

## True belief statement

Once we have explored the evidence, I invite the person with the limiting belief to write out an empowering statement that reflects the truth, at the same time as no longer limiting them. In this example they might write:

**'I have only ever experienced adult life when I have been drinking. I have no evidence to know how much fun I will have without alcohol. I would like to find out and discover the truth for myself.'**

I call this process 'LET' as in 'let's look at the evidence' because the three steps to changing a limiting belief are:

Limiting belief – what is it?

Explore the evidence – like a defence and prosecution in a court case.

True belief statement – write it out and ensure it is totally true.

If you find yourself running into a limiting belief, such as 'I can't change, I am destined to be this way forever', take the time to work through it and unlock the truth using this process. If you are unsure whether a belief is limiting you or not, ask yourself: 'Does this belief allow me to be the best version of myself? Is it holding me back? Does it add to my self-esteem and sense of self-worth? Is it stopping me from being my true-self?'

# We get what we expect

You might have taken steps to heal your trauma in the past and on these occasions you may not have achieved the outcome you had hoped for. But that doesn't mean that you are destined to never make any progress or that you should hang on to a limiting belief that will hold you back.

We usually find that what we expect is exactly what we get. If you approach the process of dealing with past trauma already believing that you are unable to change, then the chances are that this is exactly what will happen. If you can keep an open mind and even become motivated and excited by new breakthroughs and what you are discovering about yourself, then you are far more likely to notice positive changes steadily happening.

# Secrets and lies

One part of the healing process that can keep people well and truly stuck is becoming totally honest, no longer keeping secrets and making a commitment to not lying. In other words, becoming totally authentic and radically honest. When we live our lives in a web of lies, deceit, false-personas and secrets, it causes us and those around us pain.

Think about how you can start moving towards a place where you can be totally honest and authentic. It might feel hard at first, especially if you have become used to bending the truth to avoid punishment or to get your own way since you were a child. But like learning any new skill, it simply takes practice and commitment.

When you commit to living a life of authenticity, you will feel liberated and will no longer have the worry or guilt that comes with lying to the people you love. It really is a huge step towards overcoming the issues from your past and no matter how challenging it feels, please try and avoid dismissing this part of the process.

If you are unable to be honest and authentic with other people then you will never be able to be truly honest and authentic with yourself.

It would seem there are three types of people:

- Those who are mostly honest but tell the odd lie when they believe they need to. They may also sugar-coat the truth, omit details or bite their tongue in order to avoid hurting people's feelings.
- Those who lie compulsively, exaggerate most of the time and keep big secrets, usually from their partners – for example, affairs, financial problems or addictions.
- Those who used to be one of these people, but have since committed to becoming radically honest by no longer lying or keeping secrets, no matter how hard it feels to speak the truth at times.

Before I became conscious and woke up to my behaviour, I was someone who was mostly honest but would tell the odd white lie when I needed to. I would exaggerate and show off too, especially on social media. I would usually feel a compulsion to lie in order to gain approval and acceptance from other people and would commonly bend the truth if it allowed me to avoid a conflict or confrontation or enabled me to get my own way. I also had my secrets. Don't we all?

I changed. I committed to no longer lying about anything and promised myself that I would always speak the truth and tell people what I really felt in any given situation. There have been times when it has been hard, and a few occasions where I have slipped up, but, over time, it has become a new normal and life is so much easier when you don't carry around a heavy bag full of bullshit.

Making a commitment to no longer lie is easy, even if you have done it for a long time. Start to become mindful whenever you fail to tell the truth and log it in your journal, along with any negative consequences that might be attached to the behaviour. As you begin to pay more attention to the downsides of being untruthful, noticing how often you lie and what you are lying about, you will naturally find yourself changing and considering what you say before you speak.

You can become radically honest with yourself and the people around you by learning how to effectively express yourself and facing any fear of saying what you really feel. It is important not to hurt other people with brutal comments and to practice compassion as you begin communicating without lies and secrets. Start to practise this new skill and get curious about what changes in your life.

When you make this change, something incredible happens. Not only do you feel empowered, you also find that other people are more connected to you as they notice that you speak the truth, even when it is difficult. They begin to see you as someone with integrity, who can be trusted; you might even find that people begin to share personal information with you, or ask you for advice as someone who is safe and authentic.

While it is usually straightforward to bring your attention to the occasions when you lie, for some people it can be more of a challenge. When we become used to a habit of lying over many years, and when it has served us in childhood for dealing with difficult parents or siblings, it can be harder to break as a pattern of behaviour.

I guarantee that, after you have read this chapter, you will begin catching yourself when you lie. You might not adapt your behaviour right away but you will definitely start to notice it. This awareness is the first step towards changing your behaviour.

## What counts as a lie?

It is important to be clear about what the word 'lie' actually means. Many people will try and convince themselves that they aren't really lying by distorting the truth and will let themselves off the hook; in other words, they fail to take responsibility for their own actions. For example, someone who lies by leaving out important details in a conversation might convince themselves that they haven't actually lied because the person they were talking to didn't ask them a specific question directly.

Quite simply, a lie can be defined as: *keeping something secret that you know the person you are deceiving would want to be aware of.* Or, *making a false statement with the intention of misleading another person.*

Personally, I think 'keeping secrets' pretty much covers all aspects of lying. Whether you make a false statement, omit to tell the whole story or simply keep quiet, it falls under the umbrella of lying, and of failing to be honest and authentic.

There are several different types of lies. Sometimes we might distort the truth to protect another person and, on other occasions, we may cover something up to get our own way, or exaggerate the truth in order to gain a sense of approval.

It is hard to be really honest with yourself if you have a habit of lying, but remember, nobody is judging you, apart from you. Simply acknowledging that there are occasions when you have lied and being truthful with yourself about your behaviour is enough to start taking steps to break free from this unhelpful habit.

Becoming aware of an unhelpful behaviour is an enormous part of moving towards changing it.

## The different types of lies

Can you identify with any of the following types of behaviour?

**Lying by omission**: Some people adopt an 'if you didn't ask me, I'm not lying' approach and will leave out important information, often through guilt, shame or fear.

**Exaggerating:** People often embellish the truth in order to gain favour, acknowledgement or approval from others. Social media is one of the best places to witness exaggerations on a global scale.

**White lies:** People often tell what they consider to be harmless, subtle or trivial lies. These are often used to protect other people and avoid hurting them, to exaggerate and impress others, or to avoid commitments and social events that they don't want to be part of but are afraid to decline through fear of causing offence.

**Lies with a capital 'L':** These are the big lies that people intentionally use to deceive another person in order to keep them from knowing the truth. These are among the most deceptive types of lies and they actually cause the people who tell them the most suffering as they are forced to carry the guilt, shame and fear of being found out.

# Tips for breaking a lying habit

There are consequences when we lie, not only for the people we lie to, but also for ourselves as we carry the pain of deceit with us forever. Don't be too hard on yourself though; almost everyone tells lies on occasion and most people are unable to ever admit it. If you have acknowledged this behaviour, you should celebrate the fact that you are becoming much more honest and connecting with the real version of yourself.

Start to notice when you next catch yourself lying, or feeling compelled to tell a lie. Pause for a few moments before you deceive anyone, and pay attention to whether anything or anyone is triggering you to be deceitful in the situation. It could be people, places, situations, feelings or emotions that are your triggers. If you can identify patterns to your lying then you are able to take steps to address the behaviour, perhaps by putting boundaries in place, or considering a different way to respond to people with whom you struggle to be truthful.

If you find it a challenge to stop telling lies straight away, start by dropping the small deceits and slowly build up to letting go of lying altogether as you begin to feel more confident in your new skill. Sometimes we lie without even thinking about it; if you can bring a mindful awareness to the behaviour then you will soon discover you become more focused and comfortable in being truthful. If you find yourself in a situation where you are struggling to be honest, it is sometimes best to say nothing at all until you feel ready to start speaking the truth.

Be sure to gather data in your journal about how people respond to you when you tell the truth. Notice whether you seem to be gaining more respect and inviting more honesty into your life because you are radiating the same outwards.

If you feel happy to make a firm commitment to stop lying, then go ahead and do it now. Write it down in your journal and feel empowered in making an incredibly positive change to your life. If you don't feel ready to take this step right now, come back and revisit it when the time feels right.

Take some time to think about the benefits associated with being truthful. Consider how much lighter you will feel without the burden of deceit and think about whether your lies may have caused problems in the past, and whether you feel people really trust you if they know that you are prone to lying. Try and make a list that will provide you with plenty of good reasons to change this behaviour, once and for all.

There will be occasions where speaking the truth feels uncomfortable and you have to face a challenging situation. It is far better to be truthful, even when it feels hard, so that you come away from the conversation with the knowledge that you kept your integrity.

Try and make honesty a value that you live by, but don't just say it, believe it because you see the benefits that being truthful will bring to your life. People who are honest experience less loneliness, better friendships and greater connection in their intimate relationships. They also feel light and at peace, without having to live with the worry, guilt, fear and shame of deceit.

The more you experience the discomfort caused at the times when it is hard to tell the truth, the quicker you will learn that people will respect you for being honest. When you get comfortable with the things that feel uncomfortable, you are making great progress.

# What to do with your secrets

Hopefully you will start to practise being truthful and honest and discover how much of a positive difference it makes to your life. But what do you do if you have secrets from the past that you worry about someone discovering? If you continue to keep them as secrets, does it mean you are still lying and not being authentic and honest?

Part of becoming wholly authentic is to lighten your load. Secrets can destroy families and close relationships and they rarely ever serve people in a positive way. If you plan on practising being honest and telling the truth as you go forward, you won't find yourself having to hide secrets from people. But you may have pre-existing secrets that are already weighing you down and feel that you need to do something with them in order to be authentic.

Can you think of a time in your life, maybe when you were much younger, when secrets that other people have kept hurt you? My mother and step-father decided after five years of marriage that they no longer loved each other, but decided to stay together for financial reasons and to prevent me from being abandoned by another father. They kept this secret from me for over two decades and it wasn't until I moved out of the family home, when I was 25 years old, that they finally shared the secret with me. It broke my heart.

Since I began my journey of self-discovery, I have found many more secrets that were kept from me by my parents: they were both involved in relationships with other people, they had money problems, and my mother even had a boyfriend who was often at the house when I returned home from school (I was told that he was a handyman and didn't join up the dots until I was much older and wiser).

The traits of adults who have suffered CEN and trauma can often see them acting out behaviours that they feel shameful about, the thought of telling another person what they have done might fill them with dread. It is important to give serious thought to the benefit of wiping the slate clean and disclosing your secrets, but you also need to give consideration to the impact your revelations will have on you and the people you love.

The reality is that most secrets usually come out at some point, whether through the uncovering of a lie, or whether it is because living with the feeling of guilt eventually becomes unbearable and we feel compelled to end the pain. One way or another, dark secrets seem to have a habit of bringing themselves into the light eventually and the longer we carry them around, the more damage they cause us. The last thing you want is to let the mistakes from your past define the future version of you.

Becoming able to share your secrets will allow you to feel liberated and free of their burden. But tread carefully and ensure you take advice before disclosing them. Secrets can often cause major problems, especially when they involve affairs, lies about money, children, family, illness or addiction.

Before you do anything with your secrets, please ensure you read Chapter 18 about sharing our experiences safely, as it will help you understand more about the impact of holding onto anything that is causing pain and will provide additional advice and guidance.

# Affairs and infidelity

Should you tell your partner if you have committed a major breach of their trust, such as having an affair, hiding an addiction or engaging in sexual encounters without their knowledge? Many marriage counsellors advise their clients that 'full disclosure' is the only way for couples to make progress. While I understand their viewpoint – in an ideal world we would all become able to confess our darkest secrets – it very much depends on your own specific situation and on how you think your partner will react. You should also consider the potential impact on your children before you make a decision about sharing a secret.

In order to heal, we need to become completely honest and truthful and find peace with any historical secrets we have been carrying, so we can give ourselves the gift of feeling truly liberated and free. Some secrets may feel relatively easy to share, while others could well hold you back from healing and keep you stuck if you are unable to be honest about them.

Let's take the example of someone who has been having an affair behind their partner's back, although you can apply these tips to any kind of secret. What are the options to be able to become free of the burden that comes with carrying such heavy deceit?

## 1 Consider telling the truth to your partner

My personal view is that you should fully disclose your past indiscretions because they are keeping you stuck and causing you to suffer. I also believe that if we respect our partner and the relationship, we owe it to them to be honest about the mistakes we have made in the past, and to show them how we intend to change by working on our shortcomings.

Simply leaving the situation as it is will likely to cause it to fester like an untreated wound and, eventually, it will become infected and start to spread. You will likely end up never feeling completely happy and will avoid ever having the opportunity to repair the problems in the relationship that most likely existed long before the affair happened. By speaking up and sharing the truth you are giving your relationship the opportunity to flourish. Or maybe it has been over for a long time and revealing the truth will set you free and allow you to start a new chapter of your life.

Carefully weigh up the pros and cons and speak to a therapist before you do anything though. You might find that disclosing what happened during a couples therapy session will be easier and safer than doing it alone.

## 2 Share it with a therapist

If you don't feel ready to tell your partner, start by talking to a therapist and share the whole truth. A good therapist will help you work through your feelings of fear, guilt and shame and enable you to reach a decision about whether or not you should disclose the affair to your partner.

## 3 Confess your sins

It is possible to create a sense of freedom from your secret by disclosing it to someone in a 'confession' setting. This could be with a priest in a church, for example. If you are certain you don't want to tell your partner the truth you could adopt a mindset that there will be no lying going forward and you will draw a line under any past indiscretions by confessing what you have done through your faith.

## 4 Share in a group

If you belong to a therapy group, this provides a perfect setting for you to practice being totally honest and authentic without fear of judgement or repercussions. It is the ideal environment to share any secrets that are causing you to suffer and you will also be able to hear the opinions and thoughts of the other group members in regards to sharing with your partner. If you are not a member of a therapy group, I highly recommend joining one as the benefits are enormous.

## 5 Think about what you would want to happen

If the situation was the other way around. If your partner had been involved in an affair, would you want to know about it? Relationships are based on the foundation of trust and openness and there is evidence that shows many couples actually end up in a happier place, with a stronger relationship, once the dust has settled from the initial disclosure of a secret. It is also worth considering whether disclosing an affair will lead to you and those affected by it ending up in a more or less happy place over the longer-term. There are countless factors to take into account and each person and situation is unique, this is one issue that it is worth paying for professional advice and support to ensure you feel absolutely confident in any decision you make before taking action.

Disclosing secrets can be one of the most difficult parts of your journey to navigate, but help is available. Avoid any urge to ignore this and let go of any hope that you won't think about it any longer. The sooner you can become authentic, honest and free of your secrets, the sooner you will move towards healing from any past issues. Don't allow this challenging part of the process to keep you stuck, seek helpful advice from safe and supportive people and make a decision that allows you to move forward and continue on the path to personal growth.

# Integrity

Part of being authentic is having integrity, this is another key attribute in becoming the true version of who you really are. Integrity means behaving in a way that aligns with your moral principles and values, even when nobody's watching. People with integrity refuse to move outside their own boundaries and will stick to what they believe, even when it feels hard to do so.

Think about when you might have heard the word 'integrity' used in the past. For example, it might have been on a news report talking about a modern extension being proposed to an old museum with historically significant architecture. Or it could be on social media when people comment about a change in the cast of a long-running popular stage show. One of the most common uses of the word seems to be around politicians who have been discovered doing something that goes against the values that they project to gain popularity and votes.

In each of these cases people will describe how 'integrity has been ruined'. The person, place, event or situation is no longer whole or complete. It is no longer possible to trust it, as it is not authentic.

The exact same principle applies to our own lives. When we live with integrity, we have a strong moral compass and will follow it no matter how much of a challenge it seems. Although it may sound hard, we create a peaceful and happy life when we stay well away from any behaviours that go against what we truly believe.

*Having integrity means doing what we say we will do.*

The good news is that, just like making a commitment to no longer lying, living with integrity is all about becoming aware and waking up to your own behaviour so you can make adjustments that allow you to live your life in line with the values and principles that reflect who you really are, without a mask and without being false.

I want to be explicit here. I am not suggesting that you start living your life as a saint and never do anything fun, and I am not asking you to stop partaking in the activities or behaviours that you enjoy or want to do. I am simply saying that you should be honest about how you want to live your life and drop the need to hide anything you feel shame or fear about, by sticking to doing what you say you will do. People who love you unconditionally will accept you for exactly who you are. We all have flaws and make mistakes. It's part of being human, own it.

## Tips for keeping your integrity

**Get really clear on your values**: Our values create the template for our integrity and we should feel proud that we want to live by them. Consider your own values and make sure they align with the person you really are. Get motivated about this process, because it could be one of the most liberating changes you ever make to your life.

**Take responsibility for yourself**: Nobody can make you have integrity, other than you. It is important to make a firm commitment and to feel motivated by understanding the benefits of changing your behaviour, and then to embrace the fact that you are responsible for yourself and you have complete control over it.

**Saying 'no' is vital**: Until you learn how to stop pleasing people and find your voice when you need to say 'no', you are going to struggle to maintain your integrity. When we are unable to say 'no' to other people, we end up doing things to please others at the expense of our own happiness. This inevitably leads to people cancelling or missing appointments, events and commitments that they didn't want to be involved in in the first place.

*When we say 'YES' to other people, we say 'NO' to ourselves.*

**Handle mistakes with integrity:** It's natural to make mistakes; don't beat yourself up when it happens. You can maintain your integrity by dealing with mistakes in the right way. Instead of simply apologizing and doing nothing more, learn what action you might need to take in order to demonstrate your true intention to put right a wrong. Be transparent and honest about what you intend to do and, most importantly, make sure your actions match your words.

**Check in with yourself:** If you are wondering whether you have stepped out of integrity, check in with yourself and consider whether you said or did the right thing in a particular situation. There is no harm in asking other people whether they felt you were out of integrity and observing what feelings come up when you hear their answers.

You can also ask yourself the following questions to ensure your integrity is intact:

- Am I taking complete responsibility for myself?
- Am I doing what I said I would do?
- Do my actions match my words?
- Would I be happy if my child acted this way?
- Am I being honest and saying what I really feel?

I had a wonderful connection with my grandmother and I would often say to myself, 'Would I do this if my grandmother was sitting next to me?' Whenever the answer was 'no', I would usually be engaging in something that went against my values and put me out of integrity.

**Surround yourself with the right people:** When you are honest, authentic and have integrity, you will find that people who have the same moral code of conduct are drawn to you. However, it can also be easy to slip back into old habits if you aren't careful. Try and make yourself accountable to safe and supportive people who will help steer you in the right direction if you start to stray towards stepping outside of your integrity. Avoid people who lack integrity and align yourself with those who share the same outlook as you.

**Be mindful about your actions:** It can be all too easy to say one thing and then do another. A great example is promising to attend an event and then making a lame excuse to get out of it at the last minute. In order to retain your integrity it is important to stick to doing what you say, ensure your actions match your values and your words and, should you need to let someone down or deliver bad news, learn how to do it with compassion while keeping your honesty and integrity intact.

As I mentioned previously, when we feel compelled to live a life with the burden of unshared secrets and lies, it drains our energy and causes us to remain firmly stuck. You can free yourself by making this powerful change and it isn't as difficult as you might think. When we stop wasting our energy on being a false version of ourselves it makes us incredibly powerful, resourceful and equipped to allow happiness to flow into our lives.

It is rare, but if you encounter anyone who judges you or comments negatively on the choices you have made for yourself and the values you want to live by, then I would invite you to explore whether they are truly supportive of you and whether they love you unconditionally – or not. Remember the 20/60/20 rule, let go of any fear of what other people might think about the way you want to live your life and start being the person you really are. If you happen to lose a few 'friends' along the way, so be it; you will make a whole lot more and those relationships will be far more meaningful when you bring integrity, honesty and authenticity into your life.

# 14 | Setting boundaries

Emotional boundaries involve us separating the responsibility for our own wellbeing from the emotions of another person. They act like a safety bubble around us and prevent us from feeling emotional pain or hurt because of someone else's negative behaviour, their issues or feelings.

You can only set effective emotional boundaries when you have:

- taken the time to understand your values and needs;
- learned what behaviours trigger a negative reaction in you;
- become authentic and able to speak the truth, especially when it comes to saying 'no' and sharing your feelings.

When we have experienced CEN or trauma, we often find ourselves putting other people's needs way ahead of our own, believing that we don't have the right to dictate what is or is not acceptable in a particular situation. We worry about damaging a close relationship and might find ourselves keeping quiet rather than creating a situation that may end in conflict.

Hopefully you are, by now, finding a new approach in the way you deal with other people and you may have already started to explore expressing your feelings in a healthy way. Perhaps you have begun explaining to people that you expect a certain type of behaviour in specific situations and noticed how they seem to respect your honesty.

As children, chances are that any boundaries we might have had weren't respected. We may have been unable to say 'no', feared asking for help, never expressed how we felt, or may have had our right to privacy and trust violated over and over again. At that time in our lives, we did the best we could with what limited resources we had available to us. Things are totally different now though, we are no longer children and we are safe to let go of any sense of being a victim.

When I set boundaries with people, I go to great lengths to avoid being aggressive or angry; the key to setting boundaries is in the way we communicate. The best outcomes have arisen when I take a calm approach, where I seek to redirect the other person's energy in order to protect myself and remain happy, instead of being triggered.

It is important to avoid rushing into setting boundaries, especially if you are still experiencing strong feelings due to the way someone else has behaved. The last thing you want is to lash out and end up in a situation where you come away feeling that you have done more harm than good. Always take a moment to ensure that it is the adult version of you who is in control, not your inner child.

We have looked at the importance of expressing our feelings and being clear about how you would prefer someone to behave in future throughout this book. This, in itself, is setting a boundary as you communicate your expectations about how you wish to be treated.

Remember the wording we looked at:

**'When people [*insert the unacceptable behaviour*]. It makes me feel [*insert how you feel, for example angry, lonely, anxious, sad*] and I prefer it when people [*insert how you want to be treated in future*].'**

Let's take an example of a work colleague who has upset you by violating your privacy and taking items from your desk without asking you. In this situation you might say:

**'When people *violate my private space*, it makes me feel *angry* and I prefer it when people *ask if they want to access any of my belongings*.'**

In that one sentence a clear boundary has been set. It avoids being overly confrontational and expresses exactly what behaviour caused anger and what is deemed to be acceptable from people going forward.

Make sure you take the time to think about exactly what boundary you might need to set when you are faced with an emotional obstacle. The goal is to ensure that the same situation cannot happen again. The more you continue putting your personal boundaries in place, the less you will encounter emotional triggers on a day-to-day basis and the more your life will improve.

As an example, my wife is someone who prefers our home to be clean and tidy (yes, I help too). It means a lot to her that our house is nicely presented and it is rare to see a mess, even with a teenager in the house! Yet my mother used to visit us and make comments if she found even the slightest mark on a work surface in the kitchen or a stain on a tea towel. This would trigger me: I interpreted it as criticism, it made me feel like I wasn't good enough for her. Why couldn't she accept me and my home just the way that it was?

Over time I noticed that this behaviour was not a one-off. I even had friends tell me how she had pointed out shortcomings when we had gatherings at our house. There was never any mention of all the effort that had gone into preparing food, and the hospitality we had extended to her.

Her behaviour was also upsetting my wife, which caused tension between us as my default position had always been to leap to my mother's defence and now I felt stuck between the two of them. Eventually I realized that I needed to tell my mother exactly how her behaviour made me feel, and to do that I would need to be very clear that my expectation was for her not to be critical when she was in our home.

I used the exact strategy in this chapter to clearly and calmly deliver my message. She looked a little shocked and said that she didn't even realize she was doing it, and that she would be more mindful in the future. She has never criticized anything in our home since. There was no conflict and, even if she had become angry or upset, I would have remained calm and simply stood my ground on the points I was making.

The delivery of your message is important. A soft, empathetic and calming tone will ensure you stay as far away from conflict as possible and I recommend you practice your approach. But bear in mind that some people may become triggered themselves if they perceive criticism, rejection or anger in your words.

As harsh as it sounds, if you have expressed your true feelings and set a boundary and someone has an emotional reaction – that is their problem. The likelihood is that they have become triggered themselves and their reaction is an attempt to get you to meet their needs by proving that you care about them. Resist any urge to jump in and rescue them, or you will undo all your hard work. Simply inform them that you're available to listen if they want to talk further when they have calmed down, then leave the situation.

Almost everyone can become triggered by certain types of behaviour and what triggers one person won't affect someone else. It is important to remember that this process is about you and protecting yourself from allowing negative emotions to flood you. If someone who you set a boundary with becomes emotional, do not back down or begin trying to appease them. You have made your expectations totally clear, it is for them to deal with their own emotions, not you; don't go there.

With all this in mind, what could I have done if my mother decided to disrespect my boundaries and continued to criticize our home?

When we have set clear boundaries and people choose to push against them, we end up back where we started unless we take further action. Decide ahead of time what you will do if your boundary is crossed. There is no need to mention what the consequences of stepping over the boundary will be when you initially express how you feel, but you should have it in your mind so you know what steps to take if it happens. This will also stop you worrying about what you need to do if your line in the sand is crossed.

Let's imagine that my mother had continued to make cutting remarks, even after I had told her how it made me feel and been explicitly clear to her about my expectations of her. I would need to reinforce the boundary, ensuring that I was clear about what I wanted to say and making sure I was calm before I spoke. I would decide what sanction I planned to impose and would then give her an ultimatum. This may sound rather brutal, nobody wants to be threatening close family and friends with ultimatums. But if people are triggering you and being toxic then you need to take action. You can't have it both ways and this process is about you putting yourself in the driving seat of your life.

A suitable sanction in this example would be to tell my mother I no longer wanted her to visit my home. I might say:

**'I did explain that when you make comments about my home, I feel angry. I said I would rather you kept these opinions to yourself. If you carry on doing this I will have to ask you not to come to my home in future.'**

Because this statement is about reinforcing the boundary, it is perfectly acceptable to adopt a stronger tone and to directly call out the person for their unacceptable behaviour. The calm and soft approach clearly didn't work, so this needs to be a little more assertive, while still taking steps to avoid conflict or anger. The likelihood is that a firm but polite reminder will cause someone to listen and take it on board and, in most cases, you would see their behaviour change for the better. If the unwanted behaviour continues, however, you need to follow through with your sanctions.

Take plenty of time before you consider reinforcing a boundary or imposing a sanction. Consider whether you are being reasonable, whether the behaviour is as bad as you initially believed and what repercussions may follow. If you are unsure, talk it through with someone safe and trustworthy.

Once you have weighed all this up you will be in a good position to decide on the best course of action. Anyone who is willing to keep stepping over a personal boundary needs managing, as they will likely be having a negative impact on your life. But only you can make the final decision based on your own knowledge of the relationship. If it feels like a dilemma, ask yourself what the real reason is behind your hesitation. You will probably find that it has nothing to do with the specific boundary and that it is coming from your long-held fears and insecurities about how the other person might react and how that reaction will make you feel.

We have a duty of care to ourselves to prevent toxicity from seeping into our lives. You might feel that you are being strict by imposing boundaries on someone you love, but failure to do it will keep you trapped and prevent you from loving and respecting yourself. You will find that once you become able to speak the truth, express your feelings and set boundaries, your life will start to feel much easier and people will generally respect you and your feelings much more.

If you had a young child and one of their classmates was treating them unreasonably at school and making hurtful comments that were upsetting them, would you leave it and do nothing? I doubt you would; you'd take action and make your feelings known so you could resolve the situation. This is exactly how you need to start looking after yourself too.

If you struggle to identify whether or not someone is toxic, take a moment to notice exactly what feelings they cause when you encounter the behaviour that triggers a reaction in you. Use these identifiers as a guide as to whether another person is toxic or not.

- Do they prefer speaking to you rather than listening to you?
- Do they talk over you or interrupt you?
- Do they shame or embarrass you?
- Do they blame other people for their own problems?
- Do they try and out-do you when you have good news?
- Do they seek attention on social media or in the real world?
- Do they have firm opinions that are not open to debate?
- Do they bend the truth, exaggerate and lie?
- Do you feel you are unable to trust them, and that they are dishonest?
- Do they fail to provide you with emotional support when you need it?
- Do they have an excessive amount of drama in their lives?
- Do they take more than they give?
- Do they gossip and stir up situations?
- Do they complain a lot?
- Do they judge and criticize other people?

If you found yourself answering 'yes' to most of the questions above, then you have a good indicator that this person is toxic. Use this as a guide only – learn to trust your own instincts before you take any action around setting boundaries.

The more you recognize your triggers, identify the causes and set boundaries, the more your life will improve.

# 15 | Intimate relationships

CEN and trauma can have a devastating effect on our most intimate relationships. We can end up with unsuitable partners or push away perfectly good people because of our own destructive behaviour.

My wife has stood by me for over twenty years, but my journey from discovery to recovery brought with it a huge number of challenges to our relationship. I asked her about the behaviours she observed in me before I started becoming self-aware, open and authentic. This is what she wrote:

- Constant mood-swings and regular sadness
- Paranoid and jealous at times
- Things were usually about you, not 'me' or 'us'
- Needy, you were like a son at times, not a husband
- Controlling behaviour
- Emotional blackmail to get your own way
- Emotionally distant
- Avoidant of sex
- Lack of empathy and caring
- Lack of real intimacy.

Over the years my behaviour caused us to become disconnected. We experienced a lack of intimacy and found that much of what we talked about was superficial. We didn't share our true feelings and held things back from one another through fear of conflict. The issues stemmed from my inability to be authentic, honest and loving to myself. Once I started to express my feelings and speak the truth, everything fell into place and our relationship changed dramatically for the better.

The turning point came when I was able to begin communicating openly and honestly. I started to share my deepest feelings and no matter how uncomfortable it felt, I made a personal commitment to express everything that came up inside me. I also took the time to understand what her personal values were and she did the same with mine; this was a hugely beneficial exercise in becoming more connected, and learning what really mattered to each other.

Michelle has always been incredibly supportive and when she learned about my past she felt very sad. The more I opened up to her, the more she understood, and it helped her make sense of the way I sometimes behaved.

You've heard the term 'soul mates', of course. I believe that some people are drawn together due to their past experiences of trauma and emotional neglect – the term 'wound mates' might be more appropriate. They believe that their partner will meet the needs that were never fulfilled when they were children. When I began to work on myself and started to learn how to overcome my past trauma and CEN, I believed that I was the responsible party and that all the damage and disconnection in our marriage was down to me. But the more I explored, the more I realized that it wasn't the case, we were 'wound mates'.

As I became more open, honest and vulnerable with Michelle, she began to open up to me about her own childhood. She shared how she was bullied at school when she was younger, and talked about how she became self-sufficient and guarded when her siblings began entering the world when she was seven years old. She talked about the deep pain she felt from the trauma of her baby brother dying at four months old.

As she too became vulnerable, it felt like we had both unlocked the door to being open with each other as a couple, and our conversations were becoming more meaningful as we continued to delve into the stories of who we both really were. The more we spoke like this, the more connected we seemed to become.

On one occasion, we were discussing how I had relied on Michelle to meet many of the needs that were never met in childhood. As we talked, I realized I had allowed her behaviour to control my emotions and that my happiness had become largely contingent on how she acted. In turn, Michelle told me how important it is for her to feel liked. She adapts her behaviour to ensure nobody ever thinks badly of her. As she dug into this she realized that this was driven by the episodes that had happened in her childhood. She wanted to feel loved, cared for and accepted, because she was made to feel the exact opposite when she was younger.

In this moment I realized that we were 'wound mates', and that our relationship had elements of co-dependency. Michelle had been drawn to someone who would rely on her and make her feel worshipped, and I had been attracted to someone to whom I gladly handed over complete control of my emotions, because I believed she would meet my childhood needs and never reject me. When we realized that we had both been reliant on the other person for trying to meet our respective needs, we knew we both needed to change. Neither of us had anything 'wrong' with us, we just needed to learn how to adapt, become responsible for ourselves and stop putting unrealistic expectations on each other.

Relying on someone else to meet our needs can bring pain, when they don't behave in the way we want. We believe it is their responsibility to soothe us and the frustration can be intense when we don't get what we want.

Within a co-dependent partnership, the negative behaviour often affects specific areas of the relationship. This might be money, work, sex, friendships or children, for example. You may have identified certain parts of your own relationship that have been impacted already, but have you ever considered whether you and your partner were drawn together through your equal desires to have your unmet needs fulfilled?

The key to changing your relationship for the better is to become vulnerable and to begin communicating with honesty. Talk to your partner about the work you are doing, but don't place any expectations on them. Begin practising being much more open and sharing what is within you; you will notice how you start to receive the same back in return as they begin to feel safer.

A great exercise you can use to improve communication and connection in your relationship is for you and your partner to each make a list of the following:

- Your individual personal values and needs
- What triggers a strong negative emotional reaction
- What you love and admire about your partner
- Behaviours you feel don't benefit the partnership (in either of you)
- Anything you feel shame or guilt about.

Once you have a list, take the time to discuss your answers together. Try and become vulnerable and open and notice how you will be able to make adjustments to the relationship and find a deeper level of connection.

It can be all too easy to slip into a co-dependent or avoidant style of existing, where both partners play specific roles in order to try and get what they want from each other. Elements of co-dependency are remarkably common with some estimates suggesting that low-level dependencies may exist in as many as 90 per cent of people. If you recognize any of the areas in this chapter in your own relationship, it is important to know that you are far from being alone and there is much support available to help you change for the better.

# Improving your relationship

With an emotionally disconnected relationship, it is common for each partner to adopt a default role. One will usually be the 'needy' one and the other is the 'saviour'. The way in which this happens is usually very subtle, to the point it will normally go unnoticed. If, however, we don't take steps to move out of the roles we find ourselves in, we won't ever feel truly happy in the relationship.

Our instinct is to fight against the behaviours and feelings we experience, but this only serves to increase tensions and make matters worse. Instead of fighting the symptoms, it is necessary to go deeper within ourselves to find real peace, love and happiness.

We need to put ourselves at the centre of our own lives and let go of any desire to control other people. Being realistic and accepting that people do not change just because we want them to is essential. It allows us to shift our expectations and to love our partner exactly as they are, without any demands or conditions.

Consider the following questions to get an indication of whether your relationship may need some work, and write the answers in your journal:

1. Is your relationship equal? Do you and your partner have a share of the power, or is it balanced in one person's favour?
2. Do you and your partner both feel like independent adults?
3. Do you both learn from the relationship and learn from each other?
4. Do you both feel like you are constantly evolving in the partnership? Do you both help each other grow, or do you use each other to stay stuck in your respective comfort zones?
5. Does one or both of you use controlling behaviour to get what you want? This might include emotional blackmail, manipulation, lying or attention seeking.

## The 'needy' one

The needy partner feels like they could not live without the other person; their entire life revolves around them. Despite their huge need for their partner, they can be abusive towards them, especially if they feel disrespected. The dynamic of the relationship creates untold pain and feels like a wound that can't heal. This has an impact on the individual's self-esteem and needy partners can end up losing all respect for themselves, over time, as they remain trapped in a cycle of fighting to get their needs met by their mate.

At the root of the needy behaviour is fear, coming from a belief that there is no life without the partner in it. Because needy partners are totally focused on meeting their needs, they place unrealistic expectations on the other person. They also give up their personal power to them, so instead of feeling comfortable with who they are, they project their energy outwards on to their partner because they believe that this person is their saviour. They become weak and disempowered, which creates an imbalance of power and over time can cause cracks to appear in the foundations of the partnership.

## You can heal

The co-dependent relationship is an illusion, but needy partners cannot see it. I have been in this place and the only way out was to face up to reality. I accepted that I was responsible for my own happiness and meeting my own needs.

I vowed never to give away my personal power again, never to disrespect myself and to put 'me' at the centre of my life. To this day I work hard on cultivating a healthy relationship and I have seen dramatic positive changes.

# The 'saviour'

The 'saviour' believes their partner can't survive without them. The saviour feels that they are incredibly important and that their partner requires their energy and presence in order to exist. But this all comes at a cost. The saviour is never able to be the true version of themselves and has to alter their behaviour in order to enable and support the demanding needs of their partner. The saviour may end up feeling as if they are sacrificing their happiness because their mate needs them so badly. They would feel awful if they left the relationship and let their dependent down, but thoughts of leaving often cross their mind.

The saviour is in a vicious cycle, they take on their partner's responsibilities as well as their own and they often find that they have to be the 'grown up' in the relationship, dealing with their partner's challenging behaviour.

Problems arise – there is only so much negativity a saviour can bear, and eventually it builds up to such a point that they snap, with an explosive outburst or some other form of acting out. Snapping at their needy partner causes the saviour to feel intense guilt, so they commit to becoming even more responsible for their mate's happiness, which causes them further negativity. The cycle continues.

The saviour is never happy, but they have a strong need to be at the centre of someone else's life and they get significant satisfaction from another person relying on them. This desire is usually down to a lack of self-esteem from trauma or CEN, they have an emotional blockage that prevents them being able to love and admire themselves.

People who find themselves in this position are usually in a disrespectful and negative relationship so they can feel good about themselves. They want the hold their needy partner has over them just as much as their mate needs them. But it comes at a cost, they spend much of their time and energy protecting their partner from life at their own expense, preventing the saviour from growing, being whole and loving their own life. Over time, the dynamic in the relationship becomes toxic as both partners poison each other without ever realizing it is happening. Both parties in the relationship feel weak and powerless as it lacks the strength and foundations of a healthy partnership. When we look closely at a troubled relationship it is not unusual to find an element of co-dependency in one or more specific areas.

# Healing co-dependency and emotionally disconnected relationships

If you have recognized any of the elements I have described in your own relationship, please don't lose heart. If anything you should celebrate it because you have just discovered an area of your life that could have continued causing you pain for a long time by keeping you stuck. Now you can reclaim the power and do something positive.

When Michelle and I recognized that these traits were playing out in our marriage, we both decided to write down our answers to the following questions:

- What is it that I expect from my partner?
- What is it that I can offer my partner?

I recommend you do the same and spend some time evaluating your answers. Make the list as long as you like, there are no right or wrong answers, and I would encourage you to list whatever comes to mind.

Everything we have covered in the book so far will have set you up for success in your intimate relationships. You will find that you naturally become able to notice and express your feelings and speak openly and honestly about whatever is on your mind, without judging yourself or your partner. You are already a long way to making many of the changes required to enjoy a fulfilling intimate partnership.

The key to change is for both partners to take complete responsibility for themselves, including their own happiness and their own negative emotions. You can only do this if you learn to respect yourself and make a complete commitment to become loving and supportive to yourself. When we do this, we get the same back from our partners; we cultivate real love, respect and support.

The relationships we have with others are a mirror of the internal relationship we have with ourselves, If we don't change our inner relationship we will never be able to experience a truly fulfilling partnership with someone else.

Put the work into loving yourself, stop projecting your power and energy outside yourself and ensure it stays within you, where it will enable you to feel good about who you are. This energy will cause people to see you in a different light, as a stable, independent individual.

Learn to be happy on your own, become independent and free so you are able to stand in the centre of your own world. It is here where we find ourselves equipped to create the most healthy, joyful and respectful relationships.

Look back at the answers you gave to the questions about your expectations of your partner and what you believe you can offer them. Ask yourself:

- Do I give the same to myself as I expect from my partner?
- Do I give to myself what I offer to my partner?

The answer to these two questions will give you some clear direction in terms of what you need to be doing in order to stop relying on your partner to meet your needs. A healthy relationship should not place expectations on other people to make someone feel good or to meet their needs. Learning to accept your perfectly imperfect partner just as they are, and letting go of any urge to change them, is where you will find peace. But at the same time it is vital to learn how to look after ourselves and become responsible for meeting our own needs and finding our own happiness, because nobody else can do it for us.

Of course, there may be times where one, other or both parties are unable to love or accept their partner for who they are, or to stop putting unreasonable expectations on them. They may refuse to be happy unless they have a level of control over their mate and, in this case, it is sensible to question whether staying in the relationship is beneficial for either person.

# Breaking the trust

When relationships suffer due to the negative effects of CEN or childhood trauma, it can result in one, or both, partners breaching the sacred boundaries of trust. When affairs or unacceptable behaviours happen it can cause so much pain that it can feel impossible to ever repair the damage.

If one partner has become emotionally disconnected, has unrealistic expectations or carries out controlling behaviour they are, in effect, pushing their significant other away by giving a message that 'I can't love you the way you are, for who you are'.

It can be easy for someone who feels unloved, unwanted, disrespected and not 'good enough' to become caught in the trap of 'limerence' with another person or with obsessive unhealthy behaviour. They believe that this will provide them with the emotional needs that don't currently exist in their relationship.

Limerence is a dangerous false fantasy that feels like an obsessive love, but people who experience it will not be told otherwise – they are in love (either with another person or an unhealthy habit) and there is no arguing about it, they *need* the limerent object. When limerence involves another person it can overlap with love, but the main difference is that limerence is less about caring for and loving the other person, and more about obsessively securing the other person's attention and affection. It stems from a desire to be acknowledged, validated and wanted without judgement, controlling behaviour, demanding expectations or fear of rejection. Limerence can be compared to the feelings of a powerful childhood crush and it is often at the root of destructive behaviour, affairs and seeking love outside of a relationship. People often risk everything for the limerent object of their obsession.

I have experienced limerent feelings throughout my life and I am now very aware of them, making sure I put boundaries in place long before they cause problems. My relationship with my wife is my priority.

Limerence is dangerous because people who are caught in the trap cannot see reality and risk sacrificing everything they have for an illusion of love. They fail to see that what they really need is right in front of them. If only they and their partner could change their behaviour and start taking responsibility for themselves they would have no desire to start relationships with other people or act out unhealthy behaviours, because they would be fulfilled and feel loved completely.

# Acting out

Due to higher levels of testosterone, men in particular can feel drawn to sexual encounters in order to feel wanted and validated, as though they have had their needs met. Short-term gratification might provide a high in the moment, but after the event most people are left with feelings of guilt, shame and regret. Resisting these temptations, even though it may feel hard, and putting our energy into fixing what we already have so we can create a fulfilling relationship, is without doubt the best path to follow.

Sexually acting out can take many different forms and it is very often our unmet needs from childhood that cause us to sexualize specific kinks and allow them to hold power and control over us. We use these activities to avoid uncomfortable feelings and keep ourselves as far away from looking inward as possible.

Just like the co-dependent relationship dynamic, we can become addicted and obsessed with specific sexual activities and use them as a form of escapism and self-soothing, even when we know they are damaging to ourselves and those around us. The irony is that sexually acting-out is often symbolic of the very feelings and memories we are attempting to avoid. For example, someone might visit a dominant sex worker to beat and spank him because it replicates the humiliation and abuse he endured in childhood from his own abusive mother. Another example might be someone who finds herself unable to say 'no' to men who try and talk her into bed, even though she is rarely physically attracted to them. She is replicating how she could never say 'no' to her narcissistic and abusive father.

One of the most common examples of sexually acting out is from people who never felt acknowledged, praised or 'good enough' as a child. This can lead to them seeking as many sexual partners as possible in adulthood in order to obtain the validation they subconsciously crave.

Many people who suffered CEN or trauma find themselves turning to addiction in order to soothe their internal pain, and sex can become an addictive behaviour causing us to become trapped in an unhealthy cycle that we feel compelled to continue with, even though we know it has negative consequences.

Acting out sexually might involve masturbating, watching porn, using sex workers, using chat lines or having affairs and one night stands. The first step to making a positive change is to acknowledge that it has become a problem. Only the person who has become addicted will know if it is an issue or not. A good measure to identify any kind of addictive behaviour is to ask whether you have control over it, or whether it has control over you.

Almost without exception we find that shame lives at the root of this type of behaviour. The antidote for feelings of shame is to bring them out into the light by sharing them in a safe space, such as a men's or women's group or in one-to-one therapy.

# Reconnecting with your partner

If your relationship has been damaged due to past trauma or neglect then I am pleased that you are reading this chapter, because it means you and your partner can reconnect and enjoy a healthy and loving partnership that will allow you to both feel fulfilled, loved and happy. Perhaps you have started to feel more like a brother and sister than a husband and wife – in this case, you can take action now and prevent yourselves from drifting apart any further than you already have.

It can be all too easy to blame our disconnect on our circumstances in life, such as having busy careers, looking after the kids or financial challenges. These things can certainly contribute, but at the heart of the problem there is rarely one big incident or situation to blame. Drifting apart happens gradually over time; with each small interaction we have with our partners and every opportunity we avoid to feel closer and more connected to each other, we take one small step in the opposite direction.

We have hundreds of opportunities every single day that allow us to move further along the path to a closer connection and intimacy. Every small choice we make can either bring people closer together or push them further apart. When we become aware of this, we naturally begin to pay much more attention to each other and learn to stand in the other person's shoes so we can consider how they feel when we speak or act in a particular way.

You might recall how we broke down the word 'intimacy' and said it out loud so it became 'in-too-me-see'. This really is the perfect explanation for what intimacy is and how it can help people heal. Intimacy is about allowing our partner to see what is inside us on the outside with no secrets, no falseness and no lies. When we nurture true intimacy in a relationship by opening our hearts and letting our partners in, we can enjoy the most fulfilling and happy relationships we have ever experienced.

While intimacy is an important part of repairing a relationship when people have drifted apart, I want to be clear that there are some elements of yourself that may be private to you and best shared in an alternative safe space, such us in a men's or women's group or with a therapist. The goal is not to know every single thought or feeling your partner experiences, but to allow them in so that they know the true version of you, not the false-persona.

In the early stages of recognizing that a relationship needs work, it may also be appropriate to seek couples' counselling as this will provide a structure for growth and a safe space where both parties can be heard and acknowledged without judgement or fear.

# Shit-testing

Although my relationship with my wife Michelle was, on the surface, a strong one, I didn't open my heart fully to her until recently when I was able to become self-aware, and I started working on healing the deep wounds left by my childhood. I couldn't see it at the time, but my behaviour was controlling, passive/aggressive and narcissistic, and I understand now that it was so I could stay in the driving seat of the relationship, confident that she would not reject me.

I had to have a sense of control and I did all I could to give Michelle a wonderful lifestyle on a material level, so she wouldn't be tempted to leave me. My thinking was completely flawed – what she really needed was love and connection, not money and possessions. Had she found someone who met those needs while I was emotionally unavailable, then there was every chance she may have abandoned me, regardless of the lifestyle we had.

Whenever Michelle and I argued, my reactions were childlike rather than those of a rational adult and I would often find myself testing whether she really loved and cared for me. There were occasions when we would argue and I would storm out of the house and tell her I wasn't coming back. In those moments what I really wanted was for her to follow me, to make me feel desired. I never had any intention of not returning, it was a test. Michelle is a stable grown-up who has her emotions in check and she never followed; she would allow me to cool down and eventually I would walk back through the door with my tail between my legs, full of apologies for my outburst, another of my 'love tests' failed.

'Shit-testing' is when someone attempts to test another person so they can judge their emotional reaction, usually to obtain validation, confirmation or approval. It isn't exclusive to intimate relationships and you may encounter it in a work, social or educational environment. The behaviour is manipulative and controlling and people who get caught up in the drama of the 'shit test' will often relinquish their power to the person who instigated the test.

Neither of us really noticed my subtle, toxic behaviour and, over the years, my drinking took centre stage alongside bringing up our son and the growth of our business. Life was too busy, we were always on the go, there was no time to pause and take a look at who we really were, or what we were doing to enhance our relationship and intimate connection.

If you find yourself on the receiving end of a 'shit test' it is important to pause and choose your response. Your partner might be threatening divorce, but if deep down you know that they often make empty threats and this is another one, it is essential you don't get caught up in the drama and instead consider how you can respond in a rational, supportive way that avoids you becoming embodied in the emotion of the episode.

Michelle would often say to me, 'Simon, you're emotional right now, take a time-out, you know I'm here for you if you want to talk. We can explore the reasons behind what you said together, when you feel ready.' I recommend using this approach as it worked for her every single time I shit-tested.

Shit-testing is as much about being heard as it is about controlling someone to soothe a subconscious fear. By asking gentle questions and reassuring the 'tester' that we are there to listen whenever they feel ready, we are validating them and letting them know we care and have heard what they are saying. The key is to do it calmly and without any emotional reaction.

If you are prone to shit-testing, begin to notice when you are doing it. When you spot that your behaviour is unhelpful, give yourself a time-out. In the heat of these moments our wounded inner-child has taken over and we need to give ourselves some space until the rational adult returns. Once the adult version is back in control, take a deep breath and return to whoever you were shit-testing and explain that you have realized what you were doing and apologize if it is appropriate.

Try and time the length of any time-outs and see if you can work on reducing how long you spend in your inner-child mode. The more awareness you bring to the times when your adult-self goes offline, the sooner you will get back on track.

Surprisingly Michelle and I didn't have huge numbers of fights or arguments, but I would shit-test at any opportunity in the hope she would give me the attention I craved and prove her love to me. It almost always failed and I regularly found myself in incredibly low moods, experiencing childlike tantrums when my attempts to manipulate and control her didn't work out. Even on the rare occasion when one of my tests succeeded, I would analyse her every word and action as I continued to try and prove that she didn't really love me and was bound to abandon me at some point.

Fast-forward a decade and the crack in our relationship had become a gaping crevice. With every week that passed we grew further apart. Michelle had suffered twenty years of my controlling behaviour. She was sick and tired of being with a man who was emotionally absent and needy. Yet I was stuck inside my head trying to feel safe and control any threat that I might be rejected or abandoned. On top of that, my drinking was worse than ever.

Thankfully, I was able to quit alcohol and eventually managed to understand what was going on in my head. I was able to make changes and work on healing before Michelle packed her bags and left me. As I began to understand the impact of the issues from my past, she became my biggest supporter and helped me on the journey to overcoming it all for good.

I committed to working on myself and became able to understand who I really was. I learned what my life story looked like and made sense of how I had been shaped since childhood. The more I tuned into my emotions and feelings and became able to share them safely, the more I felt a sense that I was becoming authentic. I felt the warmth of respect and love for myself growing within me like a beautiful but delicate flower. I knew that I needed to nurture this precious gift as it was the key to becoming whole and happy.

I had never loved myself and I don't think I had ever truly loved anyone else until I was able to reveal my true-self. When I found love for myself, I also felt like I had fallen in love with someone new, even though Michelle and I had been together for two decades. Our relationship changed dramatically, the negative behaviour vanished and we now openly share how we feel and speak the truth without judgement, controlling, confrontation or fear.

# Other close relationships

The same positive relationship template will serve you in all your close relationships, whether with your children or your closest friends. Don't expect to change overnight, start by noticing your own behaviour and use your journal to help you become aware of any potentially damaging traits. Then become mindful and curious without judgement about the negative impact of these behaviours. Continue to learn and make gradual changes at a pace that works for you. As you begin to experience the positive benefits, you will naturally feel motivated to keep moving forward. Avoid the urge to rush, take it slowly and you will steadily shift into a whole new way of being that allows you to feel truly fulfilled.

The fact is that many relationships suffer or end due to issues caused by CEN and trauma. This is both tragic and usually unnecessary, and I am so happy that you are reading this book in order that you can get to a place where you can experience real love and healthy relationships.

# 16 | Understanding and meeting your needs

Meeting our own needs is one of the keys to breaking free from CEN and trauma and finding happiness. In the past, you might have invested your time and energy into meeting the needs of other people and found yourself putting their needs ahead of your own. This behaviour can often result in the formation of co-dependent relationships and a misunderstanding of what we really need and want.

Predictably, the story of meeting our needs begins in our childhood. We have usually been ignored, hurt, shamed or neglected as children and the only solution was to adapt how we behaved in order that we can meet the needs of our parents (or caregivers) in what becomes a futile attempt to minimize our own suffering, while attempting to receive the love, comfort, approval and support that is usually lacking.

When our parents or caregivers are emotionally absent or unavailable, we end up sacrificing our own needs in order to protect ourselves and stay safe, especially if they are controlling, selfish, abusive or narcissistic. The way that we adapt ourselves to meet the needs of our parents or caregivers doesn't allow us to be happy; it simply enables us to survive as best as we possibly can in the circumstances.

We previously looked at your core values; hopefully, these have given you some clarity around what your needs might look like, and how to meet them in a healthy and safe way. It is important to have a clear understanding of what your own needs are. You might find that you have been meeting your physical needs perfectly well (food, shelter and clothing, for example), but you have most likely been neglecting some of your emotional needs and this is a major contributor to becoming stuck.

Our needs can be broadly broken down into five categories. Using Maslow's 'Hierarchy of Needs', it is possible to identify our most basic needs and ensure that they are being met. Once the needs at the bottom of the hierarchy are being met, we can move on to the section above and identify how we are meeting our needs in this area, before we ascend to the higher levels.

Maslow's Hierarchy of Needs

This Hierarchy of Needs is shaped like a pyramid, with the most basic needs at the bottom and the most complex needs at the top. The most basic physical needs such as the requirement for water, food, shelter and sleep are at the base of the pyramid, only once these are being met should we focus on the next level of needs.

# Overview of needs

## Physiological needs

These needs are at the very bottom of the pyramid and they are fairly obvious. They are the things we require in order to survive.

Examples of physiological needs include:

- Water
- Air
- Food
- Shelter
- Sleep.

## Safety needs

The needs in the second level of the hierarchy can be a little harder to identify than the most basic requirements for survival in the level below. On this tier, the need for security and safety are the primary focus in order that people can feel a sense of control and certainty in their lives.

Examples of safety and security needs include:

- Financial security
- Safe and secure living environment
- Job security
- Relationship stability and trust
- Medical safety, feeling protected against harm, disease and illness.

## Belongingness and love needs

Social needs sit right in the middle of the hierarchy and cover the strong bonds we form through emotional connection and relationships. These encompass love needs, acceptance and belonging in relationships with family, friends and loved ones. When they are being met in a healthy manner, it serves to ensure that we don't experience loneliness, sadness or anxiety through a lack of loving and meaningful connections.

Examples of social needs include:

- Friendships
- Family relationships
- Intimate and romantic relationships
- Social interactions and community groups.

## Esteem needs

Esteem needs are the fourth tier in the hierarchy. They cover the need to feel respected and appreciated. These needs can be motivating and drive us to accomplish more in our lives. We have an inbuilt desire to achieve more and to have our efforts noticed as we grow. We want to be acknowledged and recognized for our efforts and accomplishments in life. These needs provide us with a sense of feeling valued and respected by other people.

Many victims of CEN and trauma have problems satisfying their need for self-esteem and, instead, they will either lean towards feelings of inferiority or have inflated egos. It is essential that any esteem needs are fulfilled in a healthy way. Ensure you take your time when you consider this particular need and think about what healthy esteem needs would look like in your own life.

Examples of esteem needs include:

- Respect for others
- Self-confidence
- Humility
- Accomplishments in work or education
- Achievements in hobbies or pastimes
- Belonging to a team.

# Self-actualization needs

Self-actualization needs sit at the very top of the pyramid and we only become able to meet these needs once we have fulfilled each of the four tiers below. Self-actualization is the need for us to reach our full potential in life. People who are able to meet this need are self-aware, connected with their true-self and avoidant of ego-driven behaviour.

Maslow says that a person has become self-actualized when they are making the most of their skills and abilities and are living in a way that is personally fulfilling.

Examples of self-actualization needs include:
- Focused on personal growth
- Not overly concerned by the opinions of others
- An acceptance of things being the way they are
- Spiritual and mindful nature
- In touch with feelings and emotions
- Authentic, true and real.

The needs at the top of the pyramid are related to our personal growth and self-development. Growth needs are not met due to us lacking something in life, they are met from us having a strong desire to grow as a person by developing our spiritual awareness, acceptance, authenticity and connecting with our 'true-self'.

Becoming clear on your own needs and focusing on meeting them can be a great source of motivation, and it should make you feel like you are growing and working towards a positive goal. There are no right or wrong answers when it comes to identifying your needs. I began by writing down the 'top level' needs that I felt were relevant to a specific section, for example under 'social needs' this might have been the desire for 'friendships' and 'community'. I would then specify exactly how this need was currently being met or identify exactly how it could be met in the future. In these examples, I might write down that I wanted to make more friends and that my intention is to join a local community group or club in order to build new relationships.

It is possible for anyone to identify and meet their needs; the biggest stumbling block is when we progress up the hierarchy in the pyramid of needs without fully meeting the lower-level requirements. In some cases there might be episodes in our lives that cause us to fluctuate between the tiers due to certain needs being fulfilled or not at different times. For example, the loss of a job may impact our self-esteem and our sense of safety, which might cause us to stay stuck until we are able to satisfy these needs once again.

I have provided a list of the most common emotional needs to help you begin to identify which of them you feel are most important to you. I recommend applying between three and five of the needs in the list to the categories of needs. The list I have provided does not include basic physical needs such as water, sleep, food and shelter which you will need to identify to complete the lowest tier of the hierarchy. More comprehensive lists can be found online.

| | | |
|---|---|---|
| Able | Fairly treated | Productive |
| Accepted | Forgiven | Recognized |
| Acknowledged | Forgiving | Resourceful |
| Admired | Free | Respected |
| Appreciated | Fulfilled | Safe |
| Approved of | Helped | Secure |
| Believed in | Helpful | Seen |
| Capable | Important | Trusted |
| Cared for | Included | Trusting |
| Caring | In control | Understanding |
| Challenged | Joyful | Understood |
| Clarity of mind | Listened to | Validated |
| Competent | Loved | Valued |
| Confident | Motivated | Wanted |
| Desire | Needed | Worthy |
| Empowered | Noticed | |
| Encouraged | Powerful | |

If you can take the time to identify and understand what your needs look like, you will be taking a big step to claiming back control of your life. You will soon stop allowing your needs to be met by anyone other than yourself and will begin to notice how you are connecting with the authentic and true version of yourself.

You might find that focusing on yourself and thinking about what you want causes you to feel a sense of guilt, especially if you have spent much of your life putting other people's needs before your own. If you experience any such thoughts or feelings, you need to silence your inner critic by reminding yourself that what you are doing is part of a bigger picture. When you put your own needs first you end up radiating positivity and happiness, which impacts the people around you.

# 17 | The need to control

It wasn't until some time after I had worked through my past trauma and CEN that it became clear my mother had a need to be in control and she could be manipulative when she wanted to ensure she got her own way. I couldn't believe that I had never noticed it in the past because it now seemed so glaringly obvious.

When I found the strength to face my mother and explain how I felt she had let me down as a parent, I honestly believed she would change. I figured that it was simply a case of her being unaware of her behaviour, and that, as soon as she realized the extent of the damage she had caused me, she would get to work on becoming a caring, connected, loving mother.

When I laid my feelings bare, she expressed remorse and acknowledged her parental failings, which I respected her for. This gave me real hope that she was going to step up and that we could finally begin to have a healthy and loving relationship. After all, if she had admitted that she had done something wrong, surely she would want to put it right?

One of the hardest things to accept on this journey was that my mother had no intention of ever changing; I had spoken my truth to her and it had fallen on deaf ears. I have had to learn to accept that nothing is going to change. I stayed stuck waiting for her for a long time, then finally there was an epiphany. Telling her that I didn't think she was suitably equipped for the job of parenting was never about *her* changing, it was about *me* becoming able to be totally honest with her. I realized that if I could be honest and truthful with her, then I could do it with anyone.

*When we are able to confront the person who is our biggest trigger, we grow and instantly find previously challenging situations far easier.*

Over the months that I had been confronting my feelings about my childhood, and my mother, my wife had grown in confidence and felt safe to be honest with me. She explained how much she had concealed from me as a result of my childish reactions and controlling or manipulative behaviour. She used to hold things back through fear and would sometimes do things just to please me, so she could avoid any conflict.

As Michelle explained how she had grown with me and found her voice and her truth, it dawned on me that I was exactly like my mother. I had narcissistic tendencies, I was controlling, egocentric and even had a number of sociopathic traits. I had become my mother and I had never realized it.

Labels like 'narcissist' and 'sociopath' have a stigma attached to them. They imply a 'bad' person who is ego-driven, engages in controlling behaviour and compulsive lying, and believes that they are more important than anyone else. But we should avoid putting labels on ourselves; we are all made up of many beautiful traits, along with behaviours that can hold us back. As long as we are becoming aware, and working on changing the behaviours that limit us, we are doing the best we can and should take comfort in the fact that we are becoming our true-selves.

I knew that I had many positive traits, alongside a handful of narcissistic and sociopathic tendencies. At that time I was such a mixture of different ingredients, there was no way that one label – such as 'narcissist' – would be accurate, and it would have made me feel self-critical if I had chosen to use it. So I stuck to simply labelling myself as 'Simon, who is now conscious and working on development and change'.

Sociopathic traits, narcissism and controlling behaviour usually originate from trauma and emotional neglect when we are children, and this is exactly what happened in my case. When our parents fail to give us enough comfort, support and love, or when they flood us with too much of it and suffocate us, it can result in adults developing unhelpful behaviours in order to fulfil their unmet needs.

These traits are common among adults, especially in those who have suffered CEN or trauma as children. So please don't panic if you recognize some of the behaviours in yourself. Instead, reframe your thinking and feel pleased that you have discovered another piece of the puzzle that will lead to you becoming whole and authentic.

# How do you know if you have narcissistic traits?

Not everyone who has experienced past trauma or neglect develops narcissistic traits; in some cases people go in the opposite direction and find themselves drawn to people who exhibit these behaviours. Some people don't develop any of the traits whatsoever. Narcissistic tendencies are commonly encountered within co-dependent relationships, where controlling and manipulative behaviour have become the norm.

The following list of behaviours should give you a good idea as to whether you have any narcissistic tendencies. If you identify with any of them don't worry, we will be looking at how to change them later in this chapter.

- **You are hypersensitive:** There are two types of narcissists; one is the kind that you can tell has entered a room before you even see them because they are so loud and self-important, while the other is a more covert style of narcissism that is highly sensitive, anxious, defensive and introverted. Both types are driven by the individual's desire to put their own needs first, regardless of the impact on others.

- **You are more important:** The polar opposite to the people who are hypersensitive are those who feel 'entitled' and believe they are more important than everyone else. Their behaviour is best described as grandiose or superior and they will often feel resentment at having to sacrifice themselves for other people. For example, it may anger them when they have to wait in a queue, or deal with paperwork and red tape because they believe they should be able to skip the line or the process. They may believe that they should be receiving much more attention and recognition from other people because they deserve it, and will seek adulation or appreciation. Narcissists will ensure that they are the centre of attention and can't help talking about themselves and exaggerating their achievements.

  Learning to cultivate self-love certainly involves putting yourself first in your own life and this is a powerful and healthy habit – but there is a big difference between looking after your own needs and believing that you are in some way more important than other people.

- **You are a sore loser:** People with narcissistic tendencies don't like losing, whether that's in sport, at work or in any other competitive environment. Often they will try to show that they should have won, or that they were somehow treated unfairly. When they do win they gloat or humiliate those they have beaten.

- **You seek validation and acknowledgement:** Those with narcissistic traits need attention and feel compelled to gain the approval of others, and the more they receive the more they need. It might be subtle, for example, continually seeking attention by speaking or behaving in a particular way; or it could be much more obvious as they show off about material objects, money, careers, family and holidays to gain attention and soothe their deep insecurity.

- **You know how to charm people:** In some ways, it is a gift to be able to make other people feel important by turning on the charm. However, people with narcissistic traits expect the same in return and will be waiting for the compliments and admiration to be repaid, usually with interest.

- **You can't handle not being in control:** People with these tendencies believe that life is one big disappointment and, in order to make it better, they become compelled to control almost everything around them. They believe it is their personal right to be in control because they feel superior and entitled. When these people do not have the control they want, it can result in them becoming emotionally overwhelmed or resorting to the use of underhand tactics to gain power. This might be through manipulation, emotional blackmail, aggression or lying.

- **You lack empathy:** Narcissists think only about themselves; lack of empathy is one reason they struggle to form meaningful relationships with strong emotional connections.

- **You fear rejection:** People with narcissistic traits are defined by their fears. The thought of being humiliated, rejected or abandoned causes them to struggle with trust and in many cases, the closer a relationship becomes, the less they will trust their partner. No matter how much reassurance, approval or validation they receive, a narcissist will judge themselves harshly for not being good enough. They usually feel anxious and carry a fear of being found out that they are faking it.

- **You are never to blame:** Nothing is ever a narcissist's fault. When they do find it within themselves to apologize for something they have done wrong, they will often only be doing it for their own benefit, or will only apologize with excuses that blame someone or something else for causing their mistake.

- **You have a black and white personality:** These people tend to put everything that happens in their lives into one of two categories. Things are either good or bad: when something is bad a narcissist will blame other people for it, when it is good they will take the credit. Even the memories narcissists have are split into either good or bad, they lack the ability to find any middle ground between 'all' and 'nothing'.

# How do you know if you have sociopathic traits?

The word 'sociopath' sounds scary, and you might have visions of a psychotic serial killer when you hear it. However, rather like narcissism, trauma and neglect, sociopathic traits are on a spectrum, and some people have more than others.

Sociopaths are often intelligent and charming; people tend to warm to them quickly. They are best defined as people who have traits of an antisocial personality disorder, causing them to lack remorse and conscience for their behaviour. Sociopaths are also prone to manipulative behaviour and may find themselves lying and covering things up.

Just because you have CEN and trauma in your past, it doesn't follow that you will have sociopathic tendencies. However, as with the traits of narcissism, you may find that you relate to a number of the common behaviours that follow, or you might discover they only apply to certain aspects of your life. Do bear in mind that this process is all about bringing a newfound awareness to any unhelpful behaviours in order that you can work on changing them. If you don't know, you will never be able to change.

- **You don't feel guilt, shame or remorse:** People with sociopathic traits will rarely feel a sense of guilt, shame or remorse when they do something wrong. They may well apologize to smooth over a situation, but they will do this from a place of self-protection rather than owning it and taking responsibility.

- **People love you:** Sociopaths are very charming and people may feel drawn to them. Their charming behaviour exists on the surface as the means to an end. When someone enters a close relationship with a sociopath their true personality usually becomes quickly apparent.

- **You view situations and people as opportunities:** Sociopaths are usually on the lookout for ways that they can benefit themselves by using other people and situations to their advantage. Instead of thinking about the feelings of other people or attending a social event or commitment without an agenda, they might use their charm, ego or manipulative nature to obtain approval or acknowledgment for themselves.

- **You do things your way:** Sociopaths often have little regard for social norms or rules. They may well engage in antisocial behaviour and fail to comply with regulations when the urge takes them, they have very little concept of right or wrong. There is often no clear explanation for their behaviour and rarely any kind of remorse.

- **You tend to lack emotion:** Sociopaths appear to be devoid of any emotion. While they may be prone to angry outbursts or be incredibly happy on the surface at times, this is usually a subconscious tactic to gain attention, manipulate or control the situation. Many people with sociopathic tendencies are disconnected from their emotions due to a deep rooted block that usually relates to past trauma or neglect.

- **You tend to be either negative or positive:** Sociopaths will say whatever they believe is required in order to hide their weaknesses or to manipulate a situation. It is common for them to be full of positive statements and affirmations or to be extremely negative, there's no middle ground.

- **You take risks:** Sociopaths will often get involved in risky or reckless behaviour with little regard for their own safety or the wellbeing of other people. This kind of behaviour is impulsive and can result in serious consequences.

- **You rarely plan in advance:** People with sociopathic tendencies are less likely to plan ahead and are prone to acting on impulse. They might make expensive purchases on a whim, fail to prepare for important commitments, occasions or events and, regardless of the consequences, will fail to show remorse or take responsibility for their actions.

- **You never learn:** People with sociopathic traits rarely learn from the negative consequences they experience as a result of the mistakes they make. This keeps them stuck in a behaviour loop that repeats over and over until they are able to become aware of what they are doing and feel motivated to change.

# How do you overcome narcissistic and sociopathic traits?

The first thing is not to worry if you have recognized some of these behaviours in yourself, they are much more common than you might think and, just because you have identified a number of areas that may need work, it doesn't mean you are a bad person. In some people these traits tend to come to the surface in specific areas of their lives, for example at work, in relationships or in social settings. If you have spotted some of these behaviours in yourself, can you identify any patterns?

Pause for a moment and write down ten of your best qualities – or ask someone else to do so – and you will see that we are all made up of positive and negative traits. You could also write a list with the positive and negative traits of some of the people in your life, in order to reinforce the fact that perfection is an illusion.

True narcissists and sociopaths will never change, they will never accept fault in themselves. You are different; you have put in the time and effort to identify all parts of yourself and no doubt feel motivated to work on making a positive change. This alone shows that beneath any ego- or fear-driven behaviour is a person who really does care, and who has compassion for themselves and for others.

*If you were a true narcissist or sociopath you wouldn't even have picked up this book.*

Millions of people share these characteristics, and, if we can channel the useful ones into positive areas of our lives, they can serve us and help us grow. The very fact that you may have become aware of these behaviours means that you are on the path to change and to learning how to use them in a positive way. If, however, reading about the traits of narcissism and sociopathy made you feel that you may be high on the spectrum, please don't despair. While the internet is full of articles that insist there is no specific treatment available, this is untrue. I know, because I'm a recovering narcissist who had sociopathic tendencies. I've been through the process of healing and I've come out the other side. The cure is to become conscious and aware.

Everything I have outlined in this book will help you recover. You may find it more of a challenge to become authentic and to let go of certain behaviours than someone with milder traits, but when you make it your intention to work on yourself you begin to become far more mindful. You will experience your life without the burden of these draining behaviours, which limit you from being the real version of yourself.

The good news is that narcissists and sociopaths are usually highly intelligent people, and when they see the sense in something they will channel their energy into achieving their goal and won't let anything or anyone get in the way. Use this superpower to your advantage on your journey to recovery, become mindful of not abusing it.

You may find some traits have become so deeply ingrained that you struggle to let go of them. In these situations, I recommend seeking out a professional who has experience in those specific areas and working with them, in a one-to-one or group setting, in order to get past the blockages and continue on your journey to healing.

Many people have managed to change their narcissistic and sociopathic tendencies by making it their goal and immersing themselves in the work required to achieve it. You can do the same if you have some of these traits. There may be no scientific 'cure' for them, but becoming conscious, aware and self-reflective will allow you to cultivate empathy, authenticity, experience emotions, find healthy coping mechanisms and form positive new habits and relationships that will set you free.

# 18 | Sharing our experiences safely

Our metaphorical 'shadow' is a dark and lonely place hidden away deep within our mind, always behind us, out of view. This is the place where we keep the behaviours, thoughts, feelings and emotions that we are unable to face, such as shame, anger, sadness, regret and fear. The 'shadow' is a psychological term for everything we fail to see in ourselves. We are often quick to spot faults in other people, and we will observe their shadow, but we can remain blind to our own.

Think of your shadow as the dark side of your personality. This is where your negative emotions and behaviours live – greed, hate, jealousy, desire and selfishness. Whenever you encounter something that doesn't align with your values, your conscious opinion or your attitude about yourself, it becomes part of your shadow.

You may have heard people speak about their shadow, and how damaging it can be when we keep negativity hidden. Part of this process involves you learning to become conscious of your shadow by looking into the darkness and cultivating a healthy awareness, learning to express yourself honestly and share your experiences safely.

Everything that we deny about ourselves, the parts of us that we consider weak, inferior, unacceptable or evil, all slip into the shadow. These are the aspects of us that we are unwilling to accept as being part of our positive 'true-self', the parts we disown and refuse to look at. The problem is that although we think we have denied them, they never actually leave us. They stay buried in the darkness, where they eat away at our soul and cause pain.

When we hide something by ignoring or suppressing it, we often believe that we have dealt with it adequately and that this alone is enough to allow us to be free. Our shadow, however, is like a nasty virus – the more we feed it the more it will spread and harm us. The negativity, self-criticism, behaviours, lies, emotions and feelings that we put into our shadow are the host to this virus. They allow it to thrive and grow within us. Over time, we put more and more negativity into our shadow and it becomes a huge burden that creates a very real sense of pain within our core. Eventually the weight becomes too heavy and we find ourselves cracking.

Every human needs a dark side in order to be a whole person. The problems arise when we are unable to see our shadow, and avoid keeping it light and healthy. We must honour all parts of our entire being, good or bad; ignoring our shadow is dangerous and will lead to serious problems further down the line.

When we deny specific parts of ourselves, we begin to see those parts in other people, (see 'Projection', in Chapter 10). We project what we bury within us onto others. For example, we might find that we become angry when someone appears to judge us for an opinion we have expressed on social media. The likely reason that this makes us react so strongly is because we haven't taken ownership of our own judgemental behaviour. This isn't to say that the person hasn't judged us, but if judgement wasn't in our shadow it wouldn't bother us so much. Anything that we fail to accept, own or acknowledge about ourselves is relegated into our shadow.

Exploring your shadow is challenging; nobody enjoys accepting that they have negative aspects of their personality. But it will allow you to feel lighter and free from the burden of the negativity, enabling you to nurture self-love at the same time as finding a greater acceptance for other people and their shortcomings. There is only one way to deal with a dark shadow, we need to shine light on to it.

# Shadow work

In order to become truly free it is essential that you learn to look into your shadow. It is there, in the darkness, that you will begin to find the light that will lead you to a place where you can be whole, true and happy.

I have devised a straightforward process that you can use to keep your shadow within your view. It will allow you to foster self-acceptance, honesty and authenticity. This in turn will help you move away from the issues that have been holding you back.

There are two elements to shadow work. The first is acknowledging what is within your shadow now, and the second is addressing what you might put in your shadow in the future.

## What is in your shadow now?

In order to become free, you need to look at your shadow and address what is in there at the moment. Think of your shadow as a virtual filing cabinet; every time you reject, repress or fail to acknowledge your own negative traits you add another file of information into the cabinet. When the cabinet becomes full it gets too heavy to lift, and the very surface on which it stands starts to crack, causing internal discomfort, emotional instability and leading to mental health problems.

The following steps will allow you to navigate your way into the darkness. Try and focus on emptying your internal filing cabinet using the process I have outlined. It is essential that you acknowledge everything that exists in your shadow, you should use your journal and write an absolutely true and honest account of everything outlined in the first step.

**Honesty audit**: You may have explored some of these already, but I would like you to wipe the slate clean by writing down everything that is covered by the following points. Don't hold back – you need to be totally open, honest and truthful. If you distort the truth or fail to acknowledge certain parts of your shadow then you are simply lying to yourself.

Write down, with complete honesty:

- Behaviours you keep hidden
- Behaviours you feel negative emotions about
- Secrets you keep
- Lies you have told
- Emotions you have failed to acknowledge
- Feelings you have failed to acknowledge
- Opinions of yourself
- Opinions of others
- Beliefs about yourself
- Beliefs about others.

If you have spoken openly with others about any of the areas you identify, and you have acknowledged, accepted or expressed your feelings and emotions, then the likelihood is that it does not exist in your shadow. You are looking for the parts of yourself that you have, until now, believed do not exist.

Try and think of this process rather like looking in a mirror at the aspects of yourself that you have turned away from. If it feels uncomfortable, you are looking in the right place. Embrace the discomfort, this is what will set you free.

**Get curious**: Once you have written down everything you can think of, allow yourself some time to notice if anything else from your shadow presents itself; it is likely that new insights will come to mind over the coming weeks. If you have never explored your shadow you have an entire lifetime of denial to bring out into the light, and it may take some time to obtain a comprehensive and complete list. There is no rush, take as long as you need.

The process of writing out what we have failed to acknowledge can be enough to accept the negative aspects of ourselves that we have ignored. However, I prefer to take the process one step further and I recommend that you do the same. When I completed this process, I wrote next to each item the appropriate person that I believed I needed to share it with. I identified who I considered to be the most suitable safe person (or people) for each point on my list and then I set about sharing my truth without guilt, shame or self-judgement. I simply needed to state the facts as they were, I wanted to own all parts of who I was.

This involved me sharing some behaviours, opinions and feelings that I had carried significant shame about for decades. Initially I was wary of sharing, but once I had confidence that I was getting these points out to the right person, I knew that this process was going to be a big part of my healing process and I took the leap of faith.

There was no judgement and no negativity from the people I shared my darkest self with, and every time I was able to share another part of my shadow I became lighter. After a month or two I had emptied the filing cabinet that had previously held a lifetime of shame, hatred, judgements, pain, fear, anger, sadness and worries.

I am a member of a small men's group; we encourage complete openness and honesty in our sessions and we have a policy of leaving our egos at the door and always being totally honest with each other. I was able to share plenty with the men in this wonderful group because I knew it was a completely safe space. If you are unsure where to share what you find, I recommend seeking out a suitable men's or women's group. You might also want to find a counsellor or therapist and share with them, or you may be happy to open up to close members of your family, friends or loved ones.

When we have dealt with our shadow we tend to find that our relationships improve, we become happier, more grounded and balanced as we welcome a new sense of awareness, authenticity and calm into our lives.

## Your future shadow

After you have cleared the parts of yourself that you have never acknowledged out of the filing cabinet, you should ensure that you work on keeping it as empty as possible. This will enable you to stay light and free and avoid negativity dragging you down. You will need to pay attention whenever anything is dismissed and dumped into your shadow. There will be times when things slip under your radar, but you will quickly begin to notice when this happens.

I recommend creating a set of 'shadow boundaries', these act as your internal guide for anything that you need to acknowledge or express.

This is what my list looks like:

- Behaviours that I feel shame, regret or negativity about
- All secrets – I will not keep secrets
- Lies or dishonest behaviour
- Negative emotions I fail to express
- Negative feelings I fail to acknowledge (especially shame, hate, anger, sadness and self-esteem)
- Negative opinions about myself
- Negative opinions about other people
- Negative beliefs about myself
- Negative beliefs about other people.

Once you have created your own list of 'shadow boundaries', you will become used to catching yourself whenever you experience these behaviours, thoughts, emotions or feelings. When you become aware, it is your personal responsibility to acknowledge and express yourself in a healthy and safe way in order to avoid anything slipping into the darkness.

For example, if I became triggered by someone boasting about their achievements, instead of simply ignoring it I would now explore whether I reacted emotionally because there are times when I have done the same. I would write in my journal and I would then decide where the appropriate safe place to share it might be. Depending on the circumstances this might be with the person in question, or more likely in my men's group, with a therapist or with a trusted friend or family member. The whole purpose of this process is for you to begin shining a light on everything that you have been allowing to move unnoticed into your dark side.

Finally, let's talk about shame. Shame is one of the most common negative feelings found in our shadow. It weighs us down and uses up our energy while it stays hidden in the darkness. You should deal with shame in the same way as everything else we have identified in this process. Acknowledge it, write it out and decide where you feel is the safest place to share. If it feels painful, you are looking in exactly the right place.

As soon as you begin to share anything you feel shame about, you will find that it immediately begins to lose its power. Don't avoid it or fail to acknowledge it, this is going to help you heal. You may need to find some courage in order to overcome any initial fears of sharing, but take your time to ensure you have a safe space in a group, with a therapist or with someone you trust and you will be able to use this as your go-to for anything that tries to lurk in your shadow going forward.

*Shame cannot survive in the light.*

# 19 | Dealing with discomfort

This book is designed to help you heal Childhood Emotional Neglect and past trauma. My hope is that, as you have been reading the previous chapters and reflecting on what you have learned so far, you have begun to form a new sense of self-awareness and started to acknowledge truths about yourself that you may have previously refused to consider. If so, this is a huge breakthrough. It is through accepting your own reality and becoming your true-self that you will find freedom from future suffering.

If you have already started to notice changes, that is a sure sign that you absolutely can make a lasting change if you continue to work on yourself, make the effort to show up, and invest your time into breaking free.

In most cases, people experience a feeling of transition as they move from the old version of themselves to the new, authentic, happy, free and peaceful version. We may find ourselves, as we enter this transition phase, in a grey area that puts us in between the old and new versions of ourselves. One minute we feel happier than we have felt for years, then the next minute we are emotionally overwhelmed and slip back to our default position of misery.

This is perfectly normal. Hold on to the fact that you are noticing incredible changes, and the changes are happening because you are putting in the work. You are bringing your past out from the darkness and into the light. Use your journal to write down each and every change that you notice. Pay close attention and allow your growth to be your motivation to continue moving forward with a sense of real positivity.

When I was transitioning from the 'stuck' version of myself to the version that is free and authentic, I spent a month or two in the transition phase. I kept experiencing new breakthrough moments, which were wonderful and enlightening. But I was also recalling many painful past memories which I needed to process and make sense of, causing myself more work. However, I understood that I would never heal until I stopped avoiding past negative episodes and I knew that they all had to come out into the light, to go into my journal so I could fully process them through a process of understanding, acceptance and grieving.

The transitioning period was a rollercoaster. I was emotionally up and down, things continued to trigger me, but the overwhelming reactions were beginning to soften. I took care to notice the trigger, to look within and notice what feelings came up. I would acknowledge the sadness, unworthiness or anger, instead of attempting to push it away. I sat with those feelings.

As challenging as these moments felt, they were positive because I had never previously been able to feel my emotions in such a way. I wanted to welcome the feelings in, good or bad. I accepted everything just as it was, greeting these feelings with a peaceful 'hello' in the knowledge that they would soon pass.

I would almost always turn to my journal, either when the feelings were with me or straight after they had faded away. I dug deeper with a real sense of curiosity, looking at my past for similar situations or behaviours, and it was here that I began to experience light bulb moments. I recall an occasion when I had asked my wife if she wanted to go out to dinner. She explained that she'd had a tough day at work and was looking forward to doing nothing more than having a long soak in the bath and an early night. She promised that we would head to the restaurant later in the week. I saw the dark storm clouds on the horizon and before I knew it I was triggered, overwhelmed, feeling rejected and sorry for myself.

Previously I would have firmly believed that it was Michelle who caused the storm, but I knew that most people don't react with such high emotion when someone else politely declines a dinner invitation. She had even offered me an alternative date. As the storm began to pass, the feelings started to fade and I began to write. This is copied from my journal and is exactly what I wrote:

**'I just had an emotional episode, I want to explore where it came from. It felt overwhelming and I couldn't stop it, so frustrating.**

**I asked Michelle if she wanted to go out for dinner this evening. I wanted jerk chicken. She said she didn't feel like it and even though she offered to go later this week I couldn't fight off the overwhelming feelings that followed.**

**The strongest feelings were anger and sadness.**

**I felt rejected and unwanted, it felt as though she didn't care about me and this subsequently led to further irrational thoughts about whether she really loves me. I know this is ridiculous because she does so many things that demonstrate that she absolutely does, the evidence is clear – she does love me. But I couldn't get the feelings out of my head until I had faced up to them and worked through it all.**

**This isn't about Michelle or going out for dinner, this is about me being rejected, I have felt it many times before.**

**This comes from my father abandoning and rejecting me when I was younger and multiple episodes with my mother that caused feelings of uncertainty about how important I actually was, and whether she really loved me.**

**Do your work Simon, keep bringing these things out into the light, no ignoring the discomfort!'**

I can't overstate the importance of exploring each uncomfortable situation you are faced with. If I had kept this in my head it would have continued to have overwhelmed me, but as soon as I began to write I felt like I was taking back control, becoming far more rational about what I had experienced.

From here I was able to get curious and understand exactly what the trigger was – in this case 'rejection'. Then I could trace it back to my past and make much more sense of my response.

This process will enable you to acknowledge uncomfortable feelings in a healthy way. You will no longer be pushing them away only for them to come back and bite you further down the line.

In order to help myself during the tougher moments of emotional overwhelm, I created a list of go-to tactics that I knew I could turn to whenever I needed to get back in control. I have shared the tactics that worked best for me in this chapter. You will find that some will work better for you than others; experiment with them to see what feels best for you. You can come back to this chapter and access the tactics whenever you need them.

Test these strategies before you need to use them for real, when you are feeling calm. Don't wait for an emotional episode to experiment. If you can discover which of them help you to feel calm and relaxed quickly, you will reclaim your power knowing you have the ability to move through any discomfort.

# Tactics for dealing with discomfort

## Uncomfortable thoughts

Have you ever noticed the music that plays in the background when you are in a supermarket? Do you ever pay attention to it? Maybe sometimes you hear a favourite song while you are shopping and find yourself singing as you push your trolley through the aisles. Or you might take notice when you hear a song that you don't like and experience a different feeling altogether. Most of the time I doubt you even pay attention to any music that is being played. In fact, can you even remember if your regular shop has background music or not?

This shows how irrelevant background music is to you. Of course it is there, but you probably rarely even notice it. Most of the time our intention is not to go to the shop to listen to the songs, we're there with a different purpose. We are motivated to get our shopping done and that goal is at the forefront of our minds as we dodge screaming children, slow-moving trolley pushers, and people who have no sense of spatial awareness.

Imagine if you were standing in the supermarket and it became empty: the shelves were gone, all the products vanished and suddenly there were no customers or staff. All that remained was a vast empty space and, you've guessed it, the background music. In that enormous empty space you would begin to give the background music a lot more of your attention. In fact, it would no longer be background music, it would just be 'music'. There would be hardly anything else to focus on and it would begin to become almost all you could think about (other than wondering why everything in the store just vanished, of course).

There is no way of turning our thoughts off, and even if there was, it would be a really bad idea because many of them are extremely useful; they help us learn, develop, grow and assess risk. Not all of our thoughts are useful, however, and some of them are downright uncomfortable and noisy. I had plenty of noisy thoughts when I was trying to give up drinking: 'Alcohol is the answer; pour yourself a drink, it'll relax you – you've had a few days off – go on . . .'. Trying to fight off a thought like this is draining, but giving into it is painful. Eventually it just becomes overwhelming (and having that drink might seem like the only answer to silence the noise).

But here's the thing – *you can turn your thoughts into background music*. You don't need to pay huge amounts of attention to them; no matter what the message is, you can simply accept that the thought exists and then make a decision about what you would like to do with it. Remind yourself who's in control.

Your supermarket probably has a customer service desk, right? This is where you go when you have an issue with an item or a query and it is also where you take your purchases to return them for a refund. You can do the same with your thoughts. When a thought enters your mind, you have the power of choice – but only if you are able to create a sense of awareness. If you fail to acknowledge your thoughts, you will end up blindly following some of them without any logical reason, leading to unwanted, unpredictable and even regrettable behaviour.

So before you approach the customer service desk, make sure you have acknowledged that a particular thought is with you, then decide if you would like to give it a little more airtime and listen to what it has to say – or not. If you choose you want to explore the thought deeper, that's fine. Go ahead, take a moment to become curious about the thought, consider what it is telling you and whether it is worth acting on. Take the time to consider the consequences of any actions you might take if you choose to follow the thought and then make your choice, knowing that you hold the power of choice.

Now, as you step forward to the customer service desk, you have three choices:

1. **Consciously act on it:** You have the option of keeping the thought in your virtual shopping trolley and taking it to the checkout in the store. You still have as much time as you need to change your mind, this isn't an irreversible decision. The important point is that you have made the decision

from a place of conscious awareness, rather than blindly following the thought simply because it happened to appear. This newfound awareness will serve you in many powerful and positive ways on the journey to becoming unstuck from CEN and trauma.

2. **Put the thought back on the shelf:** If, after acknowledging the thought, you feel that it is not going to serve you in a positive way, then you have the option of placing it back on the shelf. You can come back to it later if you wish, or, you can simply pass it by without paying more attention to it in the knowledge that you have looked at it, but it wasn't what you needed right now. Again, this decision is made from a place of being mindful and aware of the thought, there is no internal forcing or fighting. Simply allow the thought to be with you and if you decide it has no useful purpose, put it back on the shelf.

3. **Exchange it for something else:** As well as having the option of putting the thought back on the shelf, you also have the choice of exchanging it. You can do this by shifting your attention to something else that is with you in the present moment. There are 86,400 seconds in every day. Assuming we sleep for an average of eight hours at night, this leaves us around 58,000 seconds of consciousness each day. This means that we have a thought, on average, every second that we are awake. You are spoilt for choice in terms of what you want to exchange a negative thought for. You have the option of shifting your attention and focusing on a new thought and repeating the process, or moving your mind to something else that is with you in the present moment. Your new thought might simply be to pay attention to the background music, or focus on all customers who are wearing a certain type of clothing. Maybe you will concentrate on singing out loud, or becoming happy and playful. You can choose.

The last two choices are about making the unwanted thought fade like the background music. You do this by acknowledging that it exists, then affirming that you have no desire to interact with it at any deeper level. Sometimes it can help to say your affirmation calmly out loud or in your head, for example:

**'I am not interested in interacting with you right now; I'm moving my intention to a different thought. I might give you my attention later, when I'm ready.'**

When you become aware of the thought, make your decision. Are you keeping it, placing it back on the shelf or exchanging it for something else? Assuming that you decide not to keep the thought then you should return your focus to the present moment and release the thought – you can't control it, so let it go.

The thought might be about events from the past – you can't control those, they have already happened.

It might be a worry about the future – the future hasn't happened yet, so there is no sense in worrying about outcomes and predictions that are impossible to know.

Take a deep breath and refocus on something new that exists in the present moment.

Another good method for moving past an uncomfortable thought is to consciously choose to refocus attention on the breath. Observe your breath as it moves in and out, keeping your attention locked on the air as it flows through you. Follow it through your mind's eye. It can help to focus on a specific area as you breathe; for example, the entrance of your nose, around your nostrils where the air feels cool as it enters and warm as you exhale it out.

You can focus on your breathing just about anywhere and it can be a huge help when an unwanted thought arrives. I have used this strategy when I have been at busy events, out shopping, driving the car and even during a half marathon when I was interrupted by a couple of unwelcome thoughts around seven miles in.

The more you practise re-focusing your attention back to the present moment, the more you will claim back control over your mind. You will find that some thoughts will continue to enter your head when you try to shift your attention on to your breath. When this happens, simply notice the thought, allow it to pass and return straight back to your breath. It is a good idea to say the word 'thought' out loud or in your head, this brings about a conscious acknowledgement and will help you accept that a thought has arrived before returning your attention to your breathing. Use the breath like an anchor that holds you in a place of safety, and keep returning to it until you feel any discomfort soften.

## Get up, or you'll stay stuck

Before I share more of the tactics that worked best for me when it came to managing difficult thoughts, feelings and emotions, I want to provide you with an important piece of advice so that you are always able to use them to your advantage, no matter how tough it might feel at the time.

During my journey to healing I realized the importance of becoming aware of any discomfort that entered my mind. The simple process of acknowledging that it was with me at that moment became a healthy new habit, and I knew it was helping me by opening a previously closed door that allowed me to explore and understand more about what I was experiencing.

But there were occasions when acknowledging the feelings didn't do anything to ease them. I had been working hard, I was making good progress, but certain behaviours and people still triggered me and caused a reactive downward spiral. It was overwhelming, and sometimes I would lie on the floor, flooded with toxic feelings, often for hours.

The more I lay in that deep well of misery, the deeper it seemed to become.

My problem wasn't knowing which tactics to use in these situations, it was the struggle of moving from a place of hopelessness to getting back in charge of my mind. Eventually I found a solution and it worked perfectly. When I found myself on the floor feeling utterly dejected, I pushed my focus onto the tactic most suitable for handling the current feelings and emotions. Because I felt like I was stuck in my misery on one side of a huge canyon, and the tactic I needed to use was on the other side of that vast rocky gorge, I knew I needed to build a bridge to walk across. I have always been useless at building things, so I decided the only option was to launch myself across, instead.

I played it like a movie in my mind, imagining myself in a rocket ready to launch, to power me from one side of the canyon to the other with ease. I held that vision in my mind and began to count down out loud from ten to zero. When I hit zero, I shouted, 'MOVE!'

And that is exactly what I did. I moved as though an external force had picked me up from the floor and was giving me a firm push in the direction I needed to go. It was a game-changer. I moved straight into the tactic I needed to use and dealt with my uncomfortable feelings. I had made it to the other side of the canyon and, if you use this strategy, you will be able to get there too, whenever you need to.

I used this tactic for challenges that came up when I quit drinking and I even shared it in my book *How to Quit Alcohol in 50 Days*. Hopefully you won't need to use it too often, and you'll gain strength by knowing you have it in your arsenal.

## Using your superpowers

One thing I have noticed about many people who have suffered CEN and trauma in childhood is that most are 'all or nothing' type people. When we commit to doing something we become determined and dedicated almost to the point of obsession, we are either all in or all out.

If you have 'all or nothing' traits, this is a very special gift. You can harness it like a superpower and use it to make healing your new obsession. When we believe that something is worth working for, there is often no stopping us. We become passionate about reaching our goals, we won't stop searching for answers and putting in the work to get to where we want to be. (Don't worry if you haven't noticed traits of 'all or nothing' behaviour in yourself. You will still heal if you put in the work. I recommend consciously focusing on creating a mindset of true determination as this will serve you in an incredibly powerful way.)

As somebody who is likely to experience a great amount of negative self-talk, you probably don't believe you could ever be determined enough to make a powerful change to your life. Maybe you believe that you lack the ability to be determined.

You're wrong.

Take a moment to think about a time in your life when you made a decision to achieve something and nothing was going to stop you. Maybe you wanted to change careers, move to a new city, save for a new car, run a 10km race or half marathon, have a baby, get married or go to university. Whatever it was, you were determined to make it happen, no matter what obstacles were in your way. You will have had to face those obstacles head on, no matter how hard they seemed. Maybe you had to tell your boss you were changing jobs and you felt a huge amount of fear about it; maybe you spent hours pounding the streets alone on training runs before completing an event; maybe you had to make incredibly difficult choices when it came to moving home or city. Clearly, you already have that determination within you to do something if you really want to.

It was this sense of determination that enabled me to discover a strategy that allowed me to pick myself up from the floor when I was struggling with overwhelming emotions. In the same way, the tactics that follow will allow you to weaken any uncomfortable emotions, feelings or thoughts. Don't ignore whatever you are experiencing, acknowledge that these thoughts have come into your mind and don't attempt to fight or suppress them. I make no apology for repeating myself throughout this book - repetition will ensure the important points stick. This can feel rather like learning a new skill and you need to commit to training yourself *before* you have an emotional episode. Imagine if I were to ask you to play the violin and, instead of giving you the opportunity to practise and learn, the first time you pick up the instrument is as you walk on to the stage, alone, in a packed concert hall. It probably wouldn't end well, and the same is true if you don't prepare your tactics.

## Tactic 1: Who is in control?

An excellent tactic when you notice that you have become triggered is to pause for a moment, then check-in with yourself by taking a few slow and intentional breaths in and out through your nose. Allow a sense of calm to wash over you – even if this feels hard – and then ask yourself the following questions as you reflect on the episode that caused you to become overwhelmed:

*'How old did you feel when you became triggered?'*

The likelihood is that the reaction came from your inner child. If you can notice that you actually felt like a child at the time you were triggered, you will be in a great position to make your inner child feel safe and loved. Remember, there is no logical reason for the child within you to feel unsafe, you are looking after them now, ensuring they feel loved and protected. Make sure you remind them of this often. Inner child meditation is a great way to reinforce the positive messages.

If you found yourself reacting verbally during an overwhelming episode, use the same strategy but also ask yourself:

*'Who was doing the talking when you were triggered?'*

Was it the adult version of you, or was it your inner child? Simply recognizing that the child has taken control is often enough to snap you back into reality so you can get back in charge. At this point you need to let your child know that you can handle things from here. Say out loud:

'You are safe, you are loved and you are enough. I will deal with things as an adult from here.'

You should feel the adult version of you coming back online as you continue to provide reassurance.

## Tactic 2: Cancel, cancel, cancel!

Another excellent tactic for dealing with uncomfortable emotions and feelings is the 'cancel, cancel, cancel' technique. As with all of the tactics in this book, it is essential that you acknowledge the feeling you are experiencing then pause for a moment in order to decide how to respond. After the acknowledgement, hold the negative feeling in your mind and say either out loud, or in your head:

'Cancel, cancel, cancel!'

The more energy and volume you apply, the better. This tactic works well by reinforcing the fact that you have acknowledged the feeling but you wish to prevent it becoming overwhelming. If you feel it weakening after saying it once but it still hasn't faded completely, then repeat the process until you get back in control.

## Tactic 3: Jumping jacks

One of the best methods of getting back on track when you are experiencing your emotions and feelings starting to take over is to elevate your heart rate. Not only does this refocus your mind at the same time as enabling you to connect with your body, it also releases feel-good endorphins which will help to raise your mood. Jumping jacks are one of the best methods of achieving this. Simply acknowledge and name the feeling that has arisen within you and then get to work with 25 jumping jacks. You should feel any discomfort begin to weaken - if not, repeat the sets of 25 until it has completely gone.

## Tactic 4: Vigorous exercise

If jumping jacks aren't for you, consider an alternative way of raising your heart rate so you can dispel discomfort quickly and return to a place of calm. Some other options for you to consider include:

- Running (even running on the spot works)
- Brisk walking
- Cycling
- Swimming
- Burpees
- Mountain climbers
- Press-ups
- Sit-ups

Take some time to consider what would work best to ensure you are prepared next time you encounter unsettling feelings.

## Tactic 5: Call a friend

Talking through your uncomfortable feelings or emotions with a friend is another way to get them out of your head so you can find a new perspective. A good friend will usually be a great listener and will provide you with reassurance, as well as offering advice and approaches that you may not have yet considered. If you can meet them face to face for a coffee, all the better.

## Tactic 6: Watch the clock

Internal discomfort can often feel like it stays with us for hours, in some cases even days. This strategy will enable you to become far more mindful about how much time you allocate to uncomfortable feelings, while also getting you back in the driving seat of your life. Next time you experience painful feelings starting to rise, pause for a moment and acknowledge the feeling is with you. As always, make sure you name and label it, using the emotion wheel if required. As soon as you name the feeling, start the stopwatch on your smartphone or watch. The plan is for you to record exactly how long it stays with you for. Once the feelings have passed, end the timer and make a note of the length of time that it lasted. You will probably be surprised to find that it doesn't last anywhere near as long as you believed.

You now have a 'Personal Best' time; keep your record somewhere close to hand so you have it with you at all times. Your goal is to work on reducing your 'PB' on each occasion you have a triggering encounter going forward.

If you spend 60 minutes with overwhelming feelings on the first occasion, you might challenge yourself to bring it down to no more than 45 minutes and work on reducing it from there onwards. The tactic works because you become mindful about how long you are spending with the discomfort, at the same time as feeling motivated to reduce the time spent.

## Tactic 7: Schedule a time

I used to be a compulsive worrier. I always had a worry in my mind and even if I managed to move past it, I would quickly find something else to worry about. As one worry faded I would begin to worry about what was waiting for me around the next corner, and the next one. It was draining and soul destroying. When I explored my past I recalled how my mother, who was mostly permissive as a parent, would also be irrationally overprotective and would point out danger even when none was present. If she felt that I was too close to the road, for example, she would overreact irrationally, even when the road had no traffic and I was far enough away from the edge for no accident to occur. My tendency to constantly worry about things was shaped by her behaviour when I was young. Having an understanding of where it came from helped me make more sense of it, but it didn't help much when it came to preventing it from happening.

What did help me was a tactic that works well to silence the constant chatter of worries. It also works for dealing with any kind of negative thoughts, feelings or emotions. I decided to set aside a specific time slot each day to deal with my worries. I allocated 8:30am until 8:50am each morning and committed to using this time for a 'meeting' with my worries. I even added the daily 'meeting' to the calendar on my smartphone so I received a reminder about it. Whenever worries entered my head outside this period, I would gently remind them that I didn't have time to engage with them right now and that I would be parking them in my mental 'to-do' tray until our scheduled meeting the following morning. Sometimes I would make a note of the worry so I had an agenda for the meeting with myself and my worries. At 8:30 the next morning I would sit on my own in front of a mirror and I would talk to myself about what was worrying me. It felt strange at first but, over the course of a few days, I noticed how the worries had significantly weakened by the time I came to sit down and have my 'worry meeting'. There were occasions that I didn't even need to explore a specific worry from the previous day, as it was no longer bothering me.

As I continued to put each worry on hold throughout the day and then face it head on during my meeting, it reached a point where I had almost stopped worrying altogether. In the morning meeting the worries seemed to have lost so much of the power that they originally had, and I would often have a far more rational outlook than I did at the point when they initially came into my mind. Over time, it became a wonderful new habit and I found that I was able to easily move my worries to one side in the knowledge that I wasn't ignoring them, before addressing them on my terms and at a time that suited me.

## Tactic 8: Move to centre and refocus

Another tactic that worked well for me when it came to managing emotional triggers was to centre myself and refocus using the following process:

1. I reminded myself that I am not a victim of my emotions, even though it feels like it at times. I mentally reinforced the fact that I am an adult and I have the power of control and choice in any situation.

2. I acknowledged that I had experienced an emotional reaction and I took a moment to name the feeling and label it, before exploring where it had come from.

3. Then I considered what it was that I *really* needed at that moment. For example, if I had identified the trigger had been caused because a work colleague seemed to dislike me, then I took steps to feel loved and liked by a safe person who I knew met the need for me. This meant making a call to my wife or connecting with a different colleague who is a close friend. However, this isn't always possible and you might need to meet the need using an alternative method; wait until you can, or let go of meeting the need altogether. I also asked myself how rational I was being and questioned

whether I actually had to meet the need or not. I would follow this up by asking the question:

*'How exactly would I feel if I let this go right now?'*

This quickly weakened the negative feelings and allowed me to bring about a sense of rationality.

4. If I found that I was still holding on to negativity then I worked on shifting my emotions by using a process I created called 'CALM'. I followed these simple steps allowing me to feel myself:

**C – Calming down: I closed my eyes and then breathed in and out slowly through my nose. As I breathed I noticed where I could feel tension and stress in my body. I took as long as I needed to start feeling more relaxed, usually around five minutes.**

**A – Attention shifting: The more I breathed, the calmer I became. I locked my attention on to my breath which allowed my mind to empty and become calm. This immediately detached me from any discomfort or painful feelings, as my attention had shifted away.**

**L – Lowering my attention: Once I had emptied my mind I lowered my attention from my breath down to the centre of my body, directly below my navel. This area of the abdomen holds an energy field, known as the *tanden* in traditional Zen and Buddhist practices. I focused on an imaginary glowing ball of energy within my abdomen and, as I focused, I felt warmth or tingling in this area of my body. As I concentrated I also began to breathe in and out of the same area, which heightened the physical sensations.**

**M – Mantra repetition: Keeping my attention fixed on my *tanden*, I repeated a positive mantra that reflected how I wanted to feel. Once I had repeated the mantra a few times, I visualized myself breathing the mantra into the glowing ball of energy with each inhale. On each exhale I released unwanted energy using a word or phrase that was associated with the discomfort I had been feeling.**

The calmer I became, the more I felt myself filling up with positivity and letting go of any negative energy that I had been holding on to.

Some examples of mantras that I use are:

*'I am loved, I am healthy and I am safe.'*

*'I am ok right now and that is enough.'*

*'I own my emotions, they don't own me.'*

*'I do not need the approval of others to be happy.'*

*'I control my own happiness.'*

You can create your own mantras or search online to find something suitable. Do this ahead of time and write them down in your journal before you are faced with a situation where you need to use one for real.

With practice, this tactic can allow you to be in control of how you want to feel when a challenging emotion arises. If you can work on making this a new habit, you will learn how to stop fighting emotions and experience the power of freedom from overwhelming feelings by getting back in control.

## Tactic 9: Meditate

I have mentioned the benefits of practising mindfulness and meditation throughout this book as a tool for calming your mind during even the most turbulent of times. If you already meditate, I would encourage you to practise once in the morning and once in the evening for a minimum of ten minutes. Make it a daily intention and work on keeping a streak going by recording it in your journal.

If you are new to meditation, let go of any reservations you might have about whether it will help you, and give it a try for yourself using a guided practice that will talk you through the simple steps to becoming calm and relaxed. I recommend using one of the many smartphone apps for meditating, or search for free guided meditations on YouTube. Be committed to making meditation part of your daily routine and you will soon be able to use it to eradicate uncomfortable feelings.

## Tactic 10: Track your mood

If you have a smartphone, there are several excellent mood tracking apps available for you to download. You can use a tracking app to notify you at different points during the day and prompt you to enter your current mood at that time. The best apps will also allow you to enter notes associated with the mood as you log the information.

In addition to responding to prompts to enter your mood, you can also manually enter them as and when you notice a change in the way you are feeling. This process not only allows you to gather data and notice patterns around your moods, it also enables you to express any emotions through the note taking function.

## Tactic 11: Sit on the beach

Not a real beach, sadly, but the one that exists in your mind when you use this tactic. The process is simple:

1. Before you begin, remind yourself that you are always feeling some kind of emotion. Good, bad or indifferent; you are never without them. Emotions are like the tides, they come and go, and they change all the time. Sometimes

we experience big waves crashing on to the beach and on other occasions the sea is calm and serene.

2. Find a quiet space and either sit with your legs crossed or lie on the floor. Close your eyes and begin breathing in and out slowly through your nose. Avoid snatching at the breath, keep it natural and light.

3. As you begin to feel calm, visualize yourself on the most beautiful beach you have ever seen. The powdery sand is pure white and the sun warms your skin as the rays of light pierce huge palm tree leaves gently stirring above you from the cooling ocean breeze. Look around the beach, savour it and continue to breathe in a steady rhythm. If your attention is interrupted by unwanted thoughts simply acknowledge them by saying 'thought' and then shift straight back to the breath and your beach visualization.

4. Focus on the beautiful turquoise ocean in front of you. The waves are rough at the moment and slamming on to the sand a few metres from where you sit. The angry waves represent your uncomfortable feelings. Notice that, even though the emotional waves are currently powerful, they can't touch you or cause you any harm as you calmly sit and observe them. You are out of reach and totally safe, no matter how strong the waves become.

5. Continue to observe the sea and enjoy the sense of calm as you maintain a steady breathing tempo. As you become calmer, notice how the crystal blue ocean is also calming, the waves are no longer crashing on to the sand, they are peaceful. Continue the practice for as long as you wish, but make sure you stay with it until your ocean calms. The waves are a direct reflection of your state of mind. Try playing with them by becoming intentionally calm and watch how the water settles down. You have control.

Savour the sensation of sitting on your beach and enjoy relaxing. You can return here any time you wish and allow yourself to simply observe your emotions as they come and then go, this is your personal and private haven. Explore this incredible mental safe space in your mind and enjoy the experience of watching the waves of emotions change like the ever shifting tides.

Take the time to practise these techniques before you experience discomfort so that you know which one will serve you best during challenging moments.

# 20 | The process of grief and letting go

The process of healing from past trauma and childhood emotional neglect involves a wide range of challenging emotions as we learn to accept our past and process the new breakthroughs and discoveries we find on our journey, as we look closer at what contributed to shaping us in adulthood. Having got this far with this book, you have no doubt already experienced a range of feelings and emotions as you worked your way through the chapters.

There are times when the negative emotions, in particular, can feel incredibly strong and you may ask why you let the genie out of this particular bottle. You might start believing that it would have been easier to have stayed stuck instead of experiencing this pain. Remind yourself that any intense emotion will pass; it is part of the process of healing.

Many people describe the process of accepting their past as 'grieving' because the emotional pain can feel similar to the loss of a loved one. However, unlike grieving a death, the suffering doesn't stay with you forever and, depending on how resilient you are, you may find you move through it very quickly, or experience minimal emotional discomfort. Traditional grief usually follows five stages:

- Denial
- Anger
- Bargaining
- Depression
- Acceptance

When it comes to grieving what we lost in childhood it can be different. Some people experience each stage intensely, while others may only encounter a few, and there are even people who are able to move directly to a place of acceptance with no grieving whatsoever.

It will help to write out the losses for which you are grieving. I wrote mine out as follows:

- I lost the ability to feel 'good enough' about myself.
- I lost my childhood.
- I lost respect for myself.
- I lost the ability to feel empathy for other people.
- I lost over three decades of my life feeling stuck.

- I lost the ability to love myself.
- I lost the ability to fully love other people.
- I lost my happiness.
- I lost the right to feel safe.
- I lost comfort, support and protection of loving parents.
- I lost my playfulness, awe and innocence as a child.
- I lost my way in life.

When I listed out what I had lost in my life, I knew that I had to allow the pain to come up to the surface and that I needed to look directly at all the past events in order to finally accept them as they were. The difference this time was that I was looking at my childhood from a place of consciousness, with an objective and inquisitive perspective. Instead of allowing my inner child to be in the driving seat, I made sure it was the rational adult observing my story with a logical and open mind.

But I still grieved. I experienced each of the five stages of grief fairly intensely and needed to remind myself that the feelings were part of the healing process and that I should give myself time to process them and allow them to pass. I did not fight them, I allowed them to be with me and I acknowledged their presence, even though it hurt at times.

While the feelings were intense and challenging, they were not debilitating. Every time a new feeling arrived I would use my journal to write down what I had noticed. The very process of paying attention to my emotions helped to soften the discomfort. On other occasions I would use one of the strategies in Chapter 19 for handling uncomfortable feelings. I knew that my goal was to find acceptance and I reminded myself that my freedom would come from looking in the darkest places.

I vowed to shine as much light on the painful events from my past as possible because I knew that the more I did this, the stronger I would become, even though it caused me short-term pain. I began to realize that I was claiming back the power that CEN and trauma had held over me for so long. As past events lost their energy I found that they were not triggering huge emotional reactions whenever I chose to look back at them. The more power I claimed, the deeper I wanted to dig so I could pull more memories out from the darkness and bring them into the light.

My grief faded over a period of a couple of months. For some people it can happen more quickly and for others it takes longer. I can recall occasions where I actually found myself thanking my feelings of grief because I knew they were there to serve me. Once the grief had faded I became able to look at the events from the past as memories that I now held the power over. I felt as though I could make the choice of how much of my mental bandwidth I would allow them to take up, if any.

# The well of grief

If you have already explored your past, it makes sense to begin diving deeper in order to reach a place where you can give yourself permission to grieve and then reclaim your power. If you haven't yet written out the story of your life (see Chapter 12), I invite you to grab your journal and a pen when you feel ready.

As well as writing out specific events and episodes that you remember from your past, take the time to describe the feelings that were with you at the time along with how these historic episodes have impacted you in your adult life. Try and be as clear as possible when it comes to 'labelling' the feelings you experienced.

Take your time with this process and allow any emotions that arise to simply be with you by naming them. Then take a look at your life and ask yourself:

- Do these feelings take up space in your current adult life?
- Do they accurately describe how you feel as an adult?
- Do you want to continue to allow these emotions to have control over your life?
- Who would you be without these feelings?

Now, make a decision that it is time to look at what happened. Accept the past for what it was, grieve if necessary and move on.

Finally, you realize now that you have the power to choose how your past features in your life; make a non-negotiable commitment to yourself.

# Make a commitment

A non-negotiable commitment is an agreement we make with ourselves that we know we will stick to, no matter what happens. It is sensible to think about what important areas of your life have been neglected due to your past, and to make a personal vow never to allow that to happen again. If you decide to create a non-negotiable commitment you have to wholeheartedly mean it. If you don't feel ready to make a commitment right now, come back to this when you do.

This is the non-negotiable commitment I wrote in my own journal after several weeks of moving in and out of grieving, when I reached a point where I was feeling close to acceptance.

**'I will no longer allow my past to stop me from loving myself and being the best father and husband I can be. I will always remind myself that I have the power and choice over what role my memories are allowed to play.'**

There were numerous occasions where my son and wife were neglected while I spent time with my painful memories, and they were also impacted by negative behaviours as I tried to avoid the hurt I held inside. My non-negotiable commitment meant that I would no longer put my past ahead of the people

I loved who were with me now. I felt an incredible strength as I wrote my commitment and it gave me a real sense of resolve as I knew that, ultimately, I was in control.

If you choose to make a commitment, it will help if you place it somewhere prominent so you can be regularly reminded of it. You could stick it on the door of your fridge or save it on your smartphone home screen, for example.

# Giving the trauma back

Another big part of my healing process was giving my trauma and neglect back to the people who I felt were responsible for causing it – my mother and biological father. Before I considered this, I clearly understood that they were shaped by their own parents who were shaped by theirs before them. Trauma and neglect pass down the line from generation to generation, until someone is brave enough to stop it flowing through the family tree.

When I realized how our parents are shaped by their parents, and how the same behaviour patterns become repeated over and over by each generation, I felt a huge sense of responsibility as I recognized that I could make a decision to end the pain – not just for me, but for future generations to follow.

I felt as though I was moving steadily through the stages of the process and had grieved the fact that I was abused, neglected, uncomforted, made to feel as though I wasn't good enough, rarely supported and allowed to do what I wanted without boundaries, which exposed me to dangers. I wanted to give my trauma back, I didn't want it any longer and as far as I was concerned I didn't cause it, so why should I carry it with me?

I started by writing two letters, one to my mother and one to my deceased biological father. The first draft was an angry rant and I ended up tossing the paper in the bin and starting again; I didn't want to be accusatory and I was keen not to create conflict or division if possible. I simply wanted to state the facts, let them know how their behaviour made me feel, and what damage it had caused me in adulthood.

I stayed objective and tried to visualize my writing as though it were about someone other than me. Eventually I had written two letters that clearly expressed:

- How I believed I had been neglected and traumatized in childhood
- How I felt my parents had let me down
- How I believed they should have behaved differently
- How it had made me feel at the time
- How it has made me feel as an adult
- How it has impacted my life.

Once I had written out the letters I noticed the intensity of my emotions already seemed to have softened. Now I was faced with a dilemma: did I share these letters with my parents? My father was dead, so there was no way of sharing anything with him, but my mother was very much alive and I was unsure what to do for the best. I decided to post the letter to my father at his last known address. It was a purely symbolic gesture, helping me feel I had sent the trauma caused by his abandonment of me back to him, because I no longer wanted it.

For several weeks, I dwelled on what to do about the letter to my mother. I realized how much she still triggered me, and how all my fears around conflict, rejection and people-pleasing stemmed from her. I felt a lot of uncomfortable emotions because I was genuinely afraid of speaking the truth to her. I also knew, however, that it was the process of facing up to her that would allow me to fully heal myself.

Simply writing a letter that you can keep to yourself, or share with safe and supportive people, is enough for now. Don't put pressure on yourself to confront your parents unless you feel totally sure that it is what you want to do. Telling your parents what you think and how you feel can cause long term damage to the relationship. You are now conscious through your work, but the likelihood is that they are still very easily triggered and will experience emotional reactions if they feel attacked or criticized.

However, I also believe that the process of telling our parents exactly how they made us feel, and what we think of the way they brought us up, allows us to rip up the root cause of our issues. When we can be totally honest with them, we find that we become able to be authentic and honest with almost anyone in our lives. Behaviours and situations that have triggered us in the past tend not to have the same impact on us.

A parent who is confronted with their adult child telling them that they feel let down due to them being emotionally absent, unsupportive or neglectful will usually deny any wrongdoing, attack or become defensive. I have heard examples of parents trying to convince their children that they have come to the wrong conclusion, and of others who have become overwhelmed with emotion or exploded with anger. Please think things through very carefully before you go any further.

Most parents tend to 'JADE':

**Justify**

**Argue**

**Defend**

**Explain**

The purpose of expressing our true feelings to our parents is not to get them to change their behaviour. Let go of any hope of that now – it is very unlikely that they will change. Likewise it is not about seeking an apology or an admission of guilt, which you are also unlikely to get; and it is definitely not about punishing them.

The point of confronting our parents is for us to know that we are able to speak the truth, regardless of how painful it feels. We gain peace from giving back our trauma by expressing ourselves honestly and overcoming any fear of facing up to our parents.

It doesn't really matter what our parents say or how they react, so long as we feel that we have said what we need to without being brutal, and that we have offloaded the pain caused by their neglectful parenting. We want to come away from any conversation knowing that we have told them the absolute truth, and in a position where we feel we are in charge of determining what kind of relationship we might want to have with them in the future.

There will be many factors in play when it comes to making your own decision about whether you want to write a letter (that you never send), or whether you decide to talk to your parents face to face, but please do consider the consequences before you take any action.

You will likely find an almost magnetic pull towards *not* confronting your parents. Children of parents who are toxic have a huge need for parental approval and we fear creating any disruption due to the risk of being rejected by them. You can change without needing to change your parents, or even to talk to them about the challenges you have faced. Your happiness is not reliant on anything your parents do (or don't do). As you become more self-aware and authentic, you will notice the feelings their behaviour causes and you will naturally begin to put boundaries in place to keep yourself safe.

The ultimate place to reach is one of forgiveness for your parents through a sense of understanding. This doesn't mean pretending that the past didn't happen or taking any responsibility for their shortcomings. It's about avoiding any desire for revenge and learning how to express your sadness and anger in a healthy way, by adopting a proactive growth-mindset. This will allow you to end the repetitive cycle of abuse that will mean the toxicity goes no further than you.

You are an individual, a totally separate adult from your parents. They no longer have any control over you, and you have grown to a point that you are able to accept and face up to the truth about your past. You no longer need their approval, the only approval you need is your own. If you feel that confronting your parents is the right thing to do then know that you already have the courage within you to take that important step on your journey to healing.

Confronting parents usually leads to one of the following responses:

- Rarely, the parent will admit their mistakes, but may later try and backtrack or play things down.

- They usually go on the offensive, justifying, arguing, defending or explaining but, after the dust has settled, they may well recognize the error of their ways and attempt to put things right and possibly even change their behaviour.
- They may cut contact with their children because they refuse to face up to the pain of the truth; this is not your fault, the problem is theirs.
- It is also common to see a mixture of these three outcomes.

I recommend carefully rehearsing what you plan to say and having your notes close to hand so you ensure you cover everything you want to get out. However, you might find that you get shut down if your parents react. In some cases parents may even cut their children out of their lives – although uncommon, be prepared for it as a real possibility.

While this sounds rather dramatic, it also makes sense. Through their own upbringing our parents lack the ability to be compassionate, empathetic or to take responsibility for their own behaviour, so there is every chance they will react like children.

No matter what happens, their reaction is not your problem. Stay strong and stick to speaking your truth without reacting to their behaviour; you will reclaim your personal power in what could be one of the most incredible moments of your life. Your parents might shout, scream, be accusatory or even violent. No matter what happens, hold strong, look them in the eye and calmly express yourself. If you are unable to speak due to their anger, simply leave your letter with them and end the conversation.

You may only have one parent to confront, but if it is both, then I recommend speaking to them separately on a one-to-one basis. It is much easier when you don't have two reactions to deal with at the same time. Once you have reclaimed your power you will control how the relationship will look going forward. You can make the rules and set the boundaries to keep yourself safe, and you no longer need to tolerate any behaviour that you find unacceptable.

Confronting my mother and breaking the toxic relationship with that part of my past was one of the hardest things I have done, but it was also one of the most powerful. It enabled me to break free from the chains of CEN and trauma that had held me down for so long. I felt fully grown-up, able to start loving myself, enjoying my life and creating meaningful, loving relationships. I was no longer a victim trapped in the pain of my past and I was no longer dependent on my mother for any kind of approval or acknowledgement.

Sometimes it is either not possible to speak to our parents, or fear prevents us from having the confrontation. This is completely understandable. In some cases, the trauma or neglect may have been caused by someone other than our parents, or the person we would need to speak to may no longer be alive. This doesn't mean you can't give your trauma and neglect back. There are a number of alternatives if you are unable, or not ready, to do so face to face:

# Write a letter

When you write a letter outlining exactly how you were let down, and the impact this has had on your life, you can choose how you wish to use it. You might decide to post it to the person if you are unable to speak to them. If it is not possible to post it you could do something symbolic that represents you giving it to them, such as sending it to a last-known address, placing it on a grave if they are dead or giving the letter to someone safe and supportive who can represent the person you are unable to speak to.

# Role play

In many therapy groups, people will have one of the other members play the role of an abusive or neglectful parent, allowing them to express their emotions in a safe environment. If there was a specific type of triggering behaviour, they might have a group member play the role of the parent to recreate this abusive situation in order to replicate the negative trigger. This allows the person who wants to speak the truth to face the image of their parent and say exactly what they need to in order to let go. This process can involve a lot of tears, anger, rage and sadness, but it always ends in a huge group hug and a sense that the painful emotional block has been removed once and for all.

# Record a video

One of the big challenges of confronting a parent is fear of their reaction, and very often it can be difficult to calmly explain everything, especially if they become angry and start talking over you, or shutting you down. A solution to this, which ensures they listen to everything you have to say, is to record a video and email it to them when you are ready. Pre-recording your confrontation will ensure you are happy with how you deliver your message and that you cover every point you want to get across.

If your parents aren't around, you can also make a symbolic gesture with a video by emailing it to a safe and supportive person who you might ask to represent one of your parents. You could even ask them to reply as your parents if you wish, rather like the role-play scenario.

There is no prerequisite that states that you have to confront your parents, but I can tell you from my own experience that it felt like the biggest breakthrough and reclamation of power on my entire journey to healing. It is another occasion where facing up to short term pain is necessary in order to reap the long term benefits.

I strongly recommend seeking professional advice before taking any action, a therapist or counsellor will be able to help you reach a decision and support you.

# 21 | Whose lane are you in?

One of the biggest causes of stress and suffering is when we end up finding ourselves outside our 'own lane' and, without even realizing, we are suddenly wrapped up in drama, conflict and other people's business. Staying in our own lane means that we consciously channel our energy into only the things we can control. When we move into someone else's lane and start trying to influence what we can't control, we usually become frustrated, confrontational and angry. The simple fact is that we can only ever control that which we have power over. If something is outside your power, don't waste your time or energy.

An excellent visual representation of leaving our own lane is demonstrated in the 'Karpman Drama Triangle', a model of how people in conflict and drama-based relationships behave. When you understand the basic principle of how we can be pulled into someone else's lane through drama, you will notice how much more aware you become in order to avoid these situations occurring in the future.

Psychiatrist Dr. Stephen Karpman perfectly described the three destructive roles that people play during conflict. Interestingly he observed that people also tend to shift from one role to another as a drama unfolds:

- **The persecutor:** The persecutor is always right and makes sure everyone else knows it. In the persecutor's eyes other people are wrong, and this isn't open to discussion. The persecutor will point the finger of blame and can become angry, controlling and authoritative when people don't agree with their way of thinking.

- **The rescuer:** The rescuer has a burning desire to save other people and solve their problems, even when the other person doesn't want their help. They are rarely in their own lane and spend much of their lives in someone else's as they go about enabling people and focusing their energy on everyone's problems but their own.

- **The victim:** The victim has a default mindset of 'poor me' and feels oppressed, criticized, hopeless and powerless. They feel unable to solve their own problems or be independently strong enough to improve a situation alone, needing instead a rescuer. Even when a victim is saved, it only serves to reinforce their belief that they are unable to be happy or make positive changes and choices without the help of others.

Getting involved in drama can have an almost magnetic pull and we can be easily seduced into an unhealthy and destructive triangle. When we are wrapped up in drama and conflict we rarely focus on logical solutions and the real issues, using instead huge amounts of negative energy as we find ourselves stuck in the triangle.

Most people have a default role on the drama triangle that they will usually adopt if a conflict arises. But in most situations the roles change as the drama persists. The key to cutting this unhealthy and draining behaviour out of your life is to begin noticing when someone is trying to pull you towards joining them in the triangle, then make a conscious choice not to get involved.

# Which lane are you in?

Noticing which 'lane' you are in is an excellent way of allowing happiness into your life. Try and think of your wellbeing as a three-lane motorway and choose which one of the three lanes will be yours.

This process will enable you to pay close attention to whether you are staying in your own lane or whether you have drifted outside of it and need to move back to where you are safe:

## Your own lane

This is where you want to stay as often as possible. If you find yourself shifting away from your lane, try and notice it has happened and move back here as quickly as possible. Your own lane should be your place of default; it is safe here, you are in control and have minimal risk of becoming involved in drama, emotional upset and conflict.

Try and imagine that you have a protective bubble around your vehicle on the motorway, but only when you are in your lane. When you stay within your lane the bubble will keep you safe. Everything inside your bubble is within your control; you have the power of choice here and if you want to change something you can. Instead of becoming involved in what you think is best for someone else, concentrate only on what is right for you.

*Example of being in your lane*: You might notice feelings of being unappreciated in your job and, when you pay attention to them, you know that the right thing to do is express them appropriately to your manager. When you face the fear and speak truthfully, your manager is accommodating and agrees to have regular meetings with you to discuss your progress within the company. You will have stepped out of your own lane and into someone else's if you begin trying to influence his actions or become frustrated with his decision, you can't control either of these.

## Someone else's lane

This is a dangerous place to be. When you find yourself in someone else's lane, there is every chance you will encounter some kind of negative reaction that will cause suffering in your life. The more time you spend in someone else's lane, the less time and energy you will be able to give to your own life. When you find yourself here, move back into your own lane as quickly as possible.

*Example of being in someone else's lane*: Your friend feels unappreciated at work and you have noticed that they have become unhappy. They have decided to find a new job, but you push them to confront their manager and talk to them, even though you know they feel uncomfortable doing it and it comes with a level of risk.

## The reality lane

This covers everything that is not included in the other two lanes of the motorway. You might dwell on episodes from the past and refuse to accept them for what they were, or you may notice yourself worrying about situations in the future that may never happen. You have no power or control over either of these. Nothing here is going to change, stop wrestling with reality, let go, and accept it for what it is – you don't have to like it or agree with it, just stop fighting it.

Beginning to notice whose lane you are in can be revelatory, you probably don't realize how often you are outside the safety of your own lane. By paying attention to this, you will find it can have the power to bring you right back to where you need to be and avoid you becoming involved in negative situations.

*Example of being in the reality lane*: You quit a job several years ago because you felt unappreciated and unvalued and now feel a sense of regret, dwelling continually on the fact that you didn't stay in the role and speak your true feelings at the time, instead of leaving. The negativity and self-talk are overwhelming as you tell yourself how you 'should' have done things differently. What happened in the past is reality – no amount of thinking, fighting or storytelling will ever change it. Leave it be, get back in your own lane and move forward.

The more I worked on myself, the more aware I became of which lane I was in. This simple concept helped me learn to take a new perspective when I paid attention to how I was reacting or becoming drawn into a situation. I was able to do this using four questions that Byron Katie recommends her readers use when they encounter challenging or uncomfortable feelings (you can read more about Byron Katie's work at thework.com):

1. Is it true?
2. Can you absolutely know that it's true?
3. How do you react, what happens, when you believe that thought?
4. Who would you be without that thought?

I also found it helpful to use my journal to answer the following questions about situations that caused me emotional upset:

1. **Describe the situation or behaviour that has caused emotional upset.** Try and be specific about exactly what is causing the uncomfortable feelings by visualizing the events like a movie in your mind, then labelling the feelings before writing down the reason you believe that you felt such strong emotions.

2. **Challenge yourself by asking if what you have written is actually true.** Consider the facts without judgement or emotional bias. Try and look at the situation as an outsider looking in. You might begin to feel that you have overreacted or that you are projecting your own insecurities onto others rather than looking within yourself.

3. **What impact is the situation or behaviour having on your life?** Try and visualize how you feel and how your behaviour has been impacted by the emotional upset. How does it impact your life or the lives of others? Have negative behaviours arisen because of this situation?

4. **What would happen if you could erase the situation or behaviour that caused the emotional upset?** Visualize yourself being free of the upset and notice how you behave and what impact it has on you and the people around you. Pay attention to whatever comes up and spend some time considering whether letting go is the right choice. You may notice that you have ended up outside your own lane, or you might need to take some kind of specific action, such as expressing your feelings to someone or enforcing boundaries.

I have used this process many times in my own life. Initially I kept these questions on my phone to ensure I always had them close to hand, but over time they stuck in my memory and became a new habit. I can recall many occasions where these questions have helped me move out of a challenging situation that might previously have sent me into a tailspin of negative emotion.

One that springs to mind was when I became triggered by my wife when I suggested we try for another baby. I have shared the notes from my journal so you can understand how this process helped me.

Describe the situation or behaviour that has caused emotional upset.

'**My wife has upset me, I want to have another baby and she rejected the idea. I have suggested it several times in the past and she says we are both too old and the idea of a new baby stresses her out because our lives are incredibly busy. I have begun to allow the negative feelings to overwhelm me and started to convince myself that she is not committed to the relationship and maybe she no longer loves me.**'

Challenge yourself by asking if what you have written is actually true.

'**Yes – It is true that she doesn't want a baby and I know the thoughts I am experiencing are strong around her level of commitment and love. Looking closer, I can see that the thoughts about her commitment and love are not** true, I have so much evidence of how she shows both of these things on a daily basis in a variety of different ways.'

What impact is the situation or behaviour having on your life?

'I feel frustrated, unloved and rejected. This makes me become moody and I tend to take it out on her, which impacts both of our happiness and causes the situation to become much worse.'

What would happen if you could erase the situation or behaviour that caused the emotional upset?

'Without this in my head I would be at peace, there would be no conflict or negative feelings.'

In this situation, I realized that we both wanted different things at this particular point in our lives, and my oversensitivity to rejection had caused me to make up stories about how much my wife loved me and how committed to our relationship she was. Simply working through these questions enabled me to gain a totally different perspective and find peace in being able to respect my wife's decision and let go of being in her business by trying to pressure or control her.

You can discover some fascinating insights into yourself by simply rewriting your original statement using the opposite of the important elements. You may need to play with different variations before you discover meaningful answers.

My example might become:

'I have upset myself. I want to have another baby and my wife rejected the idea. I have suggested it several times in the past and she says we are both too old and the idea of a new baby stresses her out because our lives are incredibly busy. I have begun to allow the negative feelings to overwhelm me and started to convince myself that she is not committed to the relationship and maybe I don't love myself.'

It all made sense, my fear of rejection and lack of self-love were driving my emotions and insecurities. Use this process to explore any uncomfortable feelings or thoughts that you encounter.

With conscious attention, we can form a new habit where we are able to stay in our own lane and significantly reduce our own suffering by exploring what is going on within, rather than reacting on autopilot and having to deal with the consequences.

# 22 | No longer a victim

Many people end up in the role of victim, subconsciously aligning with people they believe will somehow rescue them by fulfilling unmet needs. No matter how many 'rescuers' we bring into our lives the sense of being helpless rarely leaves us, and victim-like behaviour often causes people to distance themselves as they become drained of their positivity.

It is easy to feel that life has treated us unfairly. We develop a 'poor me' outlook on life and gain comfort from people feeling sorry for us. We often become wrapped up in a victim status where we fail to pause or notice the damage being caused to relationships as we give nothing back. Friendships and intimate relationships become a one-way street as we drain others' energy in a fruitless attempt to make ourselves feel better.

As well as impacting the people around us, the feelings of being a victim can cause additional internal suffering on top of what we are already having to deal with from our past. The accompanying negative mindset makes us believe that we somehow deserved to feel this way and that we will never get to a place of true happiness.

When I began to become self-aware and started to pay close attention to my feelings, and to work on becoming unstuck from my past, I also made an effort to avoid being a victim. Yes, I was dealt a bad hand in my life, but there are very many people far worse off than I.

Victim mentality is usually formed by the belief that we simply aren't 'good enough'. I had never had respect for myself or truly 'loved myself'. I projected a confident and bold image on the outside in most situations, but internally I was very much lacking when it came to kindness and compassion towards myself. I began to piece together events from my past that made me understand how I had been shaped into someone who believed he simply wasn't good enough. I started to understand how even episodes that seemed fairly minor at a young age had created neural connections in the brain that hard-wired my beliefs and behaviour in the long term.

This lack of love for myself was at the heart of my problems. I had to learn to love myself in order to become more confident, to trust myself, to be able to love others completely and to feel content and happy with who I am, regardless of my imperfections.

Self-love is your key to unlocking your happiness, exactly as you are. When you love yourself, you let go of any desire to try and be something you are not through gaining approval from other people, and you begin to put yourself first. People will notice a difference as you become more confident in yourself, more assured and, above all, happy with who you are. As the self-love grows within you it creates a magnetism that attracts positive people into your life. The way we feel and what we believe on the inside is exactly what we get mirrored back to us in the real world, and, when this is an authentic and content version of ourselves, we have a positive life experience.

That is not to say that life doesn't throw up challenges from time to time, of course it does – it's part of the human experience. But when we become whole and fill ourselves up with love, it becomes much easier to deal with the problems we encounter; we feel far more grounded and things don't knock us off balance quite so easily.

Adapting your behaviour for the benefit of other people will keep you stuck. Whether it is what you say, what you do or what you believe, if you want to break free you need to work on becoming authentic and living your life as the real version of yourself. When you become your genuine-self you will start to love yourself fully.

The likelihood is that you are already moving through the following stages that lead to loving yourself:

- I am not good enough – Stuck
- I will never be enough – Stuck
- I have had enough – Becoming aware and motivated to change
- What is enough? – Learning and developing
- I am enough – Self-love is realized

Which stage were you at before you opened this book? What stage are you at now? Use this as clear evidence of your growth and as proof that working on yourself is hugely worthwhile and something you should continue.

Over time, I began to realize that nobody is perfect and very few people accept themselves for who they are, as they are. I didn't need to wait to start showing myself unconditional love, I had it within me all the time, and my newly discovered awareness allowed me to fully connect with it. You have this too.

In the book *The Art of Happiness*, the Dalai Lama shares a technique that he uses to feel gratitude for what he has in his life. He simply asks himself the following two questions:

1. I wish I was . . .
2. I am glad I am not . . .

These were the answers I wrote down when I was still stuck:

1. I wish I was more popular, and had more friends than I do now.
2. I am glad I am not lonely/alone.

When I wrote my answers, I found that the first question stirred up a feeling of envy around wishing for what I didn't have, or being something I wasn't. But the magic happens with the second question, because it made me realize that while I may be facing challenges in my life, I was also incredibly lucky and there were many people who deserved to use the term 'victim' much more than I did.

# Take a new perspective

I read books about staying positive and avoiding a victim mentality. I knew I needed to reframe and refocus my thoughts into a set of beliefs that would empower me and provide a more accurate description of where I was in my life.

It is very easy to sink into the darkness of being a victim, and to believe that we only ever have bad things happen to us and must somehow deserve them. Whenever I began engaging in any negative self-talk where I was blaming myself or adopting a victim mentality, I paused for a moment and acknowledged the thought that was with me. Once I had acknowledged the negative thought without reacting or judging myself, I gave myself a reminder that I am a survivor, not a victim. The situation was not killing me, it was helping me to learn, grow and become stronger. I looked at myself in a mirror and gave myself positive affirmations that reflected my desire to no longer be a victim.

'I am not a victim, I am working on changing my life for the better. This is what courageous and powerful people do.'

'Being a victim keeps me stuck and I am hungry to be free. I am claiming back my power by doing the work to change my life.'

'A victim stays stuck, a survivor seeks freedom and that is what I am doing.'

'I am a survivor and I am learning how to thrive in my life, if I continue to argue with the reality of my life, I will always be stuck.'

The process of not treating myself as a victim was one that took practice and patience. I knew if I remained in a place where I felt as though the world was out to reject, abandon and humiliate me I would never be able to heal.

I threw myself into learning how to reclaim a positive mindset. I wanted to be a survivor, moving forward on a personal journey of growth and I knew that I had to let go of the victim mentality that had become my go-to at times.

# Understand the cause of the victim mentality

My victim mentality had its roots in what I learned as a child. The environment I grew up in made me feel unworthy of love or attention, and I had no confidence in myself. In order to turn my victim status around, I needed to understand its cause and gather the knowledge that would allow me to take steps to heal the source of my suffering.

We have a choice: we can either remain victims, incarcerated in our own mental prison, or we can release by reaching through the bars to grab the key as we become aware of how to become brave, empowered and free.

Learning and practising new behaviours is the key, use the following steps to help yourself break free from being a victim.

# End the blame game

The process of healing is not about blame. This includes blaming yourself and blaming other people. If you become aware that you're doing so, make sure you pay attention to it, and take positive action.

Whenever I'm aware that I am blaming myself or other people I will look in a mirror and calmly ask:

**'Where is my power in this situation?'**

This enables me to view the source of my blame from a whole new perspective. I begin to look for choices and options so I can discover the most empowering way of reacting. I usually discover that I can quickly find a new approach and make a choice that puts me back in control, without blaming either myself or anyone else. The goal is to move from feeling hopeless to hopeful.

Letting go of blame does not mean that you are relinquishing responsibility for the harm that others may have caused you. Instead, you are focusing your thoughts on where you hold the power in a situation and moving away from the draining process of blaming and dwelling on what you can't change.

# Find peace in not being the victim any longer

You might discover that, as you attempt to break out of the victim mindset, you feel drawn back to it, as though it were a subconscious default setting in your brain. You have created a habit of being in this negative headspace and made it feel familiar, and you are left with the illusion that it is a safe place. Make sure you understand how damaging it is to remain stuck with an outlook that prevents you from being your best self.

You might feel as though you have lost a source of safety and comfort when you let go of thinking of yourself as a victim. Simply sit with any uncomfortable feelings and acknowledge them, they are inviting you to fill the void with positivity, and with powerful new thoughts that will serve to make you stronger.

Will you allow yourself to feel proud that you are doing something proactive, changing your life and finding peace in not being the victim any longer?

You are not alone on your journey. Find supportive online groups that will allow you to connect with other people who are facing similar challenges, so that you can share your story with positivity and pride.

# Seek out the good

Life coach Tony Robbins often asks clients who are facing a challenging situation:

**'What is good about this?'**

Even in the most difficult of times there is almost always something good we can focus our attention towards. By shifting our focus in any situation away from being a victim and on to something positive, you will become stronger. Every challenging situation in our lives comes with choices, and we always have the power to decide which choices we make. We may not always like them, but knowing there are always options can enable us to find something good to focus on.

Let's take the broad subject of childhood emotional neglect – what is good about that? It was your CEN or trauma that has powered you into reading this book, taking positive action and changing your life. You are on an incredible journey of self-discovery and growing into a whole person as you find freedom from suffering. That is definitely something good in what, on the face of it, may appear to be a negative situation.

Start to look for the good whenever you encounter a challenging situation. If you can't find it straight away, take some time to sit silently with your eyes closed while you explore deeply; you can also use your journal.

# Put your self-love first

Being a victim can bring with it a sense of self-hatred and unworthiness, a belief that we don't deserve to be happy. It is common to believe we aren't good enough. When we learn to love ourselves and accept the true version of who we really are, exactly as we are, we are able to let go of the stories and self-blaming that often come with perceiving ourselves as a victim.

I didn't love myself during the time I was stuck in the prison created by my CEN and trauma, and I realize now that by neglecting myself I was deprived of the ability to fully love other people. When I realized that this was a self-sabotaging behaviour, I knew I needed to change.

To this day I remain very aware of whether or not I am loving myself with everything I say or do. It is easy to slip back into being a victim, so I check-in with myself and stick to my commitment of putting love for myself at the heart of my life. This might sound selfish, narcissistic even; don't worry about it – if you make loving yourself your priority, then love will flow through your life and you will give and receive love unconditionally.

I use my journal almost daily and often write down an intention of having fun or doing something that will allow me to love myself. I will describe exactly how I intend to do it. Often I will fulfil my intention of bringing fun and love into my day alone as a conscious effort to be happy and comfortable in my own company. I will go for long walks, take trips to the cinema alone and I take trips to the beach by myself to watch the waves coming in and out, like my emotions.

I also began to travel alone and have now taken trips to the US, Spain and Italy by myself. At first I felt outside of my comfort zone, but these trips really helped to extend me and they were a great experience on the journey to learning to love myself again. Spending time alone is an excellent way to enhance the relationship with yourself.

Another excellent self-love tool is to become completely comfortable in your own skin. Many people are hung up on their body image due to the flood of 'perfection' they see on social media. They chase perfection and never feel happy, believing they aren't good enough. Be mindful of how you use social media. We are not emotionally equipped to be judged by hundreds of people for how we look, and posting photos of ourselves for approval is guaranteed to stir up negative feelings, especially if someone makes an unwelcome comment.

Below are some excellent techniques for feeling more comfortable in your own skin:

**Write down the things you envy in other people**: For example, 'I wish I was slim like them', or 'I wish my skin was as smooth as theirs'. Then look in the mirror at yourself and pay yourself compliments around these areas along with other parts of your body. Use a positive statement, such as:

**'I love my skin, it is perfectly imperfect and my hair looks amazing today.'**

**'Without my skin I wouldn't have my smile and today I can see happiness in my eyes.'**

Remember that most of the images you are comparing yourself to have been edited and filtered to beautify them. If you were to see the 'naked' make-up and filter-free version, that person would look very different.

**Pay attention to your strengths**: Everyone is stronger in some areas, and weaker in others. We all have unique qualities that make us different from other people, and these are often some of our most endearing features. This doesn't make us flawed, and shouldn't block us from loving ourselves. If everyone was the same, the world would be a very boring place.

Some of the people you might consider 'beautiful' are probably convinced they are ugly because they have never been able to love themselves and continually chase their own version of perfection. Start to honour your own strengths and talents, think about what you are great at and pay attention to nurturing them. This will ensure you build a more positive outlook and feel much more comfortable with who you really are.

**Surround yourself with 'radiators'**: I often use the plumbing analogy about radiators and drains. Someone who is a 'radiator' will radiate positive energy and make you feel good about yourself, whereas a 'drain' will have the opposite effect and will suck you of your energy and leave you washed out. Get rid of the drains, they are usually toxic and will bring you down with their negativity and narcissistic behaviour.

Never allow other people's opinions to define you or make you question yourself. Be comfortable with who you are and the choices you make. The modern, connected world we live in makes it easy for people to pass unwelcome judgements by pressing a few buttons; limit your exposure and create boundaries for anyone who does this. Above all, be confident that only you know what is best for you.

**Look within, this is where your happiness lives**: When you begin to feel love for yourself, you become totally comfortable with the way you act, look, smell, sound and behave, and no longer berate yourself for not matching your own, unrealistic expectations. Make sure you allow yourself time to grow your own love and focus on doing the things that are important to you. It is also important to have some quiet time to either meditate or sit in stillness so you can focus on yourself, your mind and your body.

**Take laughter seriously**: Commit to bringing laughter into your life, whether it is from watching comedy shows, being playful with friends and family, or doing something that makes you laugh out loud. Laughter is going to help you feel more comfortable with yourself and will bring more happiness into your life at the same time as reducing stressful and anxious feelings. When you are lost in laughter there is no room for self-doubt.

**Get naked**: One of the best ways to be comfortable with who you are is to spend time naked. We feel emotionally exposed when we lose our clothes and, if we have insecurities about our body, this is one of the most effective ways to start loving who you are, just the way you are. You could sit alone in front of a mirror, naked; or do things around the house without your clothes on. The more you do this, the more you will become comfortable in your own skin, even though you may feel exposed at first.

Avoid judging yourself when you are naked, simply be in the moment and embrace the joy of having a healthy and incredible body that allows you to show up in the world and do many amazing things.

As time went by and I continued working on myself, I could feel my urges to be a victim softening and the love for myself growing. The following disciplines helped me move fully from being a victim who didn't feel good enough, to someone who became whole and loved themselves completely.

# Be kind to others

Some mornings I write in my journal 'be nice today' as an intention, and I will direct my focus towards this throughout the entire day. I will allow people to go ahead of me in queues in the store, or let traffic have priority over me even if it wasn't their turn; I might be extra polite, and smile at strangers. I enjoy being nice to others and this has become a new habit. I've discovered that the nicer I am to other people, the more positive energy flows back in my direction.

Last month I saw an elderly couple sitting in the café where I was having my lunchtime coffee. When the waiter came to my table I asked if I could pay for their lunch, and asked him not to tell them it was me who had cleared their bill – because genuine kindness should not be ego-driven. The waiter took the payment for their lunch from my card and, several minutes later, I watched as he informed them that someone had already taken care of the bill. They looked both astonished and delighted, and I left quietly, feeling joy that I had brought something uplifting into their day.

I try to carry out random acts of kindness as often as possible. Try it and bask in the feeling of pure joy it gives you. Stay humble, and avoid braging about it.

# Forgive your past mistakes

As I started to experience more self-love, I also worked on forgiving myself for any past mistakes or situations where I had blamed myself. I began to cultivate a strong belief that it was acceptable to forgive and forget – yes, I had made some poor decisions in my life, but there was no benefit in allowing them to control my emotions in the present day and giving them power over my self-esteem, wellbeing and ability to heal.

The more my self-esteem grew, the more I found the ability to cut myself slack whenever I made a mistake. I accepted that nobody on earth was perfect and that expecting perfectionism from myself was unrealistic and damaging. The kinder I became, the more I found myself feeling calm, confident and happy.

# Stop saying 'yes'

As I became more confident, I became able to start saying 'no' to other people. I had always made decisions based on what I believed others wanted, driven by my fear of what would happen if they thought I had let them down. But this was bringing pain into my life and preventing me from being totally authentic.

The first couple of times I tried to say 'no' were scary. I had a massive fear of conflict and rejection. I almost crumbled and returned to the perceived safety of people-pleasing for an easy life. But I knew that it had been taking the path of least resistance in the past that had contributed to how bad I had been feeling and, in order to be authentic and loving to myself, I needed to be honest and truthful, even if it was hard to say what I felt.

Once I had got the first two or three challenging situations out of the way and calmly said 'no', I found that circumstances seemed to be turning in my favour. In one case, a client in my business was taking advantage of my kind nature by demanding more than was reasonable for the fee they paid. I declined their request and explained that we would be happy to do the extra work they wanted, but it would mean an additional fee. Pushing back caused me fear that they would reject me and take their business elsewhere, but I acknowledged that the feeling was with me and avoided repressing it.

The client didn't reject me, the opposite happened. They sent me a lovely email expressing how much they respected me for being honest and explaining the situation. They confirmed that they would be happy to pay the extra charge as they had been delighted with what I had done for them up until now.

# Ask for help when you need it

Adult children of neglectful parents often find it difficult to ask for help when they need it. We all experience challenging times in our lives and if we need help it is important to reach out to an appropriate person or support service.

Some people fear rejection, avoid responsibility, believe they will look weak, or think that they will be judged in some way by asking for help. These are all limiting beliefs that hold us back and will cause us to face our problems alone. Anyone who truly cares about you will always be willing to help when you need it.

If you need help make sure you ask for it, don't allow a false belief to hold you back. Use these eight tips to ensure you get the help you need when you need it:

- Write down your problem and identify exactly what you need help with.
- In big bold letters above the problem, write the words 'I have the right to ask for help'.
- Write down the best source of help – this could be a friend, colleague, therapist, or a support service, for example.

- Practise asking for help – use a mirror and visualize yourself confidently and clearly asking for what you need.
- Cultivate a belief that other people have good intentions and will do what they can to help you.
- No matter how uncomfortable it feels, keep reminding yourself that dealing with a problem on your own is much harder and far more painful than asking for help.
- Be patient, not everyone can provide the help you need then and there.
- Be grateful and appreciative when you receive help, for example, send a thank you card or a gift.

# Embrace the JOMO

JOMO stands for the Joy Of Missing Out – the opposite of FOMO (Fear Of Missing Out). There are times when I have had to say 'no' to an invite to an event or social function and I always embrace the joy I feel from not being there, rather than having any sense that I am missing something.

I was recently invited on a pre-wedding stag night. As someone who doesn't drink alcohol, the planned trip around the bars of London simply didn't appeal to me. I was totally honest with myself and decided I would prefer to go out for a nice meal with my wife and son instead. I politely declined the invite and embraced the JOMO as my little family and I enjoyed a wonderful steak dinner. When you learn to embrace the JOMO, you begin to feel a new sense of freedom as you claim back power in your ability to make choices that put yourself first.

For me, the path to self-love seemed to take on a power of its own. The more I paid attention to being kind to myself, the less I became plagued by negativity. As the self-love expanded I started to focus much more on taking care of myself, I started to carefully consider the consequences of any decisions I made and learned to trust myself with complete confidence in the choices I was making.

Another excellent self-love practice is to pay attention to your victories and achievements. I ensured that I wrote down each and every occasion I did something kind for myself, especially when I found my voice and was able to say 'no', instead of doing things to please other people.

Whenever you catch yourself slipping into a victim mentality, take a moment to remind yourself that you have control, and you have choices about the mindset that you want to adopt. Understand the negative effects of blaming yourself and being hampered by feelings of sadness and low self-esteem, and believe that by becoming aware and making a conscious effort to notice when you are calling yourself a victim, you can move out of it with relative ease.

Let's keep moving from victim to survivor, to thriving and alive!

# 23 | Dealing with setbacks

Any journey of change and self-improvement will inevitably come with setbacks. Instead of returning to your old habits and behaviours as soon as something throws you off balance, show yourself kindness and love by accepting that a journey of healing is rarely a straight line and that there will almost always be twists, turns and bumps along the road.

Having a setback does not make you a failure; view any setbacks as a 'data point'. A data point allows us to gather information from the setback and study it to become wiser. We should view it like a gift, because it invites us to look closely at what we learned so we can work out what to change to make ourselves stronger as we go forward, in order to prevent any repetition.

Just like anything new, don't expect to master everything at the first attempt. I am sure you wouldn't tell a child who has fallen from his bike (because he pulled the front brake instead of the back) to never get back on it again and give up. You would tell him to learn from his mistake so he avoids the same setback in the future, and to get back in the saddle as quickly as possible.

## Fall forwards, not down

If you encounter a setback and slip into old behaviour patterns, or if you find yourself overwhelmed by emotions when something triggers you, simply pause, notice what has happened and gather the data. There is no need to beat yourself up with hurtful comments that will not serve you. Don't think of it as falling down, reframe it: you have 'fallen forwards'.

When we 'fall forwards' we do so with momentum, instead of simply falling down or giving up. Falling with forward momentum involves noticing that we have slipped into our old ways, or experienced some other kind of setback, and accepting that it has happened without blaming ourselves or other people.

When you become aware that you are slipping into a negative state and experiencing a setback, give yourself permission to pause for a moment and know that you can make a choice. It is at this point that you can consciously choose to adopt an approach of 'falling forwards' and start exploring what caused the situation with curiosity by uncovering exactly what you could do better, or differently, going forwards.

When you know you can give yourself permission to 'fall forwards' you won't ever unlearn it. Whenever you run into a setback, you will find it hard not to hear a voice in your head inviting you to reframe any negative thinking and use the moment as an opportunity to propel yourself onwards, with momentum, by using the episode to learn and grow.

When we start exploring our past it is common to expect to feel some painful emotions. When I began looking closely at my own childhood, there were times when I cried uncontrollably and occasions where I thought it would be easier to give up and stay stuck than face up to the pain. But I always reminded myself that the short term discomfort was infinitely better than never healing and suffering forever.

After I had experienced the first waves of emotion from scratching the surface of my past, I noticed that any new discoveries I made about my childhood didn't have the quite the same impact on me. Instead of causing a meltdown, they would make me feel sad, unloved or angry, but not as intensely as the first few discoveries of parental incompetence. I noticed how my new self-awareness helped me to acknowledge and express what I was feeling in a safe, healthy way, and I was able to work through whatever I uncovered with a mindset of curiosity as I immersed myself in a quest to complete the puzzle of my life, as if it was my new hobby.

It took me several months to pick apart the story of my childhood. I found myself asking my parents, school friends and other relatives for information and gradually piecing together a picture that I had never before seen. Occasionally a piece of information would shake me; it would hurt to hear the brutal truth about a past episode that had shaped me negatively as an adult, but it became easier as I learned more. I was mentally toughening up.

It was as though I had to stand in a dark place for some time in order to start seeing a light of a hope. I became much more comfortable standing in those places of discomfort and my eyes became accustomed to the dark. Eventually, it changed from being pitch black, I became able to see with complete clarity and the darkness was gone.

# Take responsibility for yourself

I believe that developing a positive attitude and immersing myself in the process of becoming unstuck was vital. I got excited about the journey I was embarking on and felt motivated about how good my life would be when I had overcome the obstacles along the way. Whenever I found myself slipping into negative thinking I would immediately notice and give myself a 'can-do' statement, paying attention to what was in my control and what the positives were in any given situation.

I also took full responsibility for my own healing, recognizing that nobody other than me could change what I was dealing with on the inside. I fully understood that my recovery was in my own hands. If I put in the work, accepted that setbacks were part of the process and continued putting one foot in front of the other, I knew I would eventually get where I wanted to be.

Don't get me wrong, I didn't isolate myself and 'go it alone'. I surrounded myself with supportive people with whom I felt comfortable being totally open and honest. I shared my feelings with them and discussed where I was on my path to becoming unstuck. But I also realized that while they were supportive and wanted to help me in any way possible, the only person who was going to be able to change me, was me.

The supportive people in my life helped me when I found myself returning to past behaviours by drawing my attention to old habits and routines that were creeping back in. On other occasions I might experience an emotional meltdown following a triggering episode, and turn to a trusted friend to talk it through.

When I ran into overwhelming emotions and recognized that it was my inner child jumping into the driving seat, I would sometimes take a 'time-out'. If I was around other people I made it clear that it was nothing to do with anything they had done or said. Instead, I indicated that something had triggered me and I needed to step away for a few minutes to get back into my adult headspace.

I let them know how long my time-out would be and then ensured that I set an alarm on my phone to alert me when the time was over. (When we fail to prompt ourselves to end a time-out it can be easy to dwell on negativity or sink into a low mood. The idea is to use time-outs to your advantage in order to clear your mind and soften your inner child's emotional state).

Setbacks were a great time to check-in with myself and reflect on the progress I had made. I used these experiences as an opportunity to look at the early pages of my journal and wrote down everything that had improved since I wrote my earliest entries. This would put a setback into perspective and gave me a sense of pride about what I had achieved and how far I had come.

As well as checking in on my progress, I used setbacks as a chance to take a long hard look at my life as a whole and, in particular, my self-care routine so I could consider whether I needed to adjust anything to improve myself. Some of the areas that I would assess would be:

- Nutrition and hydration
- Exercise and fitness
- Whether I am getting enough sleep
- Work and career
- Whether any bad habits are impacting me negatively
- My financial situation

- Work/life balance
- Whether I am doing enough of what I really love
- Social life and friendships
- Family life
- Whether my boundaries were working and whether I needed to adapt or add to them
- Physical health.

I assessed each area and considered how well it was aligning with my values. If I found anything was out of alignment, I used this as an opportunity to make positive changes. I often uncovered parts of my life that could have caused a much bigger setback in the future following a less serious 'forward fall'. I was moving obstacles and pain out of my own way and had the original setback hadn't happened, I would never have paid attention.

On the inside front cover of my journal I have the letters PIES written in big blue letters. PIES is a simple but effective technique that therapist Dr David Perl (who wrote the Foreword for this book) shared with me. It allows us to perform a check-in with ourselves and notice how well we are meeting our own needs. This is another technique you could use either when you need to assess where you are following a setback, or on a more regular basis as part of your self-care routine.

# The PIES personal check-in process

Ask yourself the following questions and write your responses in your journal. If you are in an intimate relationship it can be a healthy habit to do this with your partner from time to time, to cultivate a deeper connection and level of communication.

**P – Physical:** Consider how you are feeling physically by paying attention to your overall health and wellbeing. Are you experiencing any new pains or physical discomfort, for example? Think about how your physical needs are being met and whether anything needs to change.

**I – Intellectual:** Are you keeping yourself mentally stimulated? Are you growing and learning or spending too much time watching daytime TV, using social media and filling your mind with junk information? It might be time to think about what new hobbies and activities you could take part in that will give you the level of intellectual engagement you might be craving.

**E – Emotional:** How well are your emotional needs being fulfilled? We all have a need for love and affection and we fulfil this through our close connections with our friends, family and partners. We also protect ourselves from negative emotional energy by putting boundaries in place and enforcing them if they are breached. Consider whether you need to make any changes in this area of your life.

S – Spiritual: Are you living your life in line with your values and paying attention to how you feel within? This is not specifically about exploring your religious beliefs, this is more about assessing whether you are living your life in line with your needs and what you do (or don't) believe in. We will look at spirituality in more depth towards the end of the book.

There are no right or wrong answers with this process and I recommend simply expressing whatever comes up when you address each question. All four elements of PIES will allow you to ensure you are living according to your values and enriching your life by paying attention to meeting your needs.

While the process of becoming unstuck requires us to look at our past, it is equally important not to spend too long dwelling on what you discover when you look there as this can cause overly emotional reactions that may lead to a setback. The goal is to gather the facts from the story of our life and accept them for what they are without judgement. If we end up beating ourselves up and feeling shame or guilt about the past then we need to notice our behaviour and take the appropriate steps to move out of it, as quickly as possible.

# Triggers

When you notice that you have become triggered and you start to feel unwelcome emotions, I recommend using one of the tactics from Chapter 19. Start paying attention to how long it takes you to move back into your 'adult mode'. Remember to keep a note of your best time and work on reducing this on each occasion you are triggered. Not only does this reduce how long you spend with discomfort, it also makes you much more mindful about what is happening and why.

You can also use the mirror process to identify what has triggered the emotional response:

1. Write down the circumstances that you believe caused the emotional overwhelm, for example:

   **I asked my son to clean his room multiple times and he ignored my requests, I felt angry, frustrated and rejected.**

2. Taking anyone you love out of the equation, ask yourself the following question and be really honest with your answers.

   **What do you think of a person who [add the behaviour that caused the reaction, in this example] ignores your suggestions, refuses to clean their room?**

3. Letting go of any emotional attachment to the people who may have upset you, write out a list of your answers with complete honesty. In this example they might be:
   - Ignorant
   - Selfish
   - Irresponsible
   - Immature
   - Rude
4. Once you have a list of answers, you can reflect as to whether there are times in your life that these behaviours have shown up and consider how they have impacted you. This process will allow you to obtain much more clarity around the reasons why they trigger you.

When we become triggered the issue is almost always within us, not the person who we believe caused it. See these episodes as a gift that we are being invited to explore.

Try to ensure you are fully prepared for setbacks on this journey, it is almost inevitable that you will encounter some potholes on the path to healing. Remember to ask the question, 'What is good in this situation?' if you encounter a setback. Focus on the positive steps you are taking in the present moment, consider how much better equipped you are through what you have learned, and think about how good the future will be as you continue your journey of growth.

Setbacks do not represent failure. There are countless examples of sports teams who have lost over and over, only to come back stronger than ever and claim victory. This analogy is not restricted to sports teams, it happens in every walk of life. People experience setbacks all the time, but they do not allow it to block them from becoming stronger and achieving their goal.

A setback is your opportunity to create an incredible comeback; we only fail when we stop trying.

# 24 | Hacks for happiness

Finding 'happiness' is the main purpose of human existence. However, it is a divisive topic. Some people firmly believe that, if we focus too hard on the pursuit of happiness, we end up becoming disconnected from the present moment and feeling constantly unfulfilled as we strive to reach a perceived paradise. Other people seem to have mastered the art of happiness and live rich, fulfilled lives in a state of peace, calm and contentment. Very often these people have few material possessions, and they avoid unhealthy habits and behaviours that provide only short-term gratification. They have usually learned to become happier by using their minds, breath and bodies and understand how to focus their thoughts towards happiness and away from negativity.

While it is true that we shouldn't become obsessed with being happy, I also believe that happiness is a basic need for human beings, and if we aren't happy for a reasonable amount of time then we need to take steps to change. Instead of treating happiness as a 'black or white' goal, it is far more beneficial to make it part of our core intentions, habits and values, and maintain a happiness mindset in the choices that we make.

It is possible to live with an intention of happiness and to make choices that contribute to our long-term fulfilment. We can weave the habit of happiness into our lives and make changes and decisions that ensure we maximize the chances of allowing positivity to flow in, at the same time as creating personal boundaries to keep negativity out.

I have previously talked about my work in the field of sobriety; consider the following two behaviour statements and think about which one would add to long-term happiness, and which one would bring short-term gratification and potentially damage our happiness in the future.

- 'I need to drink alcohol every day, because it makes me happy.'
- 'I spend time quality with my family at least twice a week, because it makes me happy.'

Of course, spending time with our family and the people we love most will contribute to our happiness over the longer term, whereas drinking alcohol might give a sense of pleasure in the short-term but, after the effects have worn off, you will usually end up feeling less happy than before you began drinking.

I like to think of 'happiness' as a savings account in an internal 'happy bank'. Whenever I engage in something that brings me true joy and adds to my long-term sense of happiness, it adds credits to my bank balance. On the other hand, if I partake in activities that only bring short-term gratification for a limited period of time, then I treat them as though they will deduct credits from my account.

It is important to make choices that protect us from behaviours and activities that might take away from our balance and, when we use this approach, it can be simple to ask ourselves if what we are considering engaging in will add or take away from our account. If it is a 'fleeting pleasure' activity and will take away from our happiness, then we should consider finding a better use of our time.

## Activities that provide short-term gratification

- Consumerism and making purchases for the sake of it
- Binge eating and poor nutrition
- Gambling
- Excessive exercising
- Sexually acting out
- Overuse of social media, messaging, internet and online chat services
- Video gaming to excess
- Using pornography
- Over-working
- Use of alcohol and drugs
- Hoarding and collecting.

It is important to be clear that some of these activities are perfectly healthy and even necessary in moderation, but they can cause people to detach themselves from real-life and become trapped in addictive behaviours, if they are taken to the extreme. When an activity stops providing pleasure and we find ourselves thinking about it often, and putting it ahead of other important things in our lives, it is a signal that it is out of hand and becoming an addiction.

These things reduce our happiness 'bank balance' if we partake excessively in them, as they serve only to provide us with instant gratification. They will cause us to want more of the same thing, leading to dependency and obsessive thoughts while we fight urges to repeat the behaviour.

We have a basic human desire to avoid pain and seek pleasure. If we have experienced CEN or trauma it is tempting to become drawn towards unhealthy behaviours that allow us to temporarily escape our suffering. In the western world there are vast numbers of readily available unhelpful sources of escape - but if we can become attuned to the risks these present, we can train ourselves to engage in more fulfilling pursuits instead.

While it can feel difficult to let go of unhealthy behaviours, I would encourage you to explore an experiment. Take a 30-day break from any damaging behaviours, and keep a journal to track all the positive changes that happen. It is normal to experience cravings or urges to return to the habit but the more time you put between you and the compulsive acts, the easier it becomes to let go of them.

If you are struggling with addiction or feel that taking a 30-day break from an unhealthy habit is impossible, please seek professional help.

The following are examples of activities that add to 'happiness bank accounts' and I always consider which category a behaviour or activity falls into before I choose whether to partake in it or not, even if it means finding my voice and saying 'no' when I need to do so. This requires discipline initially, especially when we have relied on a habit for a long time. But we have to put our recovery first and if it requires some short term pain as we adjust our behaviours, it is a small price to pay for no longer being stuck and suffering.

## Activities that add to our long-term happiness

- Exercise and fitness in moderate amounts
- Random acts of kindness
- Walking outdoors and enjoying nature
- Volunteering and giving to others (this might be your time, expertise or money)
- Reading and writing
- Intentionally being nice to other people
- Expressing gratitude
- Listening to your favourite music
- Meditation and mindfulness practices
- Spending time with good friends and family
- Gardening and outdoor activities
- Immersing yourself in a productive activity or project
- Craft-based activities such as painting, knitting, drawing and modelling.

*Activities that create lasting memories are among the most powerful when it comes to adding to your happiness bank balance.*

You will find that when you are able to let go of unhelpful behaviours, you give yourself the right to live as your 'true-self', this will allow more happiness to flow into your life. You will make choices and have a desire to remove negative behaviours, you will be in control and feel far lighter and free from the heavy burden it causes.

Equally, when you are able to accept any past CEN or trauma for what it was and let go of fighting reality, you will begin to learn to take down the emotional brick wall that you may have created and joy will flow freely into your life.

The same applies as you make other changes that I have shared throughout the book, such as being kind to yourself, setting boundaries and noticing, naming and expressing your feelings. It can take time and practice to naturally adopt these as new habits but, over time, you will feel a powerful change and experience the joy of more happiness.

The following hacks for happiness should provide you with inspiration to accelerate your journey to a more joyful place.

# 15 Hacks for happiness

## 1 Have a vision

Create a positive vision of the life you would like. Spend some time creating it on paper and ensure it meets all your needs and aligns with your values. Make a plan to reach your goals and begin to work towards your visions by breaking them down into smaller, more achievable steps on the path to greater fulfilment.

You might want to move home, travel abroad, change career, quit a bad habit, complete a fitness challenge or have a baby . . . The choice is yours, and there is no limit on what you can do when you put your mind to it with a clear vision and a plan.

Think about what you might need to do each day in order to reach your goals – for example, if you want to run a half marathon you will need to build up your training runs to ensure you are well prepared come race day.

It can help to invest in a vision board and place it somewhere prominent so you can track your progress and remain focused on what you need to do to make your goals a reality.

Adopt a determined mindset and remind yourself that you have achieved goals in the past when you have been focused. Make sure you clearly identify occasions when you have used this mindset to make something happen and know that you have this powerful ability at your disposal whenever you choose to use it.

## 2 Use your breath

It is one of the few constants in life. We are born with it and it stays with us until the moment we die. Our breath has the ability to react to danger and change with our emotions. Slow breathing can calm us down and, with the right techniques, we can easily control it to allow ourselves to feel peace and serenity.

Our breath also provides us with a gateway to the inner-self. When we practise meditation and connect to our breath, we become able to venture within and deeply explore who we really are. I meditate twice a day and I recommend having two short sessions daily as part of your own happiness plan. You don't need to spend vast amounts of time meditating, ten minutes per session is enough to make a real difference if you commit to it daily.

## 3 Know your meaning and purpose

When I left school I had no idea which career path I wanted to follow. I went to college to further my education and ended up dropping out after a few months when I was offered a job at a local insurance company. I remained working in the same industry for well over a decade.

I didn't pause to consider whether insurance was what I really wanted to be doing with my life. I was simply happy that it was providing money and allowing me to progress through the company. I went on to run my own insurance business with my wife, which we later sold to a larger company. Since then we have built a marketing business which employs around twenty people.

I was making good money in the marketing business and to me that was what represented success. But I wasn't truly fulfilled; my life lacked meaning and purpose. It wasn't until I stepped away from the marketing company and quit drinking that I was able to discover what really brought joy into my life – this happened when I began writing, coaching and speaking about sobriety. It felt as though I had found my purpose in life.

Most people have no idea what they want to do with their lives. It took me until I was over 40 years old to work it out and, had I not quit drinking, I doubt I would ever have gained that clarity. I would have continued to work in a business that paid well, but left me feeling stuck, anxious, unfulfilled and, ultimately, miserable.

When you begin to consider the 'purpose' and 'meaning' of your life it can feel overwhelming and people often struggle to find an answer. A better question to ask yourself is:

**'Where could I invest my time and energy on things that are important and matter to me?'**

We all have our own unique purpose in life and if you are able to find your true passion you become completely fulfilled, infinitely happier and experience a strong sense of contentment with your life.

We don't have to look hard to find the answer to what will bring meaning and purpose to our lives – it exists within us already, we need only start to search for it.

## 4 Be imperfect

Accept that everyone on earth has imperfections, and most people have some level of present day challenges that are linked to their childhood or other episodes from their past. You are one of the lucky ones who has worked out the source of your pain and taken positive steps to make a change. In my eyes that makes you a pretty incredible person. Many people fail to make the connection and struggle for their entire lives.

As you become more self-aware, you might find that you begin to notice behaviour in other people that very likely traces back to their own past. You will be surprised at how much you notice it, take comfort in the fact that it isn't just you – *nobody is perfect*!

Almost everyone has their own internal challenges and, when you begin to connect with people on a deeper level and open up about your emotions and feelings, you will find they do the same with you.

Remind yourself that everybody makes mistakes and few people are happy with who they are right now. Striving for perfection only serves to damage our self-esteem. We can all find perceived flaws in ourselves if we look for them: we could all wish to have less wrinkles, to be taller, to have a better job, or more money, to be thinner or to look different in some other way. I am bald, but I no longer waste energy wishing I had hair, I am comfortable with who I am, just as I am. This type of negative thinking will block your attempts to love yourself. Start to catch yourself when you use the words 'should' or 'shouldn't' because they usually have some kind of negativity connotation attached to them.

For example:

- I should be thinner.
- I should have gone to the gym.
- I should weigh less.
- I shouldn't be so lazy.
- I shouldn't eat so much.

When you notice yourself using these kinds of statements, use them as an internal alarm bell and switch your focus to the qualities you admire about yourself. Maybe you could write out a list of your top ten qualities and keep it close to hand if you ever need a reminder of why you are perfectly imperfect, just like everyone else on the planet.

### How would it feel if you let go of worrying about what other people think?

Over time, as you focus on what thoughts you choose to give your attention to, you will begin to find that you care much less about the areas of your life that you might have previously berated yourself about.

Perfection is an illusion and if we spend our lives chasing it, refusing to allow ourselves to be happy until we get there, chances are we will have an incredibly long wait before we start smiling. Focus on being the best version of yourself, do the best you can with the support and tools you have available at the time, and accept that this is enough.

# 5 Write your daily intentions

I write my intentions for the day in my journal every morning; it is a little bit like a 'to-do list' for my personal wellbeing. By writing out my intentions I gain a much higher level of focus on achieving what I want throughout the day. I recommend you give it a try for yourself so you can experience the difference it makes.

For example, if you want to bring more happiness into your life you might write intentions to:

**'Spend time having fun today.'**
**'Make sure I laugh today.'**

In order to make it happen, you also need to specify how you intend to bring fun into your day. Next to the entry you can describe more, for example:

**'Spend time having fun today – I will take my kids to the park and go for a coffee with my friend, they always make me laugh.'**

Once you have set it as an intention you will find that you have a strong desire to stick to the commitment you have made to yourself.

Here are some of the intentions I have written in my journal over the last couple of weeks:

- I want to laugh today – watch comedy on Netflix, possibly dance around the kitchen with Michelle, too.
- Time to connect with myself and be calm – 10-minute morning and evening meditation.
- Exercise and time for myself – 45 minutes on the exercise bike.
- Time doing what I love – make time this afternoon to write a blog post.
- Remember that thoughts are just that, thoughts. I have the choice whether or not to act on them, I can simply allow them to pass. Notice my thoughts today.

You can get as creative as you want and, if you find it beneficial to add any tasks you need to get completed, it is fine to include them within your daily intentions too.

One tip that helped me become happier is to remove all the sad, downbeat songs from my online playlists and ensure I only have tracks that lift my mood. Music is incredibly powerful and if we spend time listening to depressing playlists then it will impact our mood. If we focus on feeding ourselves songs that make us sing and dance it will have the opposite effect.

# 6 Get your heart rate up

Exercise is a fantastic way to dispel negative feelings and make you feel happier. If you can get your heart pumping with a vigorous workout, you will release 'feel-good' endorphins and energy that will make you feel more positive.

I can remember numerous occasions where I was plagued with worries, low moods or anxiety and turned to exercise to overcome it. I would often head out for a run or join a spinning class at my local gym. Without exception, I always felt much better after the workout, as though the negativity had somehow been washed away.

# 7 Know what lights you up

It can be all too easy to forget what brings true joy into our lives. As adults we have busy lifestyles with commitments and responsibilities. We can end up feeling like we have no time for ourselves.

It is important to make time, even if that means getting some help or making sacrifices in other areas. Give some thought to how you can create time for you and what pastimes will really light you up.

*If it lights you up, do more of it, make it a hobby.*

Consider the activities that cause you to lose track of time when you become immersed in them because you are enjoying yourself so much. It might be something from when you were younger, I can remember painting as a child and would focus on my artwork for hours because I was so engaged in what I was doing.

You might find you become lost in your own world of enjoyment when you are:

- Outside in nature
- Cooking
- With animals
- Listening to music
- Reading
- Writing
- Painting or drawing
- Exercising
- Fishing
- Taking part in sports.

Whatever it is, make sure you know what really brings genuine joy into your life and make it your intention to do more of it. If you can't think of anything from your past that would cause you to become totally immersed then you could look for new hobbies that take your interest. Step outside your comfort zone and discover something new and exciting.

# 8 Put experiences ahead of materialism

It has been proven that experiences impact positively on our happiness much more than material things. Experiences allow us to create wonderful memories and push us to try new things. I recently saw a story about a woman who had unexpectedly come into a significant amount of money – enough for her and her husband to never have to work again. Initially she was elated, and immediately began searching for a new house and bought several new cars. The writer who shared the story caught up with her a couple of years after the huge windfall and asked how she was enjoying life. She said that her life was obviously less stressful, and the money makes things easier in many respects. However, she also said that after the initial shock and excitement of the huge influx of money, she and her husband both found that they returned to the same level of happiness that existed beforehand and she wouldn't describe herself as any more or less happy than before she came into the money.

There are many similar stories that demonstrate how money and material possessions might provide people with a short-term boost, but eventually they always return to their default 'baseline' of happiness. We all have a baseline of happiness, a default setting. This is where our brain returns us when we have either dropped below it due to negative emotions, or when we have risen above it because of intense joy or excitement.

Think about this in the context of the 'happiness bank account' I mentioned earlier in the chapter. Over time our enjoyment and satisfaction from material items reduces, yet our satisfaction and positive memories of a life experience increases. I am sure you have many fond memories of vacations, family days out and experiences, but I doubt you have the same in relation to your past purchases.

Memorable experiences are a sure fire way to add huge amounts of credit to your happiness bank balance. Make it your intention to create as many happy memories as possible.

## 9 Manage your media

The modern world constantly bombards us with media. Whether it is in the form of 'breaking news' headlines, advertising on the radio or social networks, it can seem impossible to go more than a few minutes without being force fed information of some description.

Society has become an overload of information and if we allow ourselves to take too much of it on board it can negatively impact our sense of wellbeing. By creating personal boundaries around what media we digest and how much time we spend engaging with it, we take control and generate more happiness in our lives.

When the tragic events of September 11th 2001 happened, I found myself with the television turned on from morning until night as I watched the 'breaking news' unfold. Several days later, I was still glued to the news and had the television on permanently in the background as the fear and anxiety of global terror began to seep into me.

I found myself doing exactly the same thing at the start of the global coronavirus pandemic in 2020. But this time I noticed my behaviour and realized that if I digest vast amounts of negative news, then it is sure to heighten my anxiety. I made sure I got the facts I needed, and switched the television off.

I now like to digest my media mindfully and have become selective about when and how I access news. I also ensure that I limit the time I spend on certain social media websites and take care about what accounts I follow.

When it comes to news, I am not suggesting that you avoid the facts about what is happening in the world. Instead, consider allowing yourself a limited amount of time to access the information you are interested in and ensure you use news sources that avoid sensationalizing stories. Most smartphones have settings that allow you to restrict the amount of time you spend on specific apps and it is a healthy habit to limit yourself if you want to avoid being drawn into the fear and anxiety that accompanies much of modern-day news reporting and social media sharing and comparing. There are many websites that only share positive news, how about restricting your news intake to these for the next month, and noticing what difference it makes to your life?

It is also sensible to pay attention to how much time you spend on your smartphone. Both Apple and Android devices have built in 'screen time' functions that allow you to be mindful of this, and it is a positive practice to make use of them in order that you can be fully present in the moment rather than a slave to your screen. Start to catch yourself when you are ignoring the real world because you are being distracted by notifications and online updates.

*How about setting aside an allocated time each day to go offline and unplug?*

## 10 Recharge and reset

I am writing this on my Mac desktop computer. Currently it has 14 different website browser tabs open along with several applications that are putting a strain on the computer's processor and making the machine work harder. At the end of the working day I usually forget to shut the computer down – I rarely even put it into 'sleep' mode and instead leave everything switched on and running. As well as being absent minded, I have a belief that it is quicker to get back to work the next morning if I can click my mouse once and make the screen spring back into life. However, I know that this is a false economy because every so often the computer will become, for want of a better phrase, tired and irritable, as it has been overworked without a chance to rest. It ends up freezing and then crashing, and the restart process that follows is a time consuming process.

Humans operate in a similar way – if we don't get enough good quality sleep and rest we find ourselves crashing. A lack of sleep negatively impacts our mood, energy levels, motivation and overall sense of happiness. In order to give yourself the best chances of increasing your happiness levels it is important to get around seven to eight hours of sleep every night. It is proven that getting the right amount of sleep benefits our physical health, brain functioning and emotional balance.

Pay attention to how much sleep you get each night and if you aren't having enough use the following steps to make improvements:

- Set regular times to go to bed and to wake up; try and keep them consistent even at the weekends.
- Use a sleep tracking app, or write down how much sleep you had and how refreshed you feel in your journal each morning.
- Try and keep the hour before you go to bed as a 'quiet time', avoid television, eating, drinking, loud music and bright screens.
- If you struggle getting off to sleep, try a sleep meditation before bed or read a book.
- Avoid caffeine wherever possible, particularly after midday.
- Have a relaxing bath or shower before bedtime, studies have shown that a hot bath taken around 90 minutes before bed helped people get to sleep quicker.
- Consider supplements – magnesium is recommended by some to help sleep.
- Avoid taking naps during the day.
- Avoid alcohol – even one alcoholic drink can disrupt sleep and prevent you entering the correct cycles that refresh and restore the mind and body.
- Try and exercise during the day as it will tire you out ahead of a good night's sleep.

I also recommend conducting a 'sleep audit' of your bedroom. I do this several times a year, especially when the seasons change, as it helps to ensure my sleeping environment is optimized. I suggest you check:

- The quality of your mattress – if you can feel the springs in your ribs it has probably seen better days and needs replacing.
- The comfort of your pillows.
- The quality of your bedding, in particular the quilt, as it may be too thick or thin for the time of year.
- The darkness of the room – do you need darker curtains if light is seeping in at night from nearby traffic or lighting?
- The quality of silence – if you can hear noise when you are trying to get to sleep you should consider how to shut it out.
- The temperature of your home; if it is too hot or cold it can impact on your sleep.
- The impact of artificial lighting in the room, such as alarm clocks and electronic items.

Above all, I try to ensure my bedroom has minimal light and sound polluting it and that it feels comfortable, relaxing and welcoming when the time comes to get into bed.

# 11 Declutter

If something in your home has no purpose and doesn't provide you with a 'spark of joy' then ask yourself whether you really need it.

I tend to clear out one area of my home at a time, this week I went through my wardrobe and filled up two bin bags with clothes that I hadn't worn in over a year. Next week I will be attacking my home office. Setting aside just half an hour each week and working on a specific area of your home will enable you to quickly achieve a spacious, inviting and clean living environment that you are sure to enjoy.

When we invest our time into decluttering our home, we feel a sense of accomplishment and happiness at the positive outcome.

# 12 Self-care is crucial

Our fast-paced world moves at lightning speed and it can be hard to find time for ourselves. Yet, we are the one person who we need to look after, pay attention if you are neglecting yourself and not making time for *you*.

Even the most simple activities, such as a long hot bath with bubbles and soft music or watching a favourite movie with your kids while sharing a bucket of popcorn snuggled under a warm blanket, can feel like a real treat.

Think about how you can give yourself more attention and be sure to plan it into your daily intentions so you don't forget to do it. Putting your own happiness at the centre of your life is vital, you deserve to be happy and I am sure you want to overcome any emotional blocks that have been holding you back. Remember, you weren't born unhappy or unable to love yourself, something in your early years shaped this default subconscious behaviour. Just as with learning anything new, you can overcome it, but you need to keep practising and heading into each day with the intention of smiling and growing. Start to notice the positive changes you experience and learn from any setbacks whenever old behaviours creep back in.

# 13 Practise kindness to others

If you can form a habit of being kind to other people you will allow more happiness to flow into your life, eliminating negative emotions.

There are numerous ways that you can practise being kind to other people. You might help out at your kids' school, volunteer for a charity, buy a homeless person some food, treat someone to a gift or pay for a stranger's coffee. The options are almost endless and, if you make kindness an intention, you will notice how you feel the benefit it brings you.

Being kind to other people is proven to make us happier and it also helps us reduce our stress levels. The more often we adopt an approach of kindness, the more we will find that we experience an elevated mood, feel happier and more optimistic about our lives.

What would you need to do to bring kindness to others into each day of your life? Do you think it is a habit you could create for yourself? What is holding you back?

Kindness is contagious. The more we radiate happiness and show our caring nature to others, the more we find it comes back to us, often in random and unexpected ways, you have heard of karma right?

Kindness doesn't need to be about money, although I do think it is a wonderful trait to use some of our wealth to help people less fortunate. We can use other resources to carry out acts of kindness such as our time, unwanted items we no longer use, knowledge, skills or other resources we have.

Being kind can also be as simple as paying someone a genuine compliment. How about you give it a try today and notice what happens?

# 14 Express gratitude

Using your journal each day to write down two or three things you are grateful for is an excellent way to bring more happiness into your life by focusing on the positives in your life.

When expressing gratitude, avoid writing down material possessions and instead focus on the things that money can't buy. When you practise gratitude, try and describe in detail exactly what it is about the things you chose that makes you feel this way.

For example, you might express gratitude for:

- The food you have to eat.
- The shining sun and warm weather.
- Being able to walk in nature.
- The smile and laughter of a child.
- Being fit and healthy.

But don't leave it there. You can dramatically boost the power of your gratitude practice by explaining why you are grateful for these things. For example:

**'I am grateful for the food I have to eat because I don't have to worry about being hungry, and today I enjoyed a wonderful steak dinner with my wife and my kids.'**

This extra level of detail will help you create detailed memories and ensure you direct your attention to the many positive aspects of your life.

Another powerful practice is to have a gratitude jar or box. Instead of writing what you are grateful for in your journal you can do it on a piece of paper and then place it inside. You can even decorate the container to make it reflect gratitude, how about adding some bright colours, stickers or ribbons? You will soon find that your container begins to fill up, especially if you are adding two or three new pieces of paper each day. Over time you will have a wonderful resource that you can use if you are feeling down. Whenever you need a boost, simply pull out a piece of paper and allow it to provide you with a reason to feel thankful instead of down.

If you find at any point that writing in your journal starts to become unenjoyable, try and adjust the amount of time you spend making entries. It is important to maintain motivation and you should feel like you want to do it, as opposed to feeling like you have to force yourself. There are no hard and fast rules, if once a day is too much, try writing every other day instead.

## 15 Be more sociable

Having social connections with other people helps reduce stress and anxiety and can enable us to regulate our emotions and form a new perspective on situations that may have been causing discomfort.

In some respects, we are more connected than ever with social media, email and messaging available – all at the press of button. Yet loneliness is on the increase and many people lack the face to face interaction needed to bring more happiness into their lives. Humans have an inbuilt need for connection and it may mean that we need to step outside of our comfort zone in order to make it happen. Don't disregard the importance of forming meaningful friendships with people, it can make an enormous difference to our overall sense of wellbeing.

I don't have a huge circle of friends, but I do have two or three who I am very close to and I know I can connect with at any time. We are able to talk on a deep level and share any problems, challenges or emotions we are experiencing without judgement. You don't need to have a huge group of friends; instead, focus on forming a small number of really good ones. If you already have some good friends, take the time to look after the relationship and avoid making yourself isolated or allowing the friendship to dwindle.

If you need to find new friends you can consider:

- Joining a club or group that interests you.
- Finding a workshop or course that will connect you with people who have the same interests as you.
- Getting involved in online communities that interest you and join in, you will soon make new friends and engage with people local to you.
- Offering to volunteer or help out somewhere that will connect you with new people.

- Talking to people and starting a conversation instead of keeping quiet, this might be at work or in a social setting.
- Accepting invites to go out instead of declining them. But only if you really want to go, if not, be truthful and say 'no'.
- Connecting with the friends of your friends, ask for an introduction if you need to.
- Reconnecting with old friends who you have lost touch with.
- Hosting a small dinner party, BBQ or event and inviting people who you think you might form friendships with.

As you begin to connect with more people and create strong friendships, try and make an effort to be completely authentic and honest around them. You will be amazed at the power of authenticity and how connected it will make people feel towards you. There should be no need to be fake around a real friend, they should be happy to accept you just as you are.

# 25 | How far have you come?

As you have read through this book my hope is that you have had plenty of new insights about yourself and experienced powerful breakthroughs about how you can create the future you desire as you continue moving forward. Even the simple process of becoming more aware of the reasons why you feel a particular way, and paying attention to your feelings, can make a huge difference on the journey to healing from neglect or trauma.

It is important to be clear that all the techniques, tips and recommendations I have shared will make a difference to your life, but only if you practise them and allow them to become new habits. Be gentle with yourself, it can take time, and there will likely be setbacks along the way. Don't let that hold you back; commit to creating the life you want by learning from every experience as you grow and change.

If you made entries in a journal, now is a great time to reflect on what you wrote as you started reading this book. Take some time to celebrate how far you have come since you made your first entries. Can you be specific about what you feel has changed? If you can identify particular areas where you can clearly see positive improvements, make sure you congratulate yourself.

Use the changes you have already noticed as a catalyst to continue your journey, allow this to give you the firm belief that you will continue to develop and grow, because you already have. The more you immerse yourself in the process by working on cultivating the habits that will allow you to be truly free and happy, the more you will experience positive changes.

Avoid rushing or becoming frustrated. Simply allow the process to take the time it needs to take. Learning, healing, grieving and acceptance can feel like a challenge at times, but it does get easier. Keep noticing what is happening and paying attention to everything you experience and use your journal to gather the data.

It also makes sense to revisit the 50 questions you answered in Chapter 2 and compare your responses now to the original answers you gave. This will allow you to obtain a very clear picture of how much you have improved through your own work.

You can also answer the following questions to get an indication of which areas of your life have improved now you have a much better understanding of yourself. Score each of the questions from 0 to 10, with 0 being 'not at all' and 10 being 'all the time':

1. I am noticing my emotions and feelings much more than previously.

2. I am labelling and naming my feelings when they arise and no longer suppress them or avoid them.

3. When something triggers an emotional reaction, I now explore where it came from and consider what boundaries might need putting in place to prevent a recurrence.

4. I notice when my inner child is in control and know how to get the adult back into the driving seat.

5. I understand the story of my life and no longer blame myself.

6. I understand that it is likely I will experience a period of grieving.

7. I now accept what happened in the past for what it was and understand that arguing with reality does not serve me.

8. I am working on loving myself more, accepting who I am and treating myself with kindness and compassion.

9. I am able to express my feelings to other people even when it feels uncomfortable.

10. I am no longer projecting a false version of myself into the world; I am honest, authentic and true, even when I find it difficult.

11. I no longer agree to things just to please other people.

12. I am noticing the difference between activities that bring short term gratification and those that add to my long term happiness.

13. I feel more confident in myself and believe that I am good enough exactly as I am.

14. I understand what tactics to use if I experience overwhelming emotions.

15. My partner, family and/or close friends have noticed positive changes in me.

16. I want to continue to work on myself and I am excited to keep practising what I have discovered.

17. I expect setbacks to happen, but I know that I can use them as an opportunity to learn and grow.

18. I am standing in other people's shoes and considering how they might feel in certain situations.

19. I am noticing when I am outside of my own business and trying to stay in my own lane.

20. I no longer feel like a victim and can only see myself continuing to improve.

If you haven't experienced much in the way of noticeable changes yet, don't worry. It can take some time to experience a significant shift and, depending on the severity of trauma or neglect, it might require regular practice over a longer period before you begin to create new habits and encounter big breakthroughs.

If you have severe issues from your past it may be beneficial to seek professional therapy in addition to the work you have been doing using this book.

Regardless of how much, or how little, change you have experienced in the time it has taken you to read this book, I am confident you will have discovered information, techniques and advice that you will never unlearn and, going forward, you will now have a very clear picture of which areas of your life you need to focus on in order to improve yourself.

You have begun an amazing journey and I want you to feel incredibly proud of yourself for taking such a powerful and positive step. Many people spend their entire lives avoiding ever looking into the mirror at the real version of themselves, but you have done exactly that and this is when the magic begins to happen.

I have used the term 'journey' throughout this book. To me the whole experience has felt like a journey, the further I have travelled down the path of healing, the more I have discovered and the stronger I have become. I am unsure if the journey ever ends, or whether the journey is, in fact, life.

As well as feeling proud of yourself, it can also help to ask someone who you trust whether they have noticed any changes in you. This might be your partner, a friend or a work colleague, for example. Listen carefully to what insights they give you and if they pay you a compliment, try and accept it for what it is, the truth.

No journey to healing is ever a straight line. You will always encounter twists, turns and diversions along the way, there are usually a few potholes waiting to trip us up too which is why it is important to avoid rushing blindly forwards. Become disciplined about taking your time and enjoying the process, there is no hurry. The important thing is to keep moving forward with a mindset of progress and momentum and pay attention to the fact that you are changing for the better all the time.

Above all, remember that you really are enough exactly as you are, you don't need to do anything to impress, control or change other people.

If you have found that you have made more progress in some areas and not so much in others, then it makes sense to revisit the relevant chapters and take more time to explore them further. You have been presented with a significant amount of information in a fairly short space of time and it is unrealistic to expect everything to stick after reading this book once. It may also help for you to carry out some internet research to obtain more insights on any specific topics that you feel might need more work. You will find some helpful resources towards the back of the book.

As you go forward, continue to revisit this book and refer to chapters that may serve you in a specific situation or when you encounter a challenge in your life. Be sure to journal regularly and spend time reflecting on the progress you are making as the weeks and months go by.

# Growing in spirituality

You might have already noticed how you have become far more connected to yourself, other people and the world around you. When people become spiritual, they have very likely become fully in tune with the true version of themselves and nurtured a sense of real peace, contentment and happiness in their lives.

Spirituality is a broad concept and it can mean different things to different people. In general, it involves us having a feeling that we have a meaning and purpose to our lives and that we are connected and touching all other beings with a universal experience. People who become spiritually aware and connected describe how they have a deep sense of being alive and fully in touch with people, nature and themselves. They also commonly feel a strong connection with something greater than themselves, this might be through their faith, or through a clearer understanding of humanity and the power of the universe.

Spirituality, or 'self-actualization', is the final stage of complete healing. Don't worry if you don't feel spiritual right now, it can take time to get there and the fact that you are no longer stuck in the early stages of CEN and trauma will mean you should be experiencing much more happiness most of the time.

I am also confident that when you experience triggering episodes, you are finding that you are much more aware and exploring them with curiosity in order to understand what caused them. You may well find that these negative experiences are happening far less often and even when they do arise, they don't last as long as they did in the past. If so, this is massive progress, well done.

In most cases people find themselves growing in spirituality as a result of the positive changes they have made. As new behaviours become new habits, we become able to love ourselves and love other people fully and unconditionally. We also begin to find ourselves being fully present and awake to our behaviours and the world around us.

The green shoots of spirituality may have already started to grow in you but, in order to allow them to flourish into a beautiful and strong flower, it is best to have a plan in place and follow a path that will lead you to becoming the most happy and content that you will likely have felt in decades. The following steps will allow you to move along the path to spirituality.

## Tips for becoming more spiritual

### Get clear on your beliefs

Whether you are religious or not, it is important to be really clear about what you believe, and what your principles and personal values are. Being spiritual is about living your life in line with what you believe. If you are unsure about your beliefs, take the time to look within yourself and start writing down what you discover.

# Find what brings you closer to complete contentment and happiness

Discovering a power that you truly believe is greater than yourself is the perfect way to realize that you are not at the centre of the universe, and that there are many things that have the power to take away our false belief that we are in control.

If you are religious you might find that it is easy to recognize God as your higher power, but if you don't have a faith it may feel like more of a challenge. Finding a higher power that you believe in without question will provide you with confidence and courage in the decisions you make. You will find that you become able to move forward with even more purpose in the knowledge that your faith in a higher power will always ensure the right thing happens, without any need for you to try and control situations or people. This is about taking a beautiful leap into your faith and knowing that it will always look after you.

A higher power doesn't have to be religious, it simply needs to be something you believe in that is greater than yourself. You may believe in the science around how the universe was created. You might also believe that since the dawn of time life has continued to grow and evolve, and that humans have become stronger and more intelligent with the passing of each new millennium. Your higher power in this instance might be: *the evolution of the universe and the knowledge that everything evolves into a better version of itself over time.*

Kindness and humanity is another power far greater than any individual. Think about how kindness and humanity can impact so many people and how the human experience is a common and connected one, where acts of kindness can take away pain and suffering.

Love is another power that is greater than any human, and I'm not referring only to the romantic type. Love is infinite, it is a resource that will never run out. If we live our lives with a belief that love is a power greater than us, then we become able to give and receive love knowing it can bring people together and create long-lasting happiness.

Another higher power you could put your faith in is nature. Consider the almighty power of the weather, which removes our ability to control any situation, making it a power far greater than that of any individual. Strong storms, snow, extreme heat and floods all have the ability to change our lives and remove any belief that we are the ultimate power in the universe.

You might come up with a different higher power that feels right for you and that is completely fine. There is no 'right' or 'wrong', but it does need to be something you truly believe in; don't rush this, let it come to you. You may relate to several of the examples I have given, and there is nothing wrong with believing in more than one higher power.

## Realize how connected you are

When you become spiritual, you understand how interconnected the entire human experience is and you realize that we are unable to exist alone. Take a moment to look around you now and choose an object – maybe it is the book in your hands. Think about how many people were involved in the creation of it; obviously, I wrote it, but there were hundreds, maybe thousands of other people who have touched it in some way who are rarely noticed, but without them it would never have made it into your home.

Think about the people who helped edit and proofread it, the graphic designers who created the cover, the printers who produced the copies, the people involved in making the paper to print it on and the logistical army in the infrastructure that delivered it to you. This could be a huge list; you might start by thinking about the raw materials and begin paying attention to the huge web of people intertwined in almost every experience we have. You will realize how our lives are connected to others and how, without them, we would struggle to exist.

## Spirituality is peace

People who are spiritual experience peace in their lives. In order to find true peace, it is important to cultivate it and use it as a healthy belief to live by. Peace is the opposite to conflict – we can practise peace both internally and externally by avoiding conflict, meditating, becoming self-aware and practising forgiveness. We always have the power of choice in a situation; when we take the path of peace, we tend to avoid drama and internal discomfort and find that our lives become far calmer and easier.

## Self-love is key

We have explored self-love throughout this book and I truly believe that it is one of the foundations on which happiness, contentment and peace are built. Without the ability to love ourselves, we will become stifled when it comes to loving other people or allowing ourselves to be loved, and this will create a spiritual block. Make sure you continue to focus on practising love for yourself; it will pay huge dividends.

## Stand in other people's shoes

Practising empathy and compassion for others will allow you to become more humble and less likely to allow your ego to drive your behaviour. Be careful not to begin playing the role of the 'rescuer' or ending up on the drama triangle. Empathy and compassion are about you feeling another person's suffering and being grateful for what you have in your own life.

## Drop the unhealthy habits

We explored addictions and behaviours that only serve to provide us with short term gratification earlier in the book. In order to become spiritual you need to practise self-care, and to live in line with your beliefs and values. Any kind of self-defeating behaviour is likely to conflict with your personal code of conduct and will block your path to spirituality. If you need help addressing any specific addictive behaviours, don't wait - seek out what you need, and reach out to someone who can support you to ensure you successfully change your behaviour.

## Get mindful

Mindfulness is all about being in the present moment and paying attention to it. Instead of ruminating about the past or worrying about the future, we focus on what is happening in the now by paying more attention to everything around us, and all that we experience. There are many positive benefits to becoming more mindful and it is proven to positively impact mental health. Mindfulness will allow you to feel alive and connected to other people and the world around you; it will also help you on your journey to spirituality.

## Use your journal

I am a huge advocate of journaling, even though it can feel like a challenge at times. If you want to become spiritual, you can use your journal to track your progress and to notice how you are bringing spirituality into your life on a daily basis. You will also notice occasions where you slipped up and will be able to work out what to do differently as you go forward and evolve into a more spiritual person.

You will find that reading this book has lit a fire within you to keep working until you feel complete peace and happiness in your life. I have been where you are now and the good news is that, when the fire is ignited, you will make it your mission to continue working on change until you experience a noticeable positive shift. Immerse yourself in your work as if it is your new hobby; let go of any fear, feel proud and passionate about what you are doing in the knowledge that you will make an enormous difference to your own life, and the lives of those who are closest to you.

Imagine who you would be if you let go of it all.

> *'You can't go back and change the beginning, but you can start where you are and change the ending.'*
>
> C.S. Lewis

# 26 | Common questions and concerns

**I haven't experienced a change in myself after reading this book.**

Don't worry, healing from CEN and trauma takes time. For some people it can be a matter of months, for others it can be years. There are many different factors at play, including the severity of what happened in the past, your levels of motivation and work rate.

Be kind and gentle to yourself, there is no benefit in trying to rush or force the process. Allow things to happen naturally; as long as you continue learning and moving forward then you are making progress.

Be sure to track how far you have come and pay attention to what changes over time. You may find that it helps to seek professional help from a therapist if you haven't experienced any changes after a couple of months.

**It just feels too hard to look at events from my past.**

It is common to experience discomfort when we begin to explore the story of our lives. The reason we have avoided these episodes for so long is because of the pain they cause us. It is by finally facing up to the hurt and working through the emotions and feelings that we can become free.

It is important to carefully unpackage your past if it feels uncomfortable. Think of it as a delicate flower that is tightly packed in wrapping paper. If you aggressively rip into the sheets of paper you will likely damage the flower inside, but if you unpackage it gently, slowly and methodically you will ensure the flower remains intact. If it feels too hard to look closer at the memories right now, use the following tips to help yourself:

- Explore only as far as you feel comfortable. As you become more confident you might choose to dig a little deeper.
- Avoid getting into graphic detail, simply accepting that an event happened is enough.
- You might notice different days or times where you feel stronger and more equipped to look at the past.
- Consider working through the events with someone supportive such as a friend, partner or therapist.
- If you struggle to talk about the past, consider writing it down in your journal instead.

- Use your body instead of your mind; as you recall the memory, pay attention to your body and breathe in and out of the areas where you feel the memory to help it soften.
- Close your eyes and visualize yourself in a movie theatre, know that you are completely safe here. Then watch the memories play like a movie on the big screen; you are an observer, not an actor in the drama in front of you.
- Work on having a mindset that you 'want' to feel the feelings, as you know this will help you heal.
- Consider joining an online or face to face group with other people who have experienced trauma and CEN. You will have a safe place where you can share, without judgement, and make new friends as you come to terms with the past.
- Try and understand that these memories are holding you back and, by facing up to your fears, you will start breaking free from the pain they have caused you.

## I can't remember anything from my past and it is holding back my progress

It can be a challenge to remember exactly what happened in childhood and it can feel frustrating when we have a strong sense that past episodes have led to negative experiences in our adult lives, but we can't put our finger on exactly what they were. It can leave you feeling stuck and struggling to work with what you don't know.

When we face a traumatic or highly stressful situation as children, we can repress the memories instead of accepting them. When we repress memories we find it hard to recall them in the same way we would do with a positive experience. There has been debate about the extent to which people lose memories – however, hypnosis has been shown to help people reconnect with memories that have been repressed.

I also recommend writing the memories you do have and allowing time for more information to come to the surface as you begin to stir the deep waters in your mind. Each time something new arises, get it down in writing.

## I can't identify any issues with the way my parents treated me – what should I do?

It is common for people to struggle to find issues from their past that may have shaped them in adulthood. CEN in particular can be a very subtle form of neglect and it can be extremely hard to identify or remember. People often discount past experiences that happened as children as unimportant in adulthood, but very often the way we felt at the time continues to live within us even as adults and it causes us to suffer.

Trust your instincts and the information you have gathered and continue to explore the story of your life with an open mind and a sense of curiosity. There are some cases where it is impossible to discover more than we already know. It can help to speak to people who may be able to help you fill in the pieces of the jigsaw puzzle, for example siblings, aunts and uncles or friends of your parents. Approach any conversations with care and ensure you think about what you want to say and what you would like to find out ahead of time.

If your parents are still alive and you feel comfortable and confident enough to ask them questions about your past, you have every right to find out more. Again, make sure you plan what you want to ask before you meet with them.

If you continue to struggle to find any past events or experiences that may have caused you to suffer later in life then it may be worth engaging in a few sessions with a therapist, who will help to uncover what you have been looking for by listening to the story of your childhood. If you decide to work with a professional, make sure you work with someone who is qualified and has positive feedback.

## I understand what I need to do, but what should I avoid doing?

- Avoid suppressing or bottling up your feelings. Make sure you know how to express them and set boundaries wherever it is appropriate.

- Don't become overwhelmed by doing too much work on yourself and avoid being overloaded with other commitments. Keep a healthy balance between doing the work on yourself and having time to do what you enjoy.

- Don't keep quiet; talk about your trauma or CEN little by little with people who are safe and supportive. Allow emotions and feelings to come up and work at a pace that feels comfortable.

- Don't avoid the reality of what happened, even though it can feel hard; knowing and accepting the truth about the past is far better than living with uncertainty.

- Don't jump into any huge life changes until you have given them plenty of thought. If you are considering cutting contact with a toxic person, it is sensible to give yourself a cooling off period while you consider all the options and take advice from people you trust.

- Avoid using drugs and alcohol; while they provide temporary relief from painful memories, over the longer term they will cause us to feel worse than before we used them.

- Avoid any other unhealthy behaviours that you believe are a coping mechanism for trauma or CEN. You might experience strong urges and possibly grief as you withdraw from any unhelpful habits but, before long, these will fade and you will be free from them holding you back any longer.

- Remember that healing can take time. In some cases it can be years. Notice that you are making progress and don't try to force anything. Allow it to be a natural process.

- Don't isolate yourself while you are healing, continue to lead a normal life and socialize as usual. You don't need to talk about your past all the time if you don't want to, enjoy occasions where you don't need to focus on it.

- Don't avoid asking for help when you need it, whether it is from close friends, supportive family members or a professional therapist - you have every right to reach out when you need it.

### Can I get medication to help me cope with the bad feelings?

Medication can sometimes help, usually alongside the work you have been doing and sessions with a therapist. Doctors will consider the options on a case by case basis. If you feel the symptoms are too much to cope with, please speak to a medical professional and discuss the options.

### What professional help is available and when should I get it?

There are a wealth of professional services and expert help available for people who have suffered CEN and trauma. If you have made progress and noticed yourself becoming more self-aware and changing in other positive ways as you have read this book, you might find that working with a professional will accelerate your recovery.

Take your time before choosing a professional to work with and check their credentials carefully; ideally you should obtain references from previous clients. The best professionals have personal experience of the issues that they treat, and you have every right to ask what makes them qualified to help you when you are carrying out your due diligence.

Only you will know when the time feels right to seek professional help, but if you have experienced a prolonged period where you have felt stuck and despite your own efforts to heal you don't feel you have made sufficient progress, then it may well be time to look for extra support.

You could consider some of the following options:

- **Psychotherapy:** A trained and experienced trauma therapist will help people understand themselves and work towards them cultivating a sense of love, trust and acceptance for themselves and others. Therapists provide a safe and judgement free space and will provide people with information and insights that will help them to feel a sense of momentum as they move forward on their path to recovery.

- **Hypnotherapy:** This can allow people who have experienced trauma or CEN to work through any emotional blocks and revisit traumatic events while in a hypnotic state. During the process it is possible to reconnect with the emotions and feelings that arise, and this can result in significant progress on the path to healing.

- **Group therapy:** I found group therapy to be one of the biggest contributors to my own recovery and I would encourage you to find a group that feels like a good fit, with members who have shared similar experiences to your own. Groups are often led by a therapist or a mentor and they are most effective when they are combined with one-to-one therapy at the same time.

- **EMDR:** This stands for Eye Movement Desensitization and Reprocessing and involves people focusing on a traumatic event while they follow an object, usually a light or a therapist's finger from side to side. There is some debate about the use of EMDR; however, it has been proven to be highly effective against trauma and CEN symptoms. You can also find a number of guided 'do it yourself' EMDR practices on YouTube, although I recommend approaching any 'do it yourself' guides with caution.

- **CBT:** This stands for Cognitive Behavioural Therapy and helps people who have experienced trauma and CEN cope with heightened emotions, stress and anxiety in a healthy way by enhancing their knowledge and understanding. CBT work tends to focus on the 'effect' of trauma and CEN rather than the root causes and aims to replace unhelpful, irrational and negative thoughts with a new way of thinking.

- **DBT:** This stands for Dialectical Behaviour Therapy which is a similar treatment to CBT. DBT mostly focuses on talking and is adapted to suit people who experience intense emotional discomfort. DBT aims to help people understand and accept their emotions and feelings and learn how to better manage them to help them move to a more peaceful and happier state of being.

- **Psychodynamic therapy:** Aims to help people gain insight into the real version of themselves by exploring their needs, desires and urges alongside the experiences they may have encountered in the past. Therapists look for patterns in behaviour and help people create a clear picture of themselves in order that they can move into a better state of being and enjoy a more positive outlook on life.

- **Somatic experiencing:** A type of alternative therapy that focuses on a person's bodily sensations to help relieve the symptoms of trauma and CEN. During sessions a therapist will introduce small amounts of traumatic material and will observe a person's physical responses. Based on the responses they notice, the therapist will then help the individual work through their trauma and equip them with helpful tools to regulate themselves during challenging times.

### I know I suffered trauma or CEN but I also think something else might be going on – for example anxiety or depression.

There are cases where past trauma and CEN can mask underlying depression, anxiety and other mental health problems that exist, regardless of what happened in the past. If you have any concerns please speak to a mental health professional to discuss the best options and treatments.

### Should I think about helping other people who have suffered similar issues to my own?

Yes, when you feel ready it is incredibly powerful for you to give back to people who are at an earlier stage on their own journey. You might decide to do this by contributing in an online or face to face group, starting a blog, sharing your story or even becoming a counsellor or coach in the future.

### I have read about the benefits of group therapy – how do I find a group?

You can find therapy groups by searching online – many operate via video conferencing which means you can join no matter where in the world you are located. You can also search for face-to-face therapy groups; the added dimension of being in the same room as the other group members can be incredibly powerful. Many groups are gender specific – a Google search for 'men's therapy groups' or 'women's therapy groups' will help you find what you need. Do make sure the group is relevant to your own situation before you join, check whether other members have encountered similar experiences to your own and ask the group leader whether they believe it will be a good fit for you.

### I have seen several online programmes that promise to help overcome trauma and CEN – are these worth paying for?

Just like therapy, online programmes can be beneficial, but it is essential you do your homework and find out exactly what you will get for your money. Take the time to read reviews and find out what is included in any of the programmes you are considering joining. Some programmes don't offer much more in length or content than an audiobook, yet they are priced at several hundred dollars.

Make sure you find out:

- Exactly what the content will cover – is it relevant? Does it include what you need?
- The length of the content – how many hours' worth of material is there?
- The format of the content – is it audio, video or live online?
- How often new content is added to the programme?
- What support is provided?
- Does the programme provide any extra materials such as downloadable workbooks or questionnaires?
- Does the programme have a community, such as a members-only Facebook group that you can join?
- Are you entitled to a refund if you decide the programme isn't right for you?

And don't be afraid to ask for some references so you can speak to people who have benefitted from the programme before you part with your money.

### Reading this book has helped me get a better understanding of myself – what should I do next?

My hope is that you have started to notice yourself transforming and have begun to pay attention to the areas of yourself that have previously been holding you back.

The more you continue to cultivate the new healthy habits and techniques you have learned, the more you will continue to experience positive changes.

Even after I felt as though I had reached a place where I felt happy, free of my past issues and content with who I was, I continued to read books, listen to podcasts and take part in therapy groups to ensure I kept myself on track and focused.

As you go forward, you might want to consider exploring some of the following areas as you move into a more advanced stage of your personal growth:

- Consider exploring more about spirituality and learning about bringing it into your life.
- Create a plan for maintaining the healthy habits you have learned to ensure you don't slip back into past patterns of behaviour.
- Consider joining a therapy group or working one-to-one with a professional to work through any issues that you haven't yet explored.
- Continue your growth by working on any specific areas you feel are still holding you back. It can also help to go over any chapters you might need to refresh yourself on.
- Work on building authentic connections and meaningful relationships in your life and pay attention to any toxicity that seeps in.
- Notice when you slip into being your false-self, this might be when you fail to resist an urge to feel appreciated or acknowledged, for example.
- Think about how you can help other people and pass on what you have learned on your own journey.
- Create a vision board and be clear about what you need to achieve to get where you want to be.
- Ensure you have a clear understanding of your personal values, meaning and purpose in your life. If you don't, continue to explore them so you can get total clarity.
- Keep on noticing any uncomfortable feelings, angry outbursts or childish reactions and welcome them with compassion in the knowledge that they will provide you with information that will help you continue to grow.
- Ensure you have tactics in place to deal with any triggering situations; they can catch us off guard and will sometimes appear out of nowhere.
- Continue to put boundaries in place whenever you feel it is appropriate. When it feels a challenge to do it, make sure you work on overcoming the fear.

# Resources

**Visit my websites**

simonchapple.com

besober.co.uk

**Connect with me on social media:**

Instagram: @besoberandquit

Facebook: @quitalcoholcoach

**Other books by Simon Chapple**

*How to Quit Alcohol in 50 Days*

*The Sober Survival Guide*

**Online programmes and courses**

Alcohol addiction - joinbesober.com

Healing C-PTSD - crappychildhoodfairy.com

Personal development and growth - tonyrobbins.com

**Books**

*The Art of Happiness* by The Dalai Lama and Howard Cutler

*Loving What Is* by Byron Katy

*Wired for Love* by Stan Tatkin

*Radical Honesty* by Brad Blanton

*Healing the Child Within* by Charles Whitfield

*Running on Empty* by Dr Jonice Webb

*Growing Yourself Back Up* by John Lee

**Websites to explore**

psychologytoday.com

medium.com

limerence.net

betterhelp.com

time.graphics - online timeline maker

scottjeffrey.com

thework.com

jordangrayconsulting.com

heysigmund.com

mindbodygreen.com

thinkunbroken.com

## Men's support groups

Men Speak Men's Groups: mensgroups.co.uk

Mankind Project: mankindproject.org

## Women's support groups

Support Groups Central: supportgroupscentral.com

Turn2Me: turn2me.ie

## Smartphone apps

Calm: calm.com

Headspace: headspace.com

Insight Timer: insighttimer.com

imood journal: imoodjournal.com

## Facebook communities

Trauma Thrivers: facebook.com/groups/1221929004660869/

Childhood Emotional Neglect Support Group for Survivors:
facebook.com/groups/1673285076264700/

## Documentaries

*The Work*

*Paper Tigers*

*Happy*

*Heal*

*Happy Valley*

*Generation Found*